Praise for *The Philosophy Shop*

Schools in Britain, and indeed the world over, are being subordinated to a central diktat, which values the passing of exams above any other benefit. Learning becomes a sequence of 'teaching for the test', with rote-learning replacing genuine open-ended learning. The schools become like factories, and teachers become operatives, encouraging their students along a conveyor belt. *The Philosophy Shop* is a ts heart it is encouraging young people to think, and t ok wants to see thinking for thinking's sake, the develo of learning, and the formation of enquiring minds ig to accept authority unless grounded on good argur

As a head of a secondary school, I welcome this book, and would hope that it will be used widely in schools, families and elsewhere. It is so much more conducive to stimulating thought than the pedestrian philosophical training I received at Oxford in the 1970s as part of PPE. I went up to university with my head buzzing with the kind of questions which fill the pages of *The Philosophy Shop*. Within four or five weeks, my enthusiasm for the subject had been drummed out of me by dull teachers teaching philosophy in a dull way.

Sir Anthony Seldon, Vice-Chancellor,
The University of Buckingham and author

The winner of the Educational Book of the Year in the 2013 Education Resources Awards, *The Philosophy Shop*, is an outstanding resource, which provides active engagement instead of passive receipt of information. It can be used in various subjects on all levels for development of thinking and interaction skills and for development of reasoning and language skills.

This book is is a one-stop shop for all teachers who want to engage their children, improve interaction in class and encourage students to reflect and also to express their thoughts.

Sirkku Nikamaa-Linder, educator and lecturer, Finland

I've just started a philosophy-based scheme of learning for my year nines next year, and this book will be a massive part of that. The 'works well with' suggestions for each exercise make translating the ideas in the book into a well structured sequence of lessons a joy. I completely agree that introducing core philosophical issues to students with a 'hook' that grabs them is the best way to approach the subject. I do the same with my A level groups and it enthuses them to approach the core issue in creative ways. A very practical tool for teachers.

Ian Tustin, lead teacher of religion and philosophy, Wadham School

The judges, an independent panel of experienced educational professionals, most of whom are classroom teachers, felt that *The Philosophy Shop*, a book containing numerous philosophical puzzles and challenges offered an exciting and unusual way to develop thinking at all stages of learning.

Education Resources Awards judges

This book should get anyone thinking.

Nigel Warburton, The Open University

The Philosophy Shop is a mission to bring philosophy into our schools. This book brilliantly shows how accessible philosophy is, and how fun and mind-expanding it can be, for any ages.

Jules Evans, author of *Philosophy for Life: And Other Dangerous Situations*,
co-organiser of the London Philosophy Club and
policy director of the Centre for the History of the Emotions

Provides a treasure trove of ideas to develop children's thinking in the concepts of philosophy from as young as five, along with the opportunity to 'advance' thinking for the more able children.

Karen Taylor, *Head Teacher Update*

The Philosophy Shop

The Philosophy Shop

Ideas, activities and questions to get people,
young and old, thinking philosophically

Contributors include:

Harry Adamson   Peter Adamson   Alfred Archer   Saray Ayala   Grant Bartley   David Birch   Peter Cave
Miriam Cohen Christofidis   Philip Cowell   James Davy   Andrew Day   Georgina Donati   Claire Field
Berys Gaut   Morag Gaut   Philip Gaydon   Nolen Gertz   A. C. Grayling   Michael Hand   Angie Hobbs
David Jenkins   Milosh Jeremic   Lisa McNulty   Sofia Nikolidaki   Martin Pallister   Andrew Routledge
Anja Steinbauer   Dan Sumners   Roger Sutcliffe   John L. Taylor   Amie L. Thomasson   Robert Torrington
Andy West   Guy J. Williams   Emma Williams   Emma Worley   Peter Worley

Edited by Peter Worley

For The Philosophy Foundation

First published by

Independent Thinking Press
Crown Buildings, Bancyfelin, Carmarthen, Wales, SA33 5ND, UK
www.independentthinkingpress.com

Independent Thinking Press is an imprint of
Crown House Publishing Ltd.

First published 2012. Reprinted 2016.

Originally printed in hardback.

British Library Cataloguing-in-Publication Data
A catalogue entry for this book is available
from the British Library.

Hardback ISBN 978-178135049-2
Paperback ISBN 978-178135264-9
Mobi ISBN 978-178135060-7
ePub ISBN 978-178135061-4

Printed and bound in the UK by
TJ International, Padstow, Cornwall

To all the children that The Philosophy Foundation has worked with over the past ten years who have helped to stock up this shop.

Acknowledgements

Thanks to members of The Philosophy Foundation (formerly The Philosophy Shop) for providing entries and for running new contributions with classes of children to help make sure that this book is as tried-and-tested in the classroom as possible. Specialists who 'tested' included David Birch, Andrew Day, Steve Hoggins, Rachel Kershaw and Rob Torrington. Especial thanks go to Rob Torrington and David Birch for their close reading of the entries submitted and for their comments; to Rob for his extremely useful, last-minute proofreading efforts.

Thanks to the teachers and classes who have willingly allowed us to test many new sessions with them for the preparation of this book. I must, of course, say thank you to the children who provided some excellent questions and thought experiments of their own, many of which were included in the book (and are mentioned appropriately).

I would like to thank Professor Peter Adamson for his enlightening lecture on 'Plato, Aristotle and Dialectic', which I heard him deliver to the Institute of Philosophy. It was here that the *topos* metaphor fell into place.

The section titles were inspired by a lecture given by A. C. Grayling on the value of philosophy in which he split philosophy into just two: 'what there is' and 'what matters in what there is'. I took this and ran with it.

Thanks to Ian Gilbert for his helpful guidance with the editing process and to Caroline Lenton for her encouraging words about the project and her support in helping to bring the book to print so quickly.

'Thank you!' once again to Tamar Levi for the wonderful cover and illustrations and for all her hard work and efficiency.

But most of all I must thank, with all my love, my wife Emma for her essential work on the project: her unofficial editorial work, her contributions, her thoughts, patience, encouragement, belief and love, without whom and without which it simply wouldn't be.

Preface

Philosophy Shopping

'Look at all these things I don't need!' the philosopher Socrates is said to have declared as he stood before the many stalls filling the marketplace of ancient Athens. In contrast to the stalls in the *agora* (Greek for 'marketplace'), and by engaging the citizens there with big, philosophical questions, Socrates offered an exchange of a very different kind. His currency was ideas; a wiser, more reflective person housed within a life well-lived was his aim. This anecdote shows how one can trace the origins of philosophy – as we know it in Western Europe at least – back to shopping.

We can perhaps identify with Socrates here as we too stand amid a dizzying marketplace – albeit a much larger, global one – bombarded from all sides by promises of a better life from 'pedlars of wares'. And we too may feel the need for an alternative kind of shop as an antidote to the pressures and promises of the modern-day *agora* – one that guards against the many 'snake-oils' on offer by insisting on an 'account' or 'reason' or *logos* in Greek. Perhaps we need an alternative shop such as this in order to reach that 'better life' by other than financial, consumerist means.

The Philosophy Shop stands as Socrates to the reader: sometimes beguiling, humorous and inspiring; other times irritating, like a gadfly, goading us into wakefulness; and sometimes frustratingly circular or inconclusive. But always – it is hoped – stimulating.

This book aims to guide the reader through it with as few words as possible and without the reader necessarily knowing what it is they want. One way I hope to have done this is through the structure – or topography – of the book. The main body has been divided into four sections, or 'departments', each with its own series of subheadings:

1. Metaphysics or What There Is

2. Epistemology or What Can Be Known About What There Is

3.   Value or What Matters In What There Is

4.   Language and Meaning or What Can Be Said About What There Is

Finally, there is a small collection of entries under the heading 'Afterthoughts' that may well benefit from being visited after reading through the rest of the book. That said, the entries in the book can be read in almost any order, but to help the reader/participant(s) further, I have provided a 'Works well with …' section at the end of each entry that aims to provide the reader with a multitude of thematic maps through the book (and beyond). The 'Start Questions' and the 'Questions to take you further' are also structured so as to guide the reader or participants (see 'What is this book?' on page 1 for more on this). 'Afterthoughts' contains some useful information and guidance on developing philosophical writing of different sorts: Dr John Taylor has provided some helpful notes on how to produce good philosophical writing for philosophy papers and projects; although written primarily for school projects many of the tips would be relevant for first year undergraduate students as well. David Birch introduces the writing of philosophical poetry to children and teachers; ideas that lend themselves to all kinds of development and variation at the hands of creative teachers and pupils.

Contents

We should set aside a room, just for ourselves, at the back of the shop …

From On Solitude *by Michel de Montaigne*

But, then, is this a fair exchange that you propose? You seem to me to want more than your proper share: you offer me the merest appearance of beauty, and in return you want the thing itself, 'gold in exchange for bronze'.

Socrates speaking in the Symposium *by Plato*

O dear Pan and all the other gods of this place, grant that I may be beautiful inside. Let all my external possessions be in friendly harmony with what is within. May I consider the wise man rich. As for gold, let me have as much as a moderate man could bear and carry with him.

Do we need anything else Phaedrus? I believe my prayer is enough for me.

Socrates' prayer from the Phaedrus *by Plato*

Introduction

What is this book?

A good deal of books written to introduce the reader to philosophy are *instructive*. Either straightforwardly so, in that they explain the problems of philosophy and then take the reader through the traditional debates, or they are instructive with the *appearance* of being exploratory. This is partly due to the limits of the written word: however exploratory the author would like her book to be, and however many questions she may raise, the lack of interaction seems to demand that the author provide answers of one sort or another at some point. As Plato said, real philosophy cannot be done through the written word as books can't reply to questions or clarify what is not understood. The irony of Plato's words lies in that he said them, or rather had Socrates say them, in one of his *written* dialogues – the *Phaedrus* – and today these dialogues are the only way we know of Plato's philosophy. His *written* critique of *written* philosophy encapsulates a tension of which Plato was all too aware: we can't do philosophy properly with the written word, but it seems we can't do without it either. Plato's own answer to this is his lack of one. Many of his dialogues end inconclusively and the invitation this presents for the reader is to continue with the discussions that Plato had begun. The implication which I take from this is that Plato is saying that philosophy is a continuous, on-going dialogue.

The conversational book

This book responds to this problem in a conversational, Platonic spirit. Questions are raised by the use of a controversy brought out by a story or scenario, poem or activity; yet, unlike Plato, a dialogue is not written but left to the reader or class engaged with the problem to think through for themselves. In this sense the book is meant to be *interactive*. For this reason, I shall refer to the reader as the 'participant(s)' from now on when referring to either class or group situations because this captures both the lone reader and the classes of children that may be *read to*. There is another sense in which I wish the book to be interactive. At the end of each section, and where appropriate, you will find a note on the source of the entry and also the key philosophical topics, ideas and the philosophers' names associated with them. These have been included to allow the interested reader, teacher or class to pursue some of the ideas and to find out more about the philosophers that have thought on these questions and topics throughout history. Wikipedia has some very helpful introductory entries on many of these key words but there are also some very good, more specialised philosophy websites which can be consulted, such as The Stanford Encyclopedia of Philosophy. See the back of this book for useful addresses.

Seeing controversies

It is often said that the primary and intrinsic value of doing philosophy with children is that it is enjoyable. This, of course, depends on the fact that children do enjoy doing philosophy. And on the whole I am happy to report, from my own experience and observations, that this is true. But what about those who don't enjoy philosophy? I have noticed that many of those who claim not to enjoy philosophy are unable to stop themselves engaging with a philosophical problem, once they recognise it *as* a problem.

The frames

In this book we have tried to find a 'frame' for each of the entries that is presented to the participant. The frame is the narrative or literary context in which the philosophical idea or problem is presented. Sometimes it is a short story, a thought experiment or scenario, a poem, image or even an activity. The frame helps to achieve the following:

- ❖ It aids *understanding* of what are often quite difficult ideas. Philosophy can never be made to be easy – it is by its very nature a difficult pursuit – but it can be made accessible, as well as enjoyable.

- ❖ It *contextualises* the philosophical issue so that the participants are not lost in abstractions.

- ❖ The frame *engages* the participant(s) in an enjoyable way with the problem or idea.

- ❖ It gives *meaning* to the problem; the frame provides a context that shows why the problem, and thinking about it, matters. This may, in a direct way, show how it matters to the participant or in the real world, or it may simply show why it matters 'in the story'; either way it connects the problem with value for the participant.

- ❖ The frame *motivates* the participant to solve the problem, often for narrative reasons of one kind or another. By thinking about the problem they may be helping a character or they may simply be providing the basis for the continuation of the story. It should be pointed out that many of the frames are incomplete (see 'What Goes Up…' on page 167) and this is because the sense of unresolved mystery often helps to intrigue the participant and to keep them thinking about the problem in some way.

- ❖ The frame adds *colour* to what could be very dry and colourless. Some have touches of humour here and there to give an extra element to enjoy.

- ❖ And sometimes the frame itself *contains aspects of philosophy* or it adds, in some way, to the philosophical problem in a special, integrated way. In other words, if the frame were not there, then neither would some aspect of the problem (see 'What Zeus Does When He's Bored' on page 88).

Each frame has been designed to try to illuminate the problem so that the participant can recognise it as a problem. It remains possible that not all the problems will be clear to all the participants all of the time, but sometimes all that's needed is some more time to mull over the frame until the problem comes into focus. At The Philosophy Foundation we have found that exploring the multiplicity of different perspectives afforded by a class or group is often the best way to reveal the tensions, and therefore the controversies, in these little philosophical appetisers.

Thoughtings and philosophical poetry

You will notice that some of the frames, or stimuli, for the entries in this book are in verse. Not quite poems and not quite *not poems*, they are called *Thoughtings*, as they have been written to stimulate thoughts and thinking on specific topics or problems (see the Further Reading section where you can find more *Thoughtings*). Children enjoy ideas presented in verse and they learn them remarkably quickly. Also, see David Birch's entry in 'Afterthoughts' on Philosophical Poetry (on page 299) for some inspiring ideas on how to get children writing their own philosophical poems.

Thought experiments

I mentioned that the frame may contain *thought experiments*. But what is a thought experiment? It's a device used by philosophers to get us thinking about a particular issue or concept under a certain, very specific set of conditions. It is precisely because of the way in which they attempt to control the variables using thought alone that they have been given the name 'thought experiment'. They are not used exclusively by philosophers; there are many famous thought experiments in science too, such as 'Newton's bucket', cooked up by Newton in an attempt to show that space is absolute. Even though associated with philosophers, and even though thought experiments have been used for millennia, the coining of the term itself has been credited to the scientist Ernst Mach. Sometimes the thought experiment is presented in its unembellished, original form (see 'The Flying Man' on page 152), other times the thought experiment has been wrapped up in a story (see 'Bat-Girl' on page 170).

The topic questions: Start, Further and Central

For Plato and Aristotle, 'where you start' is very important in a philosophical enquiry, and – continuing with the 'place' metaphor (or *topos* in Greek, where the English 'topic' comes from) – 'where you go' and 'how you get there' are just as important. Plato and Aristotle both used the visual image of a chariot racecourse to illustrate the progress of philosophical enquiry. An important part of helping to find *your* place, reveal the controversies and navigate around them, are the carefully chosen questions that will be found accompanying the stimuli.

I have divided these into three kinds: the *Start Question* followed by a series of *Questions to take you further* – from now on to be referred to as 'further questions' – amongst which are the *Central Questions*.

The Start Question is designed to take the participant(s) straight to the problem by asking the question that has proved, in the classroom, to best illuminate the problem in the context of the stimulus. The Start Question is usually linked to the frame; it is the question that the participants are, overall, trying to answer and it begins the discussion by being asked explicitly. You should think of the Start Question as being like a 'you are here' arrow on a map or floor-plan and as you explore the terrain it is helpful to return to this point frequently. It allows you (or the participants) to find your bearings and once you know where you are, you need to know where to go.

The further questions are then presented as questions *into* the problem or issue and often proceed gradually *out of* the story or stimulus (although it should be pointed out that you should not feel that these questions need all be asked or that they should be asked in order). Beginning with the Start Question and moving to the further questions enables the discussion to begin reasonably concretely, but to move gradually towards more abstract thinking and discourse. For example, in 'Who Gets What and Why?' on page 235, the Start Question is: 'How much of the cake should each child get?' But then among the last of the further questions is: 'What is fair?' The further questions are often the deeper, more hidden questions that lie behind the more explicit Start Question. The further questions have been chosen carefully to guide the participants and are informed by the debates, positions and arguments around that topic to be found in the standard literature. By way of analogy, if the stimulus is what you find displayed on the door, the Start Question enables you – and invites you – to open the door into the puzzle or problem; and the further questions then guide you deeper into the puzzle or problem so that you don't lose your way. It should be noted, however, that losing your way is a perfectly natural part of the philosophical process, so if you do get lost, it's often a sign that you are *doing* philosophy, not that you are failing to do it, as is often thought.

Perhaps the most central questions of all those among the further questions list are the 'What is … ?' questions, such as 'What is beauty?' or 'What is belief?' These are traditionally known as *Socratic Questions* because of the crucial role they play in Socrates' method, his philosophical pursuits and concerns. However, in order to follow the Start and further questions, and remaining with the 'place' metaphor, I have called them *Central Questions* because of how philosophically fundamental they are. They are highlighted (in **bold**) to stand out in the list.

At some point during any of the discussions around the entries in this book it is often helpful to examine a Central Question such as 'What is beauty?' This can be done by simply asking the question and discussing it. However, you will notice that the children, especially the very young ones, will often say something like 'beauty is when something is beautiful'. To help them avoid this kind of circularity, employ a strategy I've called 'Break the Circle' (see *The*

If Machine: Philosophical Enquiry in the Classroom by Peter Worley) and add the stipulation, when asking them a Central Question, that they must not say the word they are examining in their answer. So, *can they say what the word 'beauty' is, or means, without saying the word 'beauty' or 'beautiful' in their answer?* This is a beginner's version of what philosophers call *conceptual analysis*.

A note to teachers, chairs and facilitators

As a teacher, chair or facilitator it is crucial to read through – but more importantly to *think through* – the further questions, as these provide an overview of the 'thinking landscape' mapped out by the scenario. It is not important to necessarily 'have the answers' to the problems in this book but it is of the utmost importance to have thought about them for yourself to most effectively use this book with your class or students and to help them navigate their way around the topics. If you do want 'answers', then the best you can do is to learn the various lines that inhabit the canonical debates on these issues, so that you refrain from saying what *you* think is the answer but at least provide some information on what the various voices have contributed to the debate. It should be noted that you should try, as much as possible, to avoid giving any answers when chairing a Philosophical Enquiry. At The Philosophy Foundation we have noticed that the natural diversity of ideas that the children are capable of is dampened when the teacher or facilitator shares their own views. Once the children know what the teacher thinks then it is likely that they will repeat different versions of this view. Giving answers may also spoil the interactive aims of this book.

Space to think

I have also left space for your own questions and notes where you see the heading 'Your Questions'. This enables you to grow your list of further questions based on your own thoughts and reflections and/or those of the participants involved in the discussions.

Works well with ...

There is also a list of suggested companion entries that should work well with the entry that is being used, depending on the direction that the group takes. This helps to build lesson plans and schemes of work based on themes and related topics. But it should also be invaluable to the teacher if a particular entry is not working with a particular class. Maybe the issue just isn't 'biting' for them or maybe it's a little too advanced; or maybe you just need to read a new entry to keep up the pace of the session or to keep them interested. If so, then a quick glance at the 'Works well with' section should direct you to another suitable entry. The 'Time' section is a very good example of how this should work, as many of the entries are designed for short enquiries and they will easily lead on to one other. So, if you start with 'Superbaby Time!' the children are very likely to refer to something to do with the direction of clocks and the direction of time; in which case introduce 'The Big Time Experiment'. This section will also help with differentiation between groups of differing levels of ability. So if your theme is 'time and time travel' then you should be able to find entries that groups of differing levels of ability should be able to meet. In this way you may well cover three, four or more entries in one session, possibly at the same time. The 'Works well with' list should make this approach to using the book much easier for the teacher or facilitator.

Who is this book for?

This book is for anyone who picks it up and then wants to read on. It is for those who prefer the active engagement with ideas over the passive receipt of information. The book includes entries for a wide range of ages – the starting age for each entry has been included under the title. Some have been written for young children in primary school (such as the various adventures of Phil and Soph) and some would only be appropriate for older participants (such as 'Gun' on page 223) but there are plenty of examples that, though written to *include* younger children, do not preclude the participation of older people. I challenge any-aged reader to read 'Bobby the Punching Bag' (on page 189) without becoming engaged on one level or another. We have sometimes included the label 'Advanced' in entries that are thought to stretch the young mind just that little bit further. These would be suitable for able classes, groups of gifted and talented children or groups and classes that have become familiar with and adept at doing philosophy. But don't be afraid of trying more advanced entries; your class may surprise you.

There may also be more specific audiences for whom the book will be of interest.

Teachers and classes

There are a number of ways of doing philosophy with children but what they all share is the use of enquiry that is open-ended – extended discussions using questioning and reasoning – for engaging classes. Some recommend enlisting the children to formulate and select questions (Philosophy for Children, or P4C) and others recommend the use of carefully constructed questions that are put to the children, such as the start and further questions in this book. *The Philosophy Shop* can, in some cases, be used in either way but it should be noted that many of the examples have been carefully selected for their *philosophical focus*. By allowing the children to choose their own questions the focus may be lost. Having said that, many more interesting philosophical questions may be discovered by the children when they formulate their own questions based on their concerns and interests. Many of the more fleshed-out stories, such as 'The Girl from Yesterday' (see page 69), have a good deal more going on than is covered by the prepared questions. A balance between the two approaches is probably the best, so that the focus is preserved but the participants guide the discussion within the remit of the focus. Use the 'Your Questions' section in the book to write down questions that come up during discussions. The Philosophy Foundation has devised its own method of philosophical enquiry known as PhiE that attempts to achieve that balance. A short description of this is included on page 10 (for a fuller explanation of the method see *The If Machine: Philosophical Enquiry in the Classroom* by Peter Worley).

Philosophy courses, university seminar groups and tutorials

One way to introduce a philosophical topic, and the way that most philosophy courses opt to do so, is to explain the topic (e.g. epistemological scepticism) and then to set readings by philosophers who have made important contributions to the debates surrounding the topic (e.g. Descartes' *Meditations*). However, The Philosophy Foundation advocates a different approach. We recommend presenting the students with a stimulus that captures one or more of the essential concepts or problems contained in a philosophical topic. For instance, Chuang Tzu's 'Butterfly Dream' question (see page 169) introduces the concerns of epistemological scepticism (particularly the dreaming argument). The students are encouraged, first of all, to engage by themselves with the stimulus, thus providing a context of the students' own thinking on the topic. This enables the course leader to then place the ideas and philosophers into the context of the students' own thinking. This way, the students are already philosophically engaged when they meet the philosophy and philosophers. This book provides plenty of examples of stimuli for use in this way, many of which have been written by philosophers who are experienced in engaging students with philosophical problems and topics at university level.

Philosophy reading groups or discussion groups, youth groups and church groups

Many people enjoy getting together through the excuse of discussions around books. Philosophy groups, where the excuse is ideas, are also on the increase as they find favour with many people keen to think together. If a philosophy group appeals to you, then this book is the perfect resource as the entries are stimulating for all ages, but also accessible; they are designed to help anyone 'get to the philosophy' as quickly as possible without having to wade through pages of written text. That said, groups are also encouraged to use the suggestions at the end of the entries to follow up any ideas or discussions that have particularly captured the group's interest with primary source material – that's the philosophy written by the philosophers that lies behind, and which inspired, the entries in this book.

Parents with their children and after-school philosophy clubs

At The Philosophy Foundation we are often contacted by parents who would like to find resources so that they can encourage philosophical thinking in their children. There is a plethora of books for teenagers which they can read on their own and there is a reasonable amount of resources for younger children in classrooms, but there doesn't seem to be anything for younger children which would be suitable for parents to use. *The Philosophy Shop* aims to change that. Though the content of this book is wide ranging in terms of the age of the reader/participant(s), many of the entries are suitable for young children, and in some cases, very young children. You will find a recommended 'starting age' at the top of each entry underneath the title. It is recommended, however, that because of the wide-ranging material contained herein, that the parent use the book selectively with their child; it is not advisable for a parent to leave the book with their child for them to read on their own. Any parent using this book with their child will do well to note that philosophical discussions with children are often more fruitful when there is a group of children than when there is just one child. This, of course, will depend very much on the child. Parents should also take a look at the 'Quick guide to running a PhiE' (below). One way to use *The Philosophy Shop* would be to get a group of parents to run an after-school philosophy club. Combined with some games (see The Philosophy Foundation members website www.philosophy-foundation.org for game resources), and possibly some cakes and drinks, a philosophy club could be a great and fun way to get your children started on thinking philosophically.

The lone, interested reader

But don't think this book is only for groups. It should also appeal to anyone who likes to think, or who wants to think more, particularly those who like to do so without having to wade through pages of text and information. Think of each example like a Japanese haiku, but perhaps with a more European flavour. Open it up, read an entry, look at the questions, let them roll over your mind. Take it on journeys and dip in; open it up whilst waiting for a bus or sitting on the Underground, leave a copy in the loo, or use it to steer dinner party or family gathering discussions away from the same old topics. But to get the most out of this book, the lone reader is encouraged to use it to stimulate their own investigations and to pursue their own lines of enquiry. This way the reader is invited to write the second half of the book themselves.

A quick guide to running a PhiE (Philosophical Enquiry)

Whether for a discussion group at the pub, a university seminar or a classroom of primary school children, it is useful to have some hints and tips handy on how to conduct a group discussion. First of all somebody needs to be appointed 'chair' of the discussion (also known as 'the facilitator') and it is often best if the facilitator makes a commitment not to join in the discussion but to allow – and aid – the participants to follow their own discussion based on the stimulus presented. So here is a quick guide to running an enquiry around the entries in this book:

1. **Present the *stimulus***

    Read or tell the story, poem or instructions to the participants. Perhaps read or tell it more than once, using different modes of presentation if necessary and if you are able to do so with the stimulus in question (see 'Dizzy!' on page 269 for an example of different modes of presentation based on *auditory*, *visual* and *kinaesthetic* learning styles; see also 'Not Very Stationary Stationery' on page 191 for the use of drama to help with understanding; and see 'Introducing Pencil Person' on page 41 for the use of props to help bring a stimulus to life). These entries act as examples; you should be creative about how else you can help to better communicate other stimuli in the book using these entries as models.

2. **Allow *comprehension time* if necessary**

   Particularly with younger children, it may be necessary to have the participants say back to each other what they think is going on in the stimulus. For instance, if you have read 'Arete and Deon' (see page 217) you may want to begin by asking the children to list as many (salient) features of the two children in the story as they can. It may also be helpful to list the features as they are recalled under the names 'Arete' and 'Deon' on the board. This means that not only have the children processed the story better, but they will also have the important information about the characters in view throughout the discussion. This is something you may want to do with many of the entries in this book.

3. **Ask the *Start Question***

   The facilitator should make sure that they ask this question clearly. It should be written up for all to see. The exact wording of the question should be preserved as carefully as possible until the dynamic of the discussion moves towards another question. But very often if this happens it will still serve to answer the Start Question better. So keep returning to it.

4. **Allow *talk time***

   Once the group have been presented with the stimulus and have had the Start Question put to them, they will need to have a few minutes to think/talk it through with the person or people next to them. This should be done in pairs or in small groups.

5. **Run a *group enquiry* on the Start Question**

   Once asked, answering the Start Question will be the main task of the discussion, but to help keep things focused the facilitator should refocus the discussion fairly regularly by restating the Start Question. Sometimes the discussion will naturally move to one of the further questions as the focus and, in this case, refocus the group to that question instead. Some of the entries are designed to be fairly short enquiries (see 'Dizzy!' on page 269 or 'Negative Nelly' on page 278) whereas others are written to be able to extend into longer enquiries (see 'The Clockwork Toymaker' on page 81).

6. **Be *mindful* of the further questions**

   The facilitator should listen out for signs that the group has moved – or is moving – towards one of the further questions. Someone may say, 'But, what is beauty anyway?' in a discussion around 'Louis' Beauty Detector' (see page 227) clearly indicating a need to stop and consider the further question (also a Central Question), 'What is beauty?', before returning to the Start Question.

7. ***Introduce* the further questions only as and when necessary**

   Do not see the further questions as questions to be gone through in order, like a list; they are there for guidance only. You should let the discussion determine which of the further questions to introduce, and do so only where the discussion invites it.

Fill in Your Questions

At the conclusion of the discussion, note down any new questions that have occurred to you or that were introduced by the participants in the discussion.

8. ***Works well with ...***

   See what other entries in the book would provide good follow-on discussions. For instance 'Phil and Soph and the Meeting' (see page 161) works really well as a starter activity for 'Thoth and Thamus' (see page 256). Many of the entries in the 'Time' section work well as part of a pick-and-mix approach for one session based on what direction the discussion takes. You may well end up including three or four of the 'Time' entries in one session.

9. **Research the *philosophy* that can be found at the end of each entry**

   For instance, after discussing 'Empty' (see page 52) or 'Immy's Box' (see page 20) then find out more about Newton and absolute time/space, Leibniz and relational time/space, or Kant and psychological time/space.

Although this will serve to get you started, if you are a primary or secondary classroom teacher you may feel that you want to find out more about how to conduct discussions effectively. So, for a much more detailed description of how to conduct a discussion or enquiry see *The If Machine: Philosophical Enquiry in the Classroom* by Peter Worley where you will find out more about speaker management, facilitation skills and strategies for getting more good thinking in your classroom, as well as 25 more extensively detailed lesson plans. The Philosophy Foundation also provides training in questioning and enquiry skills. See www. philosophy-foundation.org for more details and more resources.

The Shop Part I
Metaphysics or What There Is

Metaphysics: Ontology (or Existence)

A Knife Idea

Peter Worley

Starting age: 10 years

A caveman called Ug has recently found a mammoth that has died naturally and so doesn't have the characteristic puncture wounds that sabre-toothed tigers leave. Winter is drawing near. He needs the skins and the meat but is unable to cut the mammoth open because knives haven't been invented yet.

Later that day whilst Ug is collecting stones to make a fire – fire-making *has* been invented! – he cuts himself on a sharp rock (a rock we now call 'flint'). This gives him an idea: he takes the sharp-edged rock and uses it to cut open the mammoth. This enables him to get to the meat and, with the help of his new tool, to remove the skin.

The following day he uses another harder type of rock to chisel the flint into a shape that has one very sharp side making his new tool even more efficient. With his new tool he is able to make himself all sorts of other things – as yet uninvented – such as bowls, a stool and a table. Later he learns how to make more of his cutting tools, which he uses either to replace them when they break or to exchange with other cavemen for goods. Soon all of his tribe has the new tool and they give it the name 'knife'.

Start Question   When did the object become a knife?

Think about the Start Question before looking at the suggestions below.

Was it …

1.   When the rock he would make it from was lying on the ground?

2.   When he cut himself on the rock?

3.   When he had the idea?

4.   When he chiselled it into shape?

5.   When he first used it?

6.   When it was first given the name 'knife'?

7.   Or at some other time? If so, when and why?

Questions to take you further

❖   When does something become what it is?

❖   What exactly is a knife? Can you define a knife?

❖   Is Ug's tool a knife or not?

❖   Does a knife have to be a certain shape?

❖   If 'the knife', 'the bowl', 'the stool' and 'the table' don't yet have names, what are they?

❖   **What is existence?**

❖   What does 'exist' mean?

Your Questions

❖

❖

❖

Works well with

✓   The Philosophical Adventures of Pencil Person pages 41–46

✓   Phil and Soph and the Ice Cream

✓   Just Testing!

✓   A Heap of Exercises?

✓   Of Fences

✓   *The If Machine:* The Chair[1]

Philosophy: Ontology, existence, being, sense and reference, Aristotle, Wittgenstein, Frege.

---

1   See *The If Machine: Philosophical Enquiry in the Classroom* by Peter Worley (Continuum, 2011).

The 2 Square
Peter Worley

Starting age: 7 years

2	2
2	2

Start Question   Take a look at the 2s above. How many numbers do you think are there?

Questions to take you further

* How many different answers can you think of?
* If someone said that there are no numbers there, can you say why they might say that?
* **What is a number?**
* Are numbers real or made up?
* Are numbers invented or discovered?
* Where can numbers be found?
* Are the symbols that you see in 'the 2 square' numbers?
* If not, what are numbers then?
* Draw a number 2 on a blank piece of paper. Now stare at it for a few minutes. Does it still look like a 2? Turn it around and look at it from different sides. What does this exercise make you think?

Your Questions

*
*
*

Works well with

- ✓ A Pageful of Nothing
- ✓ Phil and Soph and the Numbers
- ✓ Doughnut
- ✓ A Hole Load of Nothing
- ✓ Some Sums with Zero
- ✓ *Thoughtings:* Number Wonders[2]

Source: A lesson plan on Plato's Forms by Rob Torrington.

Philosophy: Philosophy of maths, fictionalism, Plato, Aristotle and Forms.

Doughnut: Experiments with a Hole
Alfred Archer

Starting age: 5 years

Props

- ❖ (Optional) A doughnut-shaped object such as a children's toy. Or a doughnut (could be a bit messy!).

- ❖ (Optional) A packet of Polo mints.

Alice holds a doughnut in her hand. She thinks about the hole in the middle of the doughnut. She asks herself a series of questions and performs some 'experiments'. Here are her questions and experiments for you to try.

Start Question Does the hole in the doughnut exist? Or (depending on the age of the participants) is the hole in the doughnut something or nothing?

---

2   *Thoughtings: Puzzles, Problems and Paradoxes in Poetry to Think With* by Peter Worley and Andrew Day (Independent Thinking Press, 2012).

Questions to take you further

- ❖ Is the hole part of the doughnut?
- ❖ Is the hole an object?
- ❖ Is the hole something, or is it nothing?
- ❖ **What is a hole?**
- ❖ *Experiment 1:* If you move the doughnut around, does the hole move too?
- ❖ *Experiment 2:* If you eat the doughnut, do you eat the hole?
- ❖ *Experiment 3:* Could you eat the hole without eating the doughnut?
- ❖ *Experiment 4:* If you break the doughnut in two where does the hole go?
- ❖ Can you have a *whole* hole?
- ❖ Can you have *half* a hole, or an incomplete hole?

Your Questions

- ❖
- ❖
- ❖

Works well with

- ✓ Immy's Box
- ✓ Empty
- ✓ The Sound of Silence
- ✓ A Hole Load of Nothing
- ✓ A Pageful of Nothing
- ✓ *Thoughtings:* A Disappearing Riddle
- ✓ *The If Machine:* Thinking About Nothing

Source: http://plato.stanford.edu/entries/holes/

Philosophy: The philosophy of holes, ontology, epistemology, reference, *entia representationis* ('as-if' entities, fictions).

Immy's Box

Peter Worley

Starting age: 10 years   Advanced

Immy has a box and he wants to empty it. But he wants to empty it *completely and utterly*. First he opens the box and finds bits and bobs in it such as a pencil, a rubber and some little toys.

[*If you are doing this with a class then use a real box with some bits and bobs in it.*]

He takes each thing out, one at a time. Finally he has taken all the objects that were in the box out of it. *But is it empty?*

Start Question 1   Is the box empty?

Questions to take you further

❖   Can you think of something that might be in it?

❖   Is 'empty' the same as 'nothing'?

❖   Can the box be full of nothing?

❖   Is the inside of the box inside the box?

❖   **What is emptiness?**

Immy will remove whatever you can think of that is still in the box. So, what *can* you think of? List it, or them (for example, the group might suggest finger prints, germs or atoms) and Immy will remove it, or them.

Once he has removed whatever you can think of, *is the box finally empty?* Or is there something else that is still in the box?

Keep going until you think Immy will be satisfied that it is finally completely and utterly empty. Can you do it?

Start Question 2   Will the box be able to be emptied completely and utterly?

Questions to take you further

❖   Is it even possible?

❖ Is there something that can never be removed?

❖ The definition of a *vacuum* is 'space entirely devoid of matter'. Devoid means 'completely without' and *matter* means 'physical stuff'. If you manage to achieve a *vacuum* in the box would the box be completely empty then? Or would there still be something you can't remove?

❖ What about the *space* the box is in – can Immy remove this?

❖ What would happen if Immy removed the space as well?

❖ What about the *time* the box is in – can Immy remove this?

❖ What would happen if Immy were able to remove time as well?

❖ Is the box in time?

Your Questions

❖

❖

❖

Works well with

✓ A Pageful of Nothing

✓ A Hole Load of Nothing

✓ Doughnut

✓ Empty

✓ Phil and Soph and the Ice Cream

✓ *Thoughtings:* Space, Time and Other Weird Things

✓ *The If Machine:* Thinking About Nothing

Source: Thanks to Ben Jeffreys and Claire Field for thinking of 'Kant's Box' as a way of introducing *a priori* space and time to classes.

Philosophy: Kant's *a priori* space and time.

A Hole Load of Nothing

David Birch

Starting age: 7 years

Mr and Mrs Owl had been married for many years. They lived in the hole of an oak tree in a pleasant corner of the forest. They slept during the day and, when night fell, they would leave the hole to hunt for dinner.

Because owls are animals of the night they need very large eyes to help them see. Yet poor Mrs Owl was entering her twilight years and her eyesight wasn't what it used to be; so for the past few months she had needed to wear glasses when they went out searching for food.

But one night, when Mrs Owl was getting dressed, she forgot to put on her glasses and she left the hole without them.

'Oh dear, Mr Owl,' she said. 'I've left my glasses indoors. Be a darling and fetch them for me.'

'Right now?' asked Mr Owl hesitantly.

'Well, yes. I can hardly see a thing. I'll fly into a hedgehog,' chuckled Mrs Owl.

'Um …' mumbled Mr Owl and fell silent.

'*Hoot hoot*, come on, Mr Owl, don't dither.'

'Must I go? Can't you?'

'Really! What is wrong with you?' said Mrs Owl irritably.

'I'm just a little … scared.'

'Scared? Scared of what?'

'It looks terribly dark in there,' answered Mr Owl.

'Mr Owl, are you telling me you're afraid of the dark?'

There was a pause. 'Yes.'

'Mr Owl! How careless of you. How could you possibly be afraid of the dark?'

'Please don't be cross with me,' pleaded the frightened owl.

'But it's our hole, our home. You know there are no scary things in there. What's to be afraid of?'

'The dark.'

'Come now, Mr Owl. The dark is just what happens when there's no light. It's, it's – just nothing,' Mrs Owl explained.

'Yes. Nothing. I'm scared of Nothing,' said Mr Owl flatly.

'You're scared of nothing? Brilliant, you can fetch my glasses, then. Honestly, Mr Owl, sometimes you ...'

'No, no. You don't understand. I am scared of something: I'm scared of Nothing.'

'Well that doesn't make sense, dear,' said Mrs Owl, furrowing her brow. 'You say one thing and then you say the opposite. Which is it?'

'Both! Please, Mrs Owl, listen. I can't go into the hole because it's dark and full of Nothing and that frightens me.'

'Oh now I see,' said Mrs Owl, trying to play along. 'Nothing scares you?'

'Yes!'

'So what are we arguing about?'

'Nothing.'

'Ex-actly,' said Mrs Owl raising her wings. 'My glasses are by the hat stand, I think.'

'Oh my,' sighed Mr Owl. 'I can't fetch your glasses. I can't.'

'And what is the problem?'

'Nothing.'

'Good – why must you go on and on like a parrot? You're not a parrot, you know, Mr Owl. You're an owl. Now hurry along.'

At the sound of the order, Mr Owl instinctively turned to go back into the hole – till he saw the blackness and remembered his fear. 'But, no, the dark ...'

And so the argument went on. Mr Owl kept insisting that he was scared of Nothing, and Mrs Owl kept telling him that was wonderful and ordering him to fetch her glasses. And the two owls are still sitting out there on the branch, arguing till this day, like a pair of parrots.

Start Question 1   If Mr Owl is afraid of the dark, then is he afraid of something or nothing?

Questions to take you further

❖   Is the dark nothing or something?

❖   **What is the dark?**

❖   Will Mr and Mrs Owl's argument ever end?

- ❖ Is there anything nice about the dark?

- ❖ **What is fear?**

- ❖ Why are we often afraid of the dark?

Start Question 2   If Mr Owl is afraid of Nothing then is he afraid of something or nothing?

Questions to take you further

- ❖ Is nothing something?

- ❖ Is it possible to be afraid of nothing?

- ❖ Can nothing be scarier than something?

- ❖ **What is nothing?**

Your Questions

- ❖

- ❖

- ❖

Works well with

- ✓ Immy's Box

- ✓ Empty

- ✓ Doughnut

- ✓ A Pageful of Nothing

- ✓ The Sound of Silence

- ✓ *The If Machine:* Thinking About Nothing

- ✓ *Thoughtings:* A Disappearing Riddle

Philosophy: Logic, ontology, existentialism and anxiety, Kierkegaard, Heidegger, Sartre, Tillich.

The Sound of Silence

Peter Worley

Starting age: 7 years

Philosophical exercise: Read the following song lyrics and sing the well-known tune silently in your head. Don't sing it out loud! If you are with a class then conduct them and mouth the words silently so that the class is 'silently singing' together. (If it is somebody's birthday then silently sing 'Happy Birthday' to them!)

Happy Birthday

Happy birthday to you,

Happy birthday to you,

Happy birthday dear *somebody*,

Happy birthday to you.

By Anonymous

Start Question   Have you just *heard* the song 'Happy Birthday'?

Questions to take you further

❖   **What is hearing?**

❖   **What is sound?**

❖   Can sound exist if it is only in your mind?

❖   The composer Beethoven was completely deaf towards the end of his life. Can he be said to have *heard* the pieces he composed whilst deaf?

❖   If Beethoven had been deaf his whole life would you answer differently?

❖   Do you think he could have composed tunes like 'Ode to Joy' if he had been born entirely deaf?

❖   Do you have to have heard sound to imagine sound?

❖   The deaf musician Evelyn Glennie feels music by its vibrations. Can she hear music in this way?

Your Questions

❖

❖

❖

Works well with

✓　'Music To My Ears!'

✓　Green Ideas

✓　Said and Unsaid

✓　The Piano Music

✓　*Thoughtings:* Between My Ears

✓　*The If Machine:* Thinking About Nothing

Source: This was inspired by 7-year-old Elena who said 'the music I hear in my head' when the class was asked to think of more examples of things they might find in their head that are not physical such as 'thoughts' rather than 'brain'. (This discussion was conducted around the *Thoughting*: Between My Ears.)

Philosophy: The phenomenology of sound, the ontology of sound/music.

A Heap of Exercises?
Peter Worley

Starting age: 7 years

Exercise 1

1.　Make a heap of something such as books, pencils, beads, etc.

2.　Now take one of whatever-it-is away. Is it still a heap?

3.　Take another away. Is it still a heap?

4.　Keep going until you think it is no longer a heap.

Start Question 1   When is it no longer a heap? And why?

Exercise 2

1.   Put one book, pencil, bead, etc. on the floor. Is it a heap?

2.   Put another of whatever-it-is on the floor with the other one. Is it a heap now?

3.   Put another one on the others. Is it a heap now?

4.   Keep going until you think you've got a heap.

Start Question 2   When will it become a heap? And why?

Questions to take you further

❖   **What is a heap?**

❖   At what point does a heap become a heap?

❖   At what point does a heap cease to be a heap?

❖   Can this puzzle be solved?

❖   When is it true that a heap is a heap and when is it false that a heap is a heap?

❖   Can it be neither true nor false?

❖   Can it be both true and false?

❖   Are the exercises on this page a heap of exercises?

Extension activity 1

1.   Place a piece of A4 paper in front of you horizontally.

2.   Draw a picture of a baby on the left hand side of the paper and then a picture of a child on the right hand side.

3.   Draw a horizontal line between the baby and the child.

4.   Place an X on the line where you think the baby becomes a child. Can you do it?

Extension activity 2

1. Start whispering.

2. Imagine that someone is turning you up as if they had a remote control with a volume switch that controls you.

3. Gradually get louder until your whisper has turned into a scream.

Start Question 3   When exactly does a whisper become a scream?

Extension activity 3

Start Question 4   Where is the edge of a cloud?

Questions to take you further

❖   What is a cloud made of?

❖   How would you find the edge?

❖   How would you know when you have found the edge of a cloud?

❖   When a cloud of steam comes out of a kettle where is the edge of the cloud of steam? (*Important*: Be very careful around steam from a kettle!)

❖   Does a cloud have an edge?

❖   When a cloud rains where does the cloud end and the rain begin?

❖   Is water or ice the same thing as a cloud?

Your Questions

❖

❖

❖

Works well with

✓   Tralse

✓   Phil and Soph and the Three-Legged Race

✓   The Txt Book

✓   Not Half the Man He Used To Be

✓   Zeno's Parting Shot

Source: The Ancient Greek Sorites Paradox (*sorites* is Ancient Greek for 'heap'); thanks to David Birch for the extension activities and 11-year-old Clarissa for the question 'Where is the edge of a cloud?'

Philosophy: Vagueness, bivalence.

Across the River and Into the Trees
Angie Hobbs

Starting age: 9 years

The day after her ninth birthday party, Lucy felt that the celebrations should continue. 'It's still my birth week,' she pointed out. As it was a beautiful warm Sunday in May, her mother suggested she invite two or three friends over, and that they would all prepare a picnic and take it to a bluebell wood nearby.

So they packed up a basket with pizza slices and chocolate cakes and strawberries and set off across the fields towards the bluebell wood. Just before they reached the wood, they had to cross a small river by an old wooden bridge, the water bubbling over smooth white stones and sparkling in the sun. They stopped for a few minutes to throw twigs into the river, to see whose stick would emerge first from under the bridge. Lucy (who was wearing boots) sat on the bridge and dipped a foot in the river, watching it swirl around her boots.

They ate their picnic beneath a huge, gnarled old oak tree, and then climbed the tree and laid a trail through the wood. Then they lay down and played games on their phones, the mother protesting. But they took no notice of her because they were happy.

Finally, they packed up the basket and returned home, crossing over the bridge again. All their sticks had long vanished, apart from one, which was still stuck in some weed. Around the stuck twig, the water eddied and swirled.

Start Question 1   When they walk over the bridge, are they crossing the same river? If so, why? If not, why not?

The following year Lucy asked to repeat the picnic trip. This time they went after school, on the Monday. They went over the bridge (Lucy dangling her foot in the water again), and saw that part of the bank had crumbled away, probably in a recent storm. They ate under the oak tree and played with their new phone apps amongst the bluebells. The mother had given up protesting and everyone was happy. They returned home, stopping on the bridge to throw twigs into the water. The mother's twig emerged first.

Start Question 2   One year on, are they crossing the same river? If so, why? If not, why not?

Questions to take you further

❖   If you think it is the same river, then what makes it the same river?

❖   If you think it isn't the same river, then why (and how) do we still call it 'the river'?

❖   Why (and how) do we still give it the same name?

❖   How can we use stable words for unstable objects?

❖   Is the oak tree under which they picnic the same oak tree?

❖   Is Lucy the same person at 10 as she was at 9?

❖   If everything is always changing in at least some respect, then what (if anything) allows it to be the same thing?

❖   If everything is always changing, then how do identities – of a river, an oak tree, a girl – form in the first place? Perhaps there is just a swirl of change and no separate things?

❖   Does it make a difference how fast or slow the pace of change is?

❖   Does it make a difference if things are simply *liable* to change, rather than actually changing all the time?

❖   **What is change?**

Questions to take you even further

❖   This story is based on a paradox of the ancient Greek philosopher Heraclitus, who said that you couldn't step into the same river twice, because different waters were always flowing. His disciple Cratylus said that you couldn't step into the same river even *once*! In a world of extreme flux, identities cannot even form. We cannot, strictly speaking, talk of a 'river' at all.

❖   Do you agree with Cratylus?

❖ Can anyone agree with Cratylus using words? Or is he giving us a picture of the world in which language cannot exist? (Cratylus apparently gave up answering questions, and just sat there silently.)

Your Questions

❖

❖

❖

Works well with

✓ Identity Parade

✓ 'Personal Identity' section

✓ Pencil Person Meets Pencil Person!

✓ *The If Machine:* The Ship of Theseus

✓ *Thoughtings:* Flow

Source: The Pre-Socratic philosopher Heraclitus and his pupil Cratylus.

Philosophy: Identity, change/flux.

Dis-ingenious
Peter Worley

Starting age: 10 years   Advanced

Ali had heard that if you rub magic lamps they release genies, and he had also heard that genies grant wishes to those who free them from the lamp.

Ali had been rubbing lamps for three weeks now, almost non-stop. He was very tired and bored and was about to give up when suddenly the lamp he had been rubbing started to glow. He dropped it with surprise, as he had long since given up thinking that such lamps existed. A blue smoke rose out of the lamp's spout and it was not long before he was looking at a genie sitting on top of a strange cloud that had formed above the lamp.

'I am the genie of the lamp,' said the genie in a booming, echoey voice, 'and I am the most *powerful* genie that you will ever have met.'

'Well, *yeah* … because you're the *only* genie I've ever met,' replied Ali facetiously.

'But even if you had met a thousand genies I would be *the most powerful*,' the genie continued to boast, 'because I am what's called "The Ingenious Genie of Omnipotence", which – by the way – means "all-powerful"…'

In fact, Ali had to listen to almost half an hour of how powerful the 'all-powerful' genie *powerfully* was and by the time the genie got around to telling him that he would grant wishes to whomever had released him, Ali was quite bored and irritated at all the boasting. He was also disappointed to discover that this genie would only grant *two* wishes when Ali had heard that genies grant *three*!

The genie came to the end of his long speech and then said, 'So, I will grant you two wishes. You can wish for anything you want, and remember: nothing is impossible for The Ingenious Genie of Omnipotence!'

Due to his irritation at the excessive boasting, Ali came up with his own ingenious wishes that he knew would shut up the genie once and for all. *Genius!* he thought to himself.

'I wish …' said Ali with a mischievous sparkle in his voice, 'for you to create a mountain you cannot move.'

'Nothing's impossible for The Ingenious Genie of Omnipotence,' said the genie and he took his wish-granting pose. In an instant there was a huge mountain that stood imperiously before them both.

'Are you sure you can't move it?' said Ali.

'Yep!' assured the genie, though Ali noticed that he didn't seem to have tried. 'Now for your second wish,' urged the genie impatiently.

'Okay. For my second wish I wish …' – his eyes sparkled even more – 'that you move the mountain you just created!'

'But … but …' the genie looked confused.

'That should teach you not to be so boastful about something you're not!' said Ali. But then Ali realised that he had wasted his wishes ingeniously outwitting the genie and was left with no wishes for himself. Oh dear! Silly Ali.

Start Question   If he can do anything, will it be possible for the all-powerful genie to grant both wishes? Here they are:

Wish 1: To create a mountain that the genie cannot move.

Wish 2: To move the mountain that the genie just created.

Questions to take you further

❖ Is nothing impossible for the genie?

❖ Is nothing impossible?

❖ What does Ali mean when he says to the genie that he shouldn't boast about something he's not? What is it that he's not?

❖ Has Ali thought of something that is impossible for the genie?

❖ Has Ali proved that the genie was not omnipotent after all?

❖ Can you think of something that is definitely impossible?

❖ What would happen if the genie was able to grant the wish?

❖ What would happen if the genie was unable to grant the wish?

❖ 'For nothing is impossible with God' (Luke 1:37). Discuss.

Your Questions

❖

❖

❖

Works well with

✓ 'Time' section

✓ Some Sums with Zero

✓ Itselfish

✓ Tralse

✓ Just Testing!

✓ *Thoughtings:* Impossibling and More Impossiblings …

Source: Ibn Rushd (known in the west as Averroes) and the paradox of omnipotence.

Philosophy: Philosophy of religion, logical possibility.

Just Testing!
Peter Worley

Starting age: 9 years   *Advanced*

Imagine that before God had created anything at all he decided, first of all, to create just one thing. He decided to create a planet, just to test out his creation skills. So he did: *kazoom!*

Start Question 1   Is the planet that God has created big?

Questions to take you further

❖   How big is big?

❖   What determines something's size?

❖   What is size?

❖   Can something be big in itself?

❖   Does size depend on comparison?

❖   If there's nothing to compare the planet to then what size would it be?

❖   What size would God be?

❖   Is big big?

❖   Is there anything that's just big and never small?

Your Questions

❖

❖

❖

Works well with

✓   Dis-ingenious

✓   The 2 Square

✓   What Zeus Does When He's Bored

✓   *The If Machine:* The Shadow of the Pyramid

✓ *Thoughtings:* Number Wonders

Source: This thought experiment was introduced in a discussion with some 11-year-olds about whether numbers are invented or discovered.

Philosophy: Relational concepts, the nature of number.

A Pageful of Nothing
Sophia Nikolidaki

Big Question

Choose a question, any question from this page. Can you answer it? (Alternatively, you could choose a number randomly between 1 and 21 and then try to answer the question.)

Start Questions

1. Can something be full of nothing?
2. Does nothing exist?
3. Is there a place of nothing?
4. Can you ever really mean that 'you are doing nothing'?
5. What does 'nothing' mean?
6. Is there anything that could replace nothing?
7. Is nothing just a word? In that case can we insist that 'there is nothing there'?
8. Can a sound ever fade into nothing?
9. Is zero nothing?
10. Can you draw nothing?
11. Can nothing ever be useful?
12. Why do we use the word nothing to praise something? (e.g. How does the sentence 'there is nothing better than a good cup of tea' make sense?)
13. Can somebody/something be nothing?
14. Can you feel/think/do nothing?
15. Do 'being unimportant' and 'being nothing' mean the same thing?

16. What was before nothing?

17. What comes after nothing?

18. Is a hallucination a form of nothing?

19. Can you hide nothing(ness)?

20. Is hiding fading into nothing?

21. Is there anything less than nothing?

Are there any more *nothing-questions*? Can you continue to fill the page?

Your Questions

❖

❖

❖

Works well with

✓ Immy's Box

✓ A Hole Load of Nothing

✓ Doughnut

✓ Empty

✓ *The If Machine:* Thinking About Nothing

✓ *Thoughtings:* A Disappearing Riddle, Where's Mr Nobody?

Philosophy: The Pre-Socratic philosopher Parmenides and nothingness, Sartre, Heidegger.

BURIDAN's Asteroid
Robert Torrington

Starting age: 9 years

For 3,141 years the Benevolent Universal Research, Identification, Definition and Navigation computer (BURIDAN, for short) had guided what remained of the human race through space in its search for a new world. Its advanced mathematics, faultless reasoning and perfect logic had kept the human race safe for millennia.

But one day, BURIDAN stopped the ship.

Exactly 100 light-years to the left was an asteroid so large that it would be suitable for human life. But exactly 100 light-years to the right was a second asteroid identical to the first. Each one was the same shape and the same size. Each was the same distance away. They were identical. In fact, if they hadn't been in two different places, you would have thought they were the same object. With no difference between the choices, and it being impossible to go in both directions at once, BURIDAN had no reason to choose one or the other. So the ship stopped.

The crew asked BURIDAN why the ship had stopped, and were told exactly what had happened.

'Just choose one, BURIDAN,' they requested.

'How will I choose?' BURIDAN replied.

'It doesn't matter – just pick one, left or right.'

'My programming permits me only to act in accordance with reason. I am free only to do what is logical. There is no reason to choose one or the other. I would be acting illogically if I choose either.'

'But it's ridiculous to sit here and do nothing. If you don't move eventually, we'll be stuck here forever.'

'Nevertheless, there is no logical way to decide.'

Start Question   Is there a logical way to decide?

Questions to take you further (according to themes)

Logic and reason

❖   What is acting logically?

❖   **What is logic?**

❖   **What is reason?**

❖   Was BURIDAN right to stop?

❖   How should BURIDAN decide what to do?

❖   Do we think like BURIDAN?

❖   Are we logical, illogical or non-logical (what's the difference between illogical and non-logical?)?

- ❖ Which would you rather be: logical or illogical?
- ❖ How important is being logical?

Freedom and thought

- ❖ BURIDAN can only do what is logical; is BURIDAN free?
- ❖ Are you free if you only do what is logical?
- ❖ When are you free?
- ❖ Are we free?
- ❖ **What is freedom?**

Identity and physics

- ❖ Is it possible for two things to be identical?
- ❖ **What does 'identical' mean?**
- ❖ Can one thing be in two places at once?
- ❖ Are some twins identical?
- ❖ Is '1 + 1' identical to '2'?
- ❖ Are you identical to you?

Your Questions

- ❖
- ❖
- ❖

Works well with

Freedom and logic:

- ✓ Other entries in the 'Freedom' section
- ✓ Charlie's Choice
- ✓ Negative Nelly
- ✓ The Accidental Confession
- ✓ Trying to Forget
- ✓ The Traffic Light Boy (3)
- ✓ *Thoughtings:* Minds and Brains and Are You Free?
- ✓ *The If Machine:* The Lie, The Frog and the Scorpion

Identity:

- ✓ Pencil Person Meets Pencil Person!
- ✓ The Copying Machine
- ✓ Identity Parade (3): Body Copy
- ✓ Across the River and Into the Trees
- ✓ *The If Machine:* The Ship of Theseus, The Rebuild
- ✓ *Thoughtings:* Flow

Source: The story of Buridan's ass, in which a donkey was unable to choose between two clumps of grass at equal distance from the donkey. The donkey starved to death! The story was invented to make fun of Jean Buridan's philosophy of free will.

Philosophy: Buridan's ass, logic, Leibniz and 'Leibniz's Law', identity, the identity of indiscernibles.

Phil and Soph and the Ice Cream
Philip Cowell

Starting age: 5 years

Sitting out the back, in the last of the sun, at the end of another long day of play, Phil and Soph were enjoying some quiet time with bowls of ice cream. 'This is so delicious!' Phil said, as he took a big scoop and lifted it to his mouth. Soph had a full spoonful herself. 'I know!' she said. 'I would love to have a chocolate ice cream *that's blue!*'

Phil thought for a second and then said, 'I would like to try an *ice-cream-flavoured* ice cream.'

Sensing a competition, and after having had another mouthful of delicious ice cream, Soph said, 'I want an ice cream with *no flavour!*'

Start Questions

1. What would a blue chocolate ice cream taste of?

2.   What would an *ice-cream-flavoured* ice cream taste of?

3.   Would it be possible to have an ice cream with *no flavour*? (Is there *any* kind of food or drink with no flavour?)

Phil looked even more thoughtful now, and a bit of thinking time later he said, 'I wonder if there's such a thing as something with no taste, no smell, no colour, no sound and no feel.'

They both fell into silence as they thought about Phil's question whilst slurpily finishing off their ice cream.

Start Question 4   Can you think of something (not just food but *anything*) with no taste, no smell, no colour, no sound and no feel?

[*Try to answer Start Question 4 before considering the suggestions below.*]

What about:

1.   Water?

2.   Air?

3.   Words?

4.   Emotions (such as love, anger, etc.)?

5.   Thoughts?

6.   Nothing (as in 'nothingness')? Question: Is nothing something? Can you think of anything else?

Questions to take you further

❖   Why does anything taste of anything?

❖   Does ice cream have colour?

❖   Could you have an ice cream that has no colour?

❖   Could you have an ice cream that has no colour, no taste, no sound and no feel?

❖   Pretend you're Phil and you want to have an ice cream as philosophically interesting as Soph's. What would your 'philosophy ice cream' be?

Your Questions

❖

❖

❖

Works well with

✓   Other Phil and Soph stories

✓   Who's the Philosopher?

✓   Bat-Girl

✓   Rose-Tinted Speculations

✓   More Colour Conundrums

✓   The Duck and Rabbit

Philosophy: The philosophy of colour and taste, qualia, the nature of thinking, paradoxes.

The Philosophical Adventures of Pencil Person

These sessions may well blend into each other as there is a good deal of overlap between the ideas. For instance, if the discussion in 'Introducing Pencil Person' turns towards the distinction between *types* and *individual things* then run 'Pencil Person Meets Pencil Person!' to help focus this.

Introducing Pencil Person
Peter Worley

Starting age: 7 years

Props: Four (or eight) pencils, a book, a ball (or any objects that can function as a 'head' and a 'body') – Pencil Person should have pencils, though, to be 'Pencil Person'.

Assembly instructions: Take four (or eight) pencils, a book and a ball. Place the book on the floor so that the book is facing you the right way up. Now place the pencils at the corners of the book to make arms and legs. Finally, place the ball at the top to make a head.

(For younger ones, before, during or after assembling Pencil Person, read or recite the poem 'Pencil Person').

Thoughting: **Pencil Person**

I'm a person all made of pencils

Well, maybe not quite *all*

I've pencils for arms and legs

A book for a body

And my head is a ball.

So, here's a question for you

To get you chewing *your* pencils:

How many things am I?

Am I *One* or *Many*?

Though clearly made of utensils.

Start Question   How many things are there here (point to the assembled Pencil Person on the floor)?

Questions to take you further

❖   Is Pencil Person one thing?

❖   Is Pencil Person many things? If so, how many?

❖   Is Pencil Person a person?

❖   How many different answers can you give to the Start Question above?

❖   Is there one thing *and* many things? At the *same time*?

❖   **What is a 'thing'?**

❖   **What is an 'object'?**

❖   Do the parts need to be connected to be one thing?

❖   Does it just depend on how we see it?

❖ Can someone be wrong about how many things there are?

❖ The philosopher Aristotle said, 'The whole is different from the sum of its parts.' What do you think he meant by this?

Your Questions

❖

❖

❖

Works well with

✓ Just Testing!

✓ The 2 Square

✓ Some Sums with Zero

✓ A Knife Idea

✓ Disappearing Pencil Person

✓ Pencil Person Meets Pencil Person!

✓ How Many Dogs?

✓ A Heap of Exercises?

✓ *Thoughtings:* Number Wonders

Source and Philosophy: Mereology, Aristotle and the problem of one-over-many.

Disappearing Pencil Person
Peter Worley

Starting age: 9 years

Note to teacher: If running this with a class you could perform the trick similarly to the magician rather than read the story.

The Magician says that he is going to make Pencil Person disappear: 'No – not just *disappear*,' says the Magician, 'I'm going to make Pencil Person *no longer exist*!' There is a collective intake of breath from the audience.

A drum begins to roll. The lights dim. The excitement of the audience can be felt by everyone. Then the Magician suddenly puts Pencil Person in a cloth bag and, in clear sight of the entire audience, he takes the bag out of the room and places it on the floor outside. He then comes back into the room, closes the door, rushes back onto the stage and says – whilst doing 'jazzy hands' – 'T'dah! *Pencil Person no longer exists*!'

After a shocked silence someone in the audience says, rather tentatively, 'But you just put Pencil Person in a bag then placed him on the floor outside the room.'

'Yeah, so?' replies the Magician to his disappointed audience.

'Well, Pencil Person *does* still exist, he's just *not in the room any more*,' says the disgruntled audience member.

The Magician begins to look irritated and he turns to the objector and says indignantly, 'You tell me then: how else can you make Pencil Person no longer exist?'

Start Question 1   What can be done to make Pencil Person no longer exist?

Questions to take you further

❖   Would burning or blowing up the pencils, the book and the ball do the trick?

❖   Is it possible to make something *no longer exist*?

❖   Can something exist in our memories?

❖   If something has existed at one time does that mean it will exist for all time, whatever happens to it?

❖   What if something *doesn't exist yet*? Does it not exist?

❖   Can you make something exist that doesn't exist now? If so, what?

After a while of arguing about whether Pencil Person still exists or not, the Magician has an idea. He leaps to his feet and brings the bag back into the room. He removes all the pencils, the book and the ball from the bag and proceeds to place each of the pencils in different people's pencil-cases that are in different parts of the room. He puts the book on a bookshelf among many other books and the ball into a box full of different kinds of balls.

'There!' he says, 'Now *surely* Pencil Person no longer exists!'

Start Question 2   Has the Magician done it? Has he made Pencil Person no longer exist?

Questions to take you further

❖   How do something's parts have to have been arranged for it to exist?

❖   If the parts still exist, does that mean that the thing the parts made up still exists?

❖   **What does 'exist' mean?**

❖   Is the man a magician?

❖   If you were to make a paper aeroplane, fly it across the room and then unfold it again, would the paper aeroplane still exist? Try it.

Your Questions

❖

❖

❖

Works well with

✓   A Knife Idea

✓   Doughnut

✓   A Heap of Exercises?

✓   'Personal Identity' section

✓   Introducing Pencil Person

✓   Pencil Person Meets Pencil Person!

✓   The Time Diet

✓   *The If Machine:* The Chair, Get Stuffed, To the Edge of Forever

✓   *Thoughtings:* Space, Time and Other Weird Things

Source: Ibn Sina (Avicenna) and necessary and contingent existence – inspired by part of his 'proof' for the existence of God.

Philosophy: Ontology, existence, concept of a thing.

Pencil Person Meets Pencil Person!

Roger Sutcliffe

Starting age: 5 years

Follow the instructions on pages 41–42 to construct *two* Pencil Persons, next to each other, so that they appear identical.

Start Question   Are they the same or different?

Questions to take you further

❖   Are they the same *sort* of thing?

❖   How many different ways can they be different?

❖   Why, if they are different in so many ways, do people agree that they are, after all, the same sort of thing?

❖   Can you look around and identify two things that are different *sorts* of things, but are 'the same' in at least one way?

❖   Can different things be the same in any way? If so, how?

❖   What makes something the same?

❖   What exactly does 'same' mean? What exactly does 'different' mean?

Your Questions

❖

❖

❖

Works well with

✓   Introducing Pencil Person

✓   Disappearing Pencil Person

✓   'Personal Identity' section

✓   How Many Dogs?

✓   The Duck and Rabbit

- ✓ Across the River and Into the Trees
- ✓ Pinka and Arwin Go Forth: Making Up Their Minds
- ✓ *The If Machine:* Yous On Another Planet, Can You Step in the Same River Twice?

Philosophy: Identity, type and token identity, universals and particulars, Plato and Forms.

Metaphysics: Time

Thoughting: A Birthday Surprise!

Peter Worley

Starting age: 7 years

I can travel backwards
Or keep going straight
I can go sideways;
Left or right.

But can I go *through* time
Forwards or backwards;
Do you think
that I might?

I wish I could
Coz then I would
Say 'Hello!' to my mummy

But for a birthday surprise
I would say 'Hello!'
just *before*
I popped out from her tummy!

By You (see A Poem By You? on page 58 to see how)

Start Question   Would it be possible, with a time machine, to travel to a time before you were born?

Questions to take you further

❖   Do you think we could travel through time like we travel through space, forwards and backwards, left and right?

❖   What would it be like to travel left or right through time? Do you think it would be possible?

❖   Would travelling to a time before you were born lead to a contradiction (i.e. that it is both true *and* false that you have not yet been born)?

❖   Will a time machine one day be built or would a time machine be impossible?

❖   Would it be possible, with a time machine, to meet yourself?

❖   If you did meet yourself when you were younger, what might you say to your younger self? Would you have any advice?

Your Questions

❖

❖

❖

Works well with

✓   A Poem By You?

✓   Itselfish

✓   The Non-Existent Hero

✓   The Girl from Yesterday

✓   *Thoughtings:* Space, Time and Other Weird Things

Source and Philosophy: The philosophy of time travel, David Lewis' paper 'The Paradoxes of Time Travel'.

The Time Diet

Peter Cave

Starting age: 10 Years   *Advanced*

Start Question 1   (to think about before reading the story): Do the past and future exist?

Samantha says, 'The past does not exist – after all, it is past, well past. It no longer exists. You can only have memories of it.'

Stanley says, 'The future does not exist – after all, it is future, so very future. It is not yet in existence. You can only guess what will happen.'

Sue says, 'Well, at least the present exists – and I live in the present. So that is all right.'

'Hold on,' say Samantha and Stanley, 'how long in time is the present? If it has any length – one hour, one minute, one second – then some of it must be in the past or in the future. So, how long is *now*?'

Start Question 2   How long is *now*?

Questions to take you further

❖   What is *now*?

❖   Where is *now*?

❖   Is *now* always moving or is *now* still?

'That's okay,' replies Sue, but now feeling very squeezed by time, getting thinner and thinner in time. 'The present is an instant, the line between past and future.'

'Ah hah,' chorus Samantha and Stanley. 'The future does not exist; the past does not exist. So, the present is just a line between things that do not exist. But that is impossible. How can there be a line, a boundary, a fence, between what does not exist?'

Sue feels herself getting thinner and thinner at this thought – so thin that she vanishes into nothing.

Start Question 1   (again): Do the past and future exist – as well as the present?

Questions to take you further

❖ What reasons can you give for why the past, the present and the future don't exist?

❖ Does the past exist, but not the future?

❖ How long does the present – does *now* – last?

❖ If the past does not exist, how can you have a memory of it?

❖ What is time like? How does it move? What is its shape? What does it do?

Your Questions

❖

❖

❖

Works well with

✓ Other entries from the 'Time' section (particularly Time-Stretching, The Time-Freezing Machine, The Time Machine, The Girl from Yesterday)

✓ Empty

✓ *Thoughtings:* From Me To You and Space, Time and Other Weird Things, especially Petering

Philosophy: Philosophy of time, St Augustine and presentism, McTaggart and static and dynamic time.

Empty
Peter Worley

Starting age: 7 years

Imagine an emptiness. There's nothing in the emptiness, just … emptiness!

Start Question 1   Is there *time* in the emptiness?

Questions to take you further

❖ If nothing happens in the emptiness, is there time?

❖ If nothing changes in the emptiness, is there time?

❖ **What is time?**

❖ **What is change?**

❖ Is time something different from change?

❖ The philosopher Aristotle thought that 'time is the measurement of change'. Do you agree with him? If no change happens in the empty space, then would Aristotle think that there is time or not?

Start Question 2   Is there *space* in the emptiness?

Questions to take you further

❖ If there is nothing *in* space, then is there space?

❖ **What is space?**

❖ What would the world be like if there wasn't any space?

❖ The scientist Isaac Newton thought that there *would* be space in emptiness because space would be needed if there was something to put in it. The philosopher Gottfried Leibniz thought that there *wouldn't* be any space in emptiness because there is only space when there is something for there to be a space between. Who do you agree with and why?

❖ The philosopher Immanuel Kant thought that there would only be time and space if there was someone to *think of them*. Do you agree or disagree?

Your Questions

❖

❖

❖

Works well with

✓ The Time Diet

✓ Immy's Box

✓ Doughnut

✓ A Hole Load of Nothing

✓ A Pageful of Nothing

✓   *The If Machine:* Thinking About Nothing

✓   *Thoughtings:* Space, Time and Other Weird Things, especially Space

Source and Philosophy: Aristotle on time, Newton and absolute space, Leibniz and relational space, Kant and *a priori* space and time, Sydney Shoemaker's 'Time Without Change'.

Superbaby Time!
Peter Worley

Starting age: 7 years

Superbaby is a superhero with super-powers but with the mind of a child. One day Superbaby is playing a computer game and he super-loses. He gets super-angry and wants to play again. Instead of just pressing 'restart game' on the controls he decides that he wants to make time go super-backwards so that he can play the game again but this time not super-lose! He flies up to the very top of Mount Everest, grabs hold of the mountain and uses his supreme super-strength to make the Earth revolve in the opposite direction so that he can make time go in the opposite direction too.

Start Question   If the world were spun in the opposite direction would this make time go backwards?

Questions to take you further

❖   Does time move?

❖   Does the earth's movement cause the movement of time?

❖   What do you think makes time move?

❖   What do you think would happen if the world suddenly spun the other way?

❖   Clearly Superbaby has super-strength but does Superbaby have super-reasoning skills as well? Is Superbaby super-right or super-wrong when he reasons that if the world spins backwards, time will go backwards?

Your Questions

❖

❖

❖

Works well with

✓ Empty

✓ The Telly-Scope

✓ The Time-Freezing Machine

✓ Time-Stretching

✓ The Big Time Experiment

✓ The Time Machine

✓ *Thoughtings:* Space, Time and Other Weird Things

Source: The film *Superman* directed by Richard Donner.

Philosophy: The direction of time.

The Telly-Scope
Peter Worley

Starting age: 11 years

Lilly loves to watch her favourite soap opera *The Zargonians*. She laughs and cries with the characters as she sees their lives unfold. Sometimes it is boring and some-times it is exciting and sometimes it is very sad. But Lilly lives in a time when soap operas are very different from how they were in your time – a time in the far future from you. They don't use actors because they don't need to. What they do is point a very powerful telescope at a distant planet and they simply watch the lives of the inhabitants of the planet in their homes on what they call a 'Telly-Scope'. Viewers learn the languages and study Zargonian culture at school. It is much more than a soap opera but people watch it and enjoy it like one.

When one of the main characters, a Zargonian boy called Noob, is very sad because of something that happens in his family, Lilly wants to contact him to comfort him. She asks her mum, 'Can I contact the Zargonians? After all, they are real aren't they?'

Her mother looks at her and says, 'Yes, they are real … in a manner of speaking …' She has a concerned expression on her face.

'What is it, mummy?' says Lilly.

'There's something I need to tell you but I'm not sure how to explain it.'

'Tell me what?' asks Lilly.

'Well,' begins her mother, 'if you look at the sun you actually see the sun, not as it is now, but as it was eight minutes ago.'

'That's weird. But how?' asks her daughter.

'It's because light travels at a certain speed. It's very fast, travelling at 299,792,458 metres per second. But the sun is so far away that it takes light travelling at that speed *eight minutes* to get here. That's why we see the sun as it was eight minutes ago.'

Lilly thinks for a moment then says, 'So if I want to see the sun as it is right now I would have to wait for eight minutes?'

'That's exactly right,' says her mother. 'We say that the sun is "eight light-minutes away" because it takes the light from the sun eight minutes to get here,' her mother finishes. Then she adds, 'But remember, Lilly: *you must never look at the sun directly – it could blind you!*'

'But what's that got to do with *The Zargonians*?' asks Lilly, not really listening to her mum's warning.

'The thing is, Lilly: Zargonia is over *ten million light-years away*.'

'So, let me see …' says Lilly thoughtfully as she looks up and holds her chin, 'that means …

[*Before reading on: what do you think it means?*]

… that if "eight light-minutes" means that it takes light eight minutes to reach Earth then "ten million light-years" must mean …' – Lilly's face darkens as she realises what it means – '… that it takes light *ten million years* to reach Earth. But that must mean that what I watch on the Telly-Scope isn't happening now at all.'

'That's right Lilly,' says her mother, trying to reassure her.

'It must have happened ten million years ago,' says Lilly. 'When I watch my favourite soap opera I'm peering into history.'

'I suppose you're right,' says her mother, slightly startled. She hasn't thought of it like that before.

Lilly is quiet and thoughtful for a few days. She feels very sad, as if there has been a death in the family, even though the people in *The Zargonians* have died millions of years ago. But then she has an idea that brightens her mood. It occurs to her that when she watches *The Zargonians* she travels through time using the miracle of the speed of light … and the Telly-Scope.

Start Question   Is watching *The Zargonians* a form of time travel?

Questions to take you further

❖   Are you time travelling every time you look at the sun (though, remember it is dangerous to look at the sun directly!)?

❖   Some stars are so far away that we are still seeing their light even though they no longer exist. When you look at old, dead stars, is that time travel?

❖   If it is not time travel, are you at least 'peering into the past' as Lilly said?

❖   Is Lilly right to feel sad about her discovery that the Zargonians lived a very long time ago?

❖   Will it change the way she watches *The Zargonians?*

Your Questions

❖

❖

❖

Works well with

✓   Superbaby Time!

✓   Empty

✓   The Time-Freezing Machine

✓   Time-Stretching

✓   The Big Time Experiment

✓   The Time Machine

✓   *Thoughtings:* Time, Space and Other Weird Things, particularly Light from Stars

Source: Einstein's theory of relativity.

Philosophy: The philosophy of time travel.

A Poem By You?

Peter Worley

Starting age: 10 years

One day, whilst you are minding your own business watching the TV in your bedroom, something very strange happens. There is a weird distortion in the air in the middle of the room. Then, through the distortion steps a person. It appears to be some kind of doorway. Odd as it may seem, it's nothing compared to who it turns out the person is. For the person is you.

They explain that they are from the future. You are being visited by a *future you*. They hand you a piece of paper. On it is a poem called 'The Birthday Surprise'. Then they say, 'You must copy this into your own handwriting so that you can win a poetry competition. If you do, then you'll be a famous poet when you grow up … like me!'

'But where did *you* get it from?' you ask your visitor.

'I got it from the book that published the winning entries from the competition. You're in loads of poetry books in the future,' the other you replies.

'But where did *they* get it from?' you ask.

'They got it from you, of course!' explains the future you. 'It's your poem after all. Or it *will be* if you enter the competition. Sorry, I've got to go before the time portal closes again!'

The future *you* steps back through the doorway – or time portal, as they called it – and then the distortion fades leaving you dumbfounded at what has just happened to you. As instructed by … *you*, you sit down, take out a piece of paper and quickly copy the poem down in your own handwriting:

The Birthday Surprise

I can travel backwards

Or keep going straight

I can go sideways;
Left or right.

But can I go *through* time
Forwards or backwards;
Do you think
that I might?

I wish I could
Coz then I would
Say 'Hello!' to my mummy

But for a birthday surprise
I would say 'Hello!'
just *before*
I popped out from her tummy!

Start Question   Who originally created the poem 'The Birthday Surprise'?

Questions to take you further

❖   Has anyone created the poem?

❖   Is it possible for the poem to have come from nowhere?

❖ Does this story lead to a paradox (an impossible situation) or do you think it could make sense?

❖ Does this scenario prove that time travel is not possible?

❖ If not, then how would time travel make sense of situations like this one?

❖ If you win the competition, would you have cheated?

❖ Who should win the competition?

Your Questions

❖

❖

❖

Will work with

✓ The Birthday Surprise

✓ The Non-Existent Hero

✓ The Butterfly Effect

✓ The Girl from Yesterday

✓ Philosophical Poetry

✓ *Thoughtings:* Archaeology and Anthology of Unwritten Poems

Source: Short story 'The Muse' by Anthony Burgess.

Philosophy: The philosophy of time travel, David Lewis' paper 'The Paradoxes of Time Travel'.

The Time-Freezing Machine
Peter Worley

Starting age: 7 years   *Advanced*

Professor Timothy Tempo has created a time-freezing machine. He takes his machine into a school to demonstrate it. He explains to the children that he can freeze time with his new machine. He turns to the class and asks them to give him a length of time for him to programme into the machine. The first child to speak says, 'Five minutes?'

'Is anyone here feeling more adventurous than that?' says the Professor.

Another hand goes up. 'An hour,' says an unsure voice.

More hands go up.

'A day.'

'A week.'

'A year.'

'Ten years!'

'A hundred years!'

'A million years!'

'Okay,' says the Professor. 'Now we're ready to try the machine. Let's freeze time for *one million years.*'

Some of the children look a little worried. He inputs the correct data into his time-freezing machine. 'When I press the red button on my machine,' explains the Professor, 'time will freeze for *one million years.*'

Some of the children hold each other's hands. The Professor leans forward and presses the red button …

Start Question 1   What do you think will happen?

Questions to take you further

❖   If time freezes for one million years, how would the children know if it has happened?

❖   Will they know?

❖   Will anything be different?

❖   Would they be any older?

Once his finger releases the button, Professor Tempo looks up and smiles to his audience. 'So, how did that feel?' The crowd look more than a little confused. No one says a word. The only sound is the clock ticking on the wall. Then, a girl in the audience bravely raises her hand. 'But, Professor, nothing has happened … everything is the same. Time has just kept on going.'

'No it hasn't,' the Professor replies. 'It's been stopped still for one million years.'

'But I can't tell any difference!' exclaims the girl, frustrated.

'Well,' muses Professor Tempo. 'How would you tell?'

Start Question 2   How would you tell if time has stopped?

Questions to take you further

❖   How do we know time isn't stopping all the time?

❖   If nothing changes, could you still think?

❖   **What is time?**

❖   What would have happened to the world outside the classroom?

❖   Does the idea of a time-freezing machine make sense?

Your Questions

❖

❖

❖

Works well with

✓   Empty

✓   Superbaby Time!

✓   Time-Stretching

✓   The Big Time Experiment

✓   The Time Machine

Source: Martin Cohen's *101 Philosophy Problems*. Thanks to Rob Torrington for part 2 of this entry.

Philosophy: The philosophy of time, Sydney Shoemaker's 'Time Without Change'.

Time-Stretching

Peter Worley

Starting age: 5 years

Little Timmy is excited about tomorrow because tomorrow is Timmy's birthday. But this week time seems to have slowed right down. Each day that he gets closer to his birthday seems to stretch out longer than the day before it. *How can that happen?* he thinks to himself, *how is it that time seems longer some days and shorter on others?*

Start Question 1   Does time slow down sometimes and speed up at other times?

Questions to take you further

* How fast does time go?

* Does it change speed?

* Imagine two children are playing together and one of them is having a lot of fun. For her an hour seems to take ten minutes. But the other child is bored – the same hour seems to take two! Is time moving at different speeds for each child?

The night before his birthday Timmy goes to bed and he thinks to himself, *I can't wait until tomorrow! I wish I had a time machine so I could get to my birthday quicker.* But then it occurs to him that he *does* have a time machine. All he has to do is go to sleep and he'll wake up in what seems like five minutes with his birthday finally arrived! … All he has to do is go to sleep!

Start Question 2   If Timmy manages to go to sleep, when he wakes up will he have time travelled as if he were in a time machine?

Questions to take you further

* Is sleep a kind of time machine? If so, why? If not, why not?

* **What is a time machine?**

* If a time machine existed what would it be like?

* Do you think Timmy will get to sleep?

* Is time something that happens in the mind or outside of it?

Your Questions

*

*

*

Works well with

✓ The Time Diet

✓ Empty

✓ Superbaby Time!

✓ The Time-Freezing Machine

✓ The Big Time Experiment

✓ The Time Machine

✓ The Girl from Yesterday

Source: This thought experiment was inspired by 8-year-old Rokas who wondered if time travels at different speeds for people having fun and those who are bored.

Philosophy: The phenomenology of time.

The Non-Existent Hero

Peter Worley

Starting age: 11 years   Advanced

Herbert was a hero to all humankind but there was a small problem. Herbert didn't exist. Here's why.

Herbert's grandfather wasn't a very nice man and he did some rather bad things to a lot of people. He was also very, very rich. Herbert hated his grandfather for what he had done to so many people. When his grandfather died at the age of 80

Herbert inherited a great deal of money from him. He used the money to invest in the invention of the first ever time machine. Once it was built he travelled back in time and sought out his grandfather as a young man, at a time before he had done any of the many terrible things Herbert knew he would go on to do.

Herbert hid himself in a park opposite his grandfather's house, prepared his rifle and waited for him to emerge. Later that day, as his grandfather stepped out of the house, Herbert lifted his rifle and pointed it at him. With his grandfather firmly in his sights he paused as the tragedy of his situation dawned on him. Yet, despite this, he decided that his own tragedy was a price worth paying for what he was about to do for humankind.

He pulled the trigger.

And that's why Herbert doesn't exist.

Start Question   Can you explain why Herbert doesn't exist?

Questions to take you further

❖   Does this story make sense? Could the events in this story have happened?

❖   Some people think that situations like this prove that time travel is impossible. Do you agree?

❖   Why is Herbert's situation tragic?

❖   Is ceasing to exist a price worth paying for ridding the world of a very bad person?

❖   This story is an example of a 'temporal paradox'. What is paradoxical about the story?

❖   **What is a paradox?**

Your Questions

❖

❖

❖

Works well with

✓   The Birthday Surprise

✓   A Poem By You?

✓   Dis-ingenious

✓   Itselfish

✓   *Thoughtings:* Puzzles and Paradoxes

Source: David Lewis' paper 'The Paradoxes of Time Travel'.

Philosophy: The philosophy of time travel, time travel paradoxes.

The Big Time Experiment
Peter Worley

Starting age: 7 years

All the governments of the world have decided to try a huge experiment with time. In fact, it's the biggest experiment that's ever been done. At exactly 12 o'clock mid-day on the twelfth day of the twelfth month of the year 2112 all the clocks of the world are to be stopped. The scientist behind this huge operation, Professor Timothy Tempo, believes that when this is done time itself will stop.

Start Question 1   Is the Professor right – will time itself stop when all the clocks in the world are stopped?

There is a second part to Professor Tempo's big experiment. After all the clocks have been stopped, he is then going to have all the clocks in the world moved back by an hour simultaneously. He says that once this has been done the entire world, and therefore everyone on it, will have travelled back in time by one hour.

Start Question 2   Is the Professor right – will moving all the clocks back by an hour mean that everyone will have travelled back in time by an hour?

Questions to take you further

❖   Clocks were invented by humans, so was time invented by humans too?

❖   Do clocks make time move? If not, what makes time move?

❖   What was time like before clocks were invented?

❖   Would time have felt different before clocks were invented?

❖ Without clocks, how would you know what time of day it is?

❖ **What is time?**

❖ Does this experiment need to be performed for us to know whether Professor Tempo is right or wrong? Or can we know what will happen just by thinking about it?

Your Questions

❖

❖

❖

Works well with

✓ Superbaby Time!

✓ The Telly-Scope

✓ The Time-Freezing Machine

✓ Time-Stretching

✓ The Time Machine

✓ The Girl from Yesterday

✓ The Pill of Life

Source: This thought experiment emerged from discussions with many primary school children about crossing different time zones.

Philosophy: The nature of time, the distinction between time and the measurement of time or 'clock time'.

Thoughting: The Time Machine
Peter Worley

Starting age: 7 years

I really could do with a time machine
I'm late for class: *it's history*!

When time is lost
Is it gone forever?
Or can we get it back
With a little endeavour?

But wait a minute
I *do* have one!
And I'm travelling in it
One second at a time.
Just think about it,
Don't look at me oddly,
My time machine is,
Well, it's my … body!

Start Question   Is your body a time machine?

Questions to take you further

❖   Does your body travel through time?

❖   Is time outside of your body or inside your mind?

❖   Can you name the three dimensions? Is time a dimension?

❖   If your body is not a time machine, then what is a time machine?

❖   What does the poet mean when he/she says, 'I'm late for class: *it's history*!'? Is it a history class they are going to?

Your Questions

❖

❖

❖

Works well with

✓   Superbaby Time!

✓   The Telly-Scope

✓   Time-Stretching

✓   The Big Time Experiment

- ✓ Tralse (first half)
- ✓ *Thoughtings:* From Me to You

Source: This came out of discussions with primary school children, some of whom made a similar suggestion themselves.

Philosophy: The nature of time travel.

The Girl from Yesterday
David Birch

Starting age: 7 years

It had been the most beautiful day of her life. To celebrate her birthday Jessica and her friends had taken a trip to a village by the sea. The sun was shining and the world was everywhere in colour.

They had visited a stables and hired horses. For hours they rode together along the shore, galloping through the sand, laughing with excitement. They rode the horses through the shallow water and became dripping wet as the ocean splashed wildly over them. They rode to exhaustion.

Later, Jessica and her friends walked into the village. They discovered a sweet shop that filled the entire street with the crazed, heart-dancing smell of sugar. They rushed in. Behind the counter an old man was weighing sherbet lemons.

'Guess what, mister?' Jessica said boastfully. 'It's my birthday!'

'Is it really?'

Jessica and her friends nodded with conviction.

'Well in that case,' said the old man, 'you can have as many sweets as you like.'

'For free?' they gasped in unison.

'For free,' uttered the old man simply, profoundly.

It had been the most beautiful day of her life and Jessica didn't want it to end. On the train home she desperately tried to stay awake, willing the day to last a little longer. But her drowsiness overwhelmed her and she was soon fast asleep.

She awoke to the sound of rain and her mother calling her to get dressed for school. 'Where did yesterday go?' she wondered in shock. She couldn't remember. One minute she was on a sun-lit train, and the next minute *this* – rain and school.

'I want yesterday,' Jessica told her mum.

'Don't worry about yesterday,' her mum said. 'It's today you ought to be thinking about.'

'But where did yesterday go? I miss it,' Jessica cried.

'There's yesterday,' said her mum pointing to a photograph Jessica's friends had taken.

'That's not yesterday. It's just a photograph. It's not real.'

Start Question 1   Where did yesterday go?

Questions to take you further

❖   Where does yesterday go?

❖   Where is the past?

❖   Does the past exist?

Jessica's heart ached for yesterday so she found her way back to the station and caught a train. She was going in search of yesterday.

She returned to the beach where she and her friends had raced madly. But yesterday wasn't there. The prints from the horses' hooves could still be seen, but were fainter, fading. And whereas the ocean yesterday was blue, today it was grey.

She walked into the village and found the sweet shop.

'You're the girl from yesterday!' chirped the old man happily as she walked in.

'No,' Jessica replied sadly, 'I'm the girl from today.'

'Why the long face?' asked the old man. 'It's the beginning of a whole new year of your life.'

'My mum said that too. She said I should stop thinking about yesterday.'

'She's right. You have such a lot to look forward to.'

'But I don't want to just go forwards. I'd like to go backwards sometimes too.' A deep sigh. 'Where did yesterday go?' Jessica asked hopefully, truly believing the old man might know.

There was a pause. 'I wonder that myself,' the old man replied, his voice deflated.

'Do you know?'

'Some days I think it's gone forever. Some days I'm not so sure.'

Gone forever. Jessica was stung by these words.

She left the old man to catch the train home, but she told herself that she would keep looking for yesterday.

As the train rocked along the tracks, Jessica's body felt heavy. She could feel sleep coming over her. She closed her eyes and dreamt. She dreamt of ocean sounds and endless shores, the shimmering sun on gilded hair; she dreamt of pounding hooves and the rising moon, and all that was that wasn't there.

Start Question 2   Will Jessica ever find yesterday or is it gone forever?

Questions to take you further

❖ Is the past inside us?

❖ Should we forget the past and only think about the present?

❖ Has the past gone forever?

❖ **What is the past?**

❖ **What is memory?**

❖ When we look at a photograph are we looking at the past?

Your Questions

❖

❖

❖

Works well with

✓ The Birthday Surprise

✓ The Time Diet

✓ Superbaby Time!

✓ The Telly-Scope

✓ Time-Stretching

✓ The Big Time Experiment

✓ *Thoughtings:* From Me to You

Philosophy: The ontology of the past, the nature of time.

The Butterfly Effect
Peter Worley

Starting age: 10 years   Advanced

It's the year 2214 and the Time-Tourist Company offers the holiday of a lifetime. TTC – as the company is known – arranges trips through time using their patented 'Time-Tourist Company Time Machine'. Customers can travel to any time they like as long as it is in the past. It costs a small fortune to do but there is no shortage of willing customers for such a unique and thrilling experience.

In order to avoid any problems that may result from changing the past, TTC are able to place a special path that hovers above the world in the past so that the tourists cannot touch anything and thereby change the past. They are also invisible to anyone in the past. So all the time-tourists are able to do is view history.

But one day, whilst a group of time-tourists are visiting the Eocene period, between 40 and 50 million years ago, one of the tourists steps from the path despite having been strictly forbidden to do so. When the time-tourist wanders off the path they accidentally step on a butterfly, killing it underfoot.

Start Question   Will stepping on the butterfly have any effect on the future? If so, what sort of effect do you think it could have?

Questions to take you further

❖   It is only a small change, so will it have any effect?

❖   Can a small change in the past have a large effect on the future?

❖   When the time-tourists return to their own time, will anything have changed?

❖   How are things through time connected?

❖   Is everything connected?

❖   The Eocene is the geological period in which the earliest butterfly, fossils have been found. If the time-tourist had ended a particular species of butterfly, what effect might that have had?

❖   Would time travel be difficult for these reasons?

Your Questions

❖

❖

❖

Works well with

✓　Other entries from the 'Time' section (particularly The Non-Existent Hero, The Birthday Surprise, A Poem By You?)

✓　The Broken Window

✓　The Traffic Light Boy (1, 2 and 3)

✓　Jean-etic

Source: A short story by Ray Bradbury called 'A Sound of Thunder'.

Philosophy: Complexity, causation, chaos theory, contingency.

Metaphysics: Freedom

The Queen of Limbs
Peter Worley

Starting age: 9 years   *Advanced*

[**Question to consider whilst reading or hearing the story**   What is Marion?]

Marion awoke and climbed out of her box. She was a performer and really enjoyed the feeling of being on stage and giving people joy. She was a comedian and laughter her currency.

Marion worked with a hand puppet called Pippa. She felt sorry for Pippa because Pippa was not her own person. She only came alive when someone put their hand inside her empty body and moved her. Pippa was not very happy because she was made to do a performance she didn't want to do. She explained to Marion that she was a 'real actor' and that she should be doing Shakespeare, but each night she was made to do silly vaudevillian comedy. 'It's beneath me!' she protested.

Although Marion was very happy doing comedy, she still felt sorry for Pippa for not being able to make her own decisions and for not being able to do what she really wanted to do. She told Pippa this. Pippa looked at Marion with an angry glare in her eyes (Pippa's puppet-face *always* had an angry glare, but right now it was the correct face to have!).

'Do you think that you are any different?' she said to Marion.

Marion was in a very different situation to Pippa – there was no hand controlling her decisions, but she thought it insensitive to say so.

Pippa continued. 'Are you able to choose what you do?'

Marion felt that she should respond. 'Of course I can, I love my job and I would still choose my job even if I could do anything else.'

'But *could you* really choose to do anything else?' asked Pippa.

'Yes!' replied Marion, 'it's just that *I don't choose* to do anything else because I love what I do.' She paused before continuing. '*I don't have a hand in me controlling my every move!*' She regretted saying these words the moment she had said them.

Though Pippa's face was unable to change it seemed that the anger in her glare had increased. 'You may not have a hand controlling you but you should take a closer look around you!' Clearly upset, Pippa left Marion in a state of bewilderment. What could Pippa have meant?

Start Question 1   Does Marion make her own decisions and choices?

Questions to take you further

❖   What is Marion?

❖   If she didn't happen to love what she did, would Marion be able to choose to do something else?

❖   Who do you agree with in the argument between Pippa and Marion?

❖   Does the fact that Marion believes that she could choose to do something else prove that she has a choice?

❖   **What is a choice?**

❖   What do you think Pippa could have meant when she said 'you should take a closer look around you'?

[**Question to consider whilst hearing the second part of the story**   What do you think it is that Marion is beginning to notice?]

That night, during her performance – a performance she had run hundreds of times, perhaps thousands – she remembered Pippa's words that she should take a closer look around her. There was a glint of light from time to time that she caught out of the corner of her eye. Now that she thought about it, the glint had always been there but she hadn't really thought about it before. *What was that glint?*

There it was again! It was the same glint that spider's webs sometimes give at certain angles in the light. *And again!* It looked like a single line of thread very close to her head. Then there were more of them. Threads all around her. Where did they lead? They came from above and ended … at her hands and arms and legs! Fine, almost invisible threads that told only one story: Marion realised with horror that she was not so different from Pippa after all.

The cause of Pippa's movements was easy to see – a clearly visible hand and arm – but the cause of Marion's movements was less easy to see. Now that she had seen them, however, she couldn't believe that she hadn't seen them before. Now that she had seen the threads that guided her arms and legs they seemed like coarse ropes hanging all around her, getting in the way.

Start Question 2   What is Marion and what has she discovered about herself?

Questions to take you further

❖   How much are we like Marion and Pippa?

❖   Are there any things that cause us to move, like Pippa's hand and Marion's threads?

❖   Are there any things that cause us to make the decisions we do, other than ourselves?

❖   Are we like Pippa and Marion – are there forces that control us – or are we different?

❖   Are we free to choose what we do? Are we free to make our own decisions?

Works well with

✓   Other entries in the 'Freedom' section

✓   Nick of Time

✓   The Wicked Which

✓   Charlie's Choice

✓   A New World

✓   *Thoughtings:* Are You Free?

✓   *The If Machine:* The Happy Prisoner, The Frog and the Scorpion, The Little Old Shop of Curiosities, Billy Bash, The Robbery

Source and Philosophy: Determinism and free will, Schopenhauer's *Prize Essay on the Freedom of the Will.*

Prisoner
Georgina Donati

Starting age: 7 years

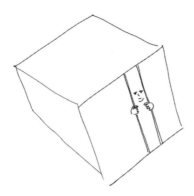

Start Question   Is this person free?

Questions to take you further

* What is it that makes them free or not free?

* What does it mean to be free?

* **What is freedom?**

* Can you be more or less free?

* Is someone in a prison free at all?

* Are people who are not in prisons free?

* If the person chose to be locked in the prison, would they be free then?

* Are there different kinds of freedom? If so, then what would they be?

* You may think the person is not real. If they aren't, then are they free?

Your Questions

*
*
*

Works well with

- ✓ Other entries in the 'Freedom' section
- ✓ Nick of Time
- ✓ The Wicked Which
- ✓ Charlie's Choice
- ✓ A New World
- ✓ *Thoughtings:* Are You Free?
- ✓ *The If Machine:* The Happy Prisoner, The Frog and the Scorpion

Philosophy: Freedom of speech, political freedom, freedom and determinism, freedom of goodness and reason.

Are There Cogs Beneath the Wind?

David Birch

Starting age: 7 years

In this story there are two worlds. One of these worlds is the Clockwork world. Every morning, before sleeping people wake, the world is wound up like a clock. Tightly, tightly it is turned and then released, making the day proceed cog-like. Everything happens predictably, nothing is accidental, the whole day unwinds in an orderly tick-tock way.

There is another world very different to this. This is the Windswept world. Every morning, before sleeping people wake, rather than being wound up the world is shaken up, as if it were a giant snow globe. The day then proceeds swirling. Everything happens randomly, little is predictable, the whole day unfurls in a disorderly swish-swosh way.

Whereas the Clockwork world is full of sense, the Windswept world if full of surprise. And although the Clockwork world is tidy, the Windswept world is a mess. In the Clockwork world laws determine what will happen, but in the Windswept world it is all a matter of luck. The Clockwork world is full of knowledge; the

Windswept world has only guesses. In the Windswept world people walk around with their fingers permanently crossed, but in the Clockwork world they believe a thorough plan is all one needs.

The Clockwork world is folded and neat. The Windswept world is tangled in heaps.

Start Question: Which of these worlds is our world most like?

Questions to take you further

❖ Is it one or the other or is it both?

❖ Which world would you rather live in?

❖ Which of these worlds is most:

    a. Happy?

    b. Dangerous?

    c. Perfect?

    d. Add to list as suggestions are made.

❖ In which world does this belong?

    a. Choice.

    b. Natural disasters, like earthquakes and tornadoes.

    c. Birthdays.

    d. Thoughts and wishes.

    e. Time.

    f. Adventure.

    g. Right and wrong.

    h. Again, add to list as suggestions are made.

Your Questions

❖

❖

❖

Works well with

✓ Other entries in the 'Freedom' section

- ✓ A Random Appetizer
- ✓ What Goes Up …
- ✓ The Broken Window
- ✓ Jack's Parrot and Wind-Spell

Philosophy: The teleological argument for the existence of God, determinism and chance.

The Clockwork Toymaker
Peter Worley

Starting age: 11 years   Advanced

Sometime in the 18th century in Switzerland there was a toymaker who made the most remarkable toys. They were so detailed no one could quite believe they had been fashioned by hand. His most famous toys were two mechanical dolls called Isaac and Gottfried who, once wound up, would move around in the most elegant dance with each other. It was amusing to watch but also awe-inspiring that one man, and his two hands, could create from nothing such elegance and complexity. Of such complexity were they that Isaac and Gottfried would never do exactly the same dance twice. There was always something, however small, slightly different from the time before.

'Where did you get the inspiration for your *little wonders*?' he was once asked by a very impressed customer.

'That's easy,' replied the toymaker, 'I simply looked to the people around me who make their own "little dances" every day to and from their places of work, to church and around each other. Always the same, yet always a little bit different,' he chuckled.

'But we people are not like wind-up toys. We are not mechanical, we can choose what we do,' objected the customer.

'I have often wondered about that,' said the toymaker. 'I have wondered whether I would be able to make a toy using only my springs and coils, cogs and pendulums, that could choose what it wanted to do.'

Start Question 1a Do you think that it is – or would ever be – possible to make a toy person using only springs and coils, cogs and pendulums?

Start Question 1b If so, could it be made to be able to choose what it wanted to do?

Questions to take you further

❖ If we have a *free will* (the ability to choose for ourselves) like the customer suggested, how does it work?

❖ Do we have a free will?

❖ What is a free will?

❖ Do you think it possible to be able to make a mechanical doll with a free will, as the toymaker supposed?

'I don't think that would be possible,' said the customer.

'But are we really as different from my toys as we like to think?' asked the toymaker. 'We are wound up at the start of our lives and we simply keep moving in all sorts of ways until we finally unwind at the end of our lives. Is that so very different from my toys?'

Eventually the toymaker grew old and one day, alas, it transpired that his toys would never again be made as he drew his last breath and died. In his will he had left instructions for his internal organs to be 'made use of for some greater purpose'. But when the surgeons opened him up to remove his organs they were shocked to discover that under his leathery skin there were the most intricate machines in place of a heart, lungs and brain and, for that matter, everything else. Under his skin they found only shining, well-oiled clockwork parts, just like the toymaker's little toys only much, much more complicated.

The surgeons looked at each other in amazement. 'But who made the toymaker?' one of them asked. 'He couldn't have made himself!' exclaimed another.

To this day, and according to his wishes, his clockwork heart still operates a clock somewhere in an old Swiss house, but where his clockwork brain is housed and what purpose it serves remains a mystery.

Start Question 2 How much are we like the toymaker?

Questions to take you further

❖ How much are humans like mechanical toys?

❖ If the toymaker were to wind up one of his toys and then let it go, is where it ends up determined by how it is started?

❖ There is an old Chinese saying, 'Endings are contained in their beginnings.' Once something begins does that mean that the end is inevitable?

❖ Is what you do at the end of your life determined by what happens at the beginning of your life?

❖ If so, does that mean that everything is planned?

❖ If the toys never dance in exactly the same way, does that mean that they are not determined?

❖ Who made the toymaker? Could he have made himself?

❖ Are some things determined and other things not?

❖ Do things happen with or without meaning and purpose?

❖ Does how the universe begins determine everything that happens in the universe?

❖ If so, would that include you and me?

❖ Is what is going to happen determined by what has already happened?

Extension activity:

It transpired that the toymaker had been knocked over by somebody running past him and not looking where they were going. When he had been knocked over something inside him had snapped and broken. That's why he had stopped working.

Questions to take you even further

❖ Had the toymaker been killed or simply broken?

❖ Should the person who had knocked him over be punished? If so, for what?

❖ Is it right that his parts were used 'for some greater purpose'?

❖ When we die should our parts (heart, kidneys, liver, etc.) be used for other people?

Your Questions

❖

❖

❖

Works well with

✓ Other entries in the 'Freedom' section

✓ Nick of Time

✓ Pinka and Arwin Go Forth, especially Of Macs and Men

✓ *Thoughtings:* Are You Free?

✓ *The If Machine:* Billy Bash, The Little Old Shop of Curiosities, The Frog and the Scorpion, The Happy Prisoner

Source: *Clockwork or All Wound Up* by Phillip Pullman.

Philosophy: Determinism, free will, Isaac Newton, Gottfried Leibniz, the problem of the first cause ('the prime mover').

Immy's Interesting Invention
Peter Worley

Starting age: 10 years

Immy is concerned that too many people lie to each other, steal from others and generally harm other people when they shouldn't. To combat this worry – a worry that many people share with him – and being also a scientist and inventor, Immy has come up with what he thinks is a solution to the problem. He has invented a tiny device that can be implanted into our heads, and once implanted will stop anyone with the implant from being able to do certain things, no matter what the circumstances. Immy suggests programming the device to stop us from doing the following things because he thinks they are things no one should ever do:

1. Lying

2. Stealing

3. Causing harm to others

That would mean that once the device has been implanted into your head you would be simply *unable* to lie, steal or cause harm to others. If you tried, then your tongue, your hands – or whatever it is – would simply stop working.

Start Question 1a   Would you have the implant with Immy's suggestions programmed in so that you would never, under any circumstances, lie, steal or cause harm?

Start Question 1b   If not Immy's, have you any of your own suggestions that you would programme into the device?

Questions to take you further

❖   Just like Immy, some people think that there are certain things you should never do, under any circumstances, such as killing. Are they right about this?

❖   Is it right that our freedom be limited so that we behave better?

❖   Is it right that we have freedom to do as we please even if others are harmed as a result?

❖   What is more important: freedom or the greater good?

❖   Would it be better if we had no power of choice but always did the right thing?

❖   If we had Immy's implant, would we always do the right thing?

Your Questions

❖

❖

❖

Works well with

✓   Other entries in the 'Freedom' section (particularly Prisoner)

✓   A Bad Picture

✓   The Wicked Which

✓   Nick of Time

✓   The Good Daleks

✓   Arete and Deon

✓   Louis' Goodness Detector

✓   *The If Machine:* The Ring of Gyges, The Ceebie Stories

✓   *Thoughtings:* Are You Free?

Source: 'The Three Laws' from Isaac Asimov's *Robot* stories.

Philosophy: Kant and the categorical imperative, moral absolutism, Mill and the harm principle.

The Otherwise Machine
Peter Worley

Starting age: 10 years   *Advanced*

Have you ever wondered what would have happened if you had done something differently?

Saheela has. And she has been busy. She has designed and built a machine, a very special machine, and it is also very big. She has had to build a huge laboratory under her house, as big as a football pitch, to house the giant and complicated super-computer with its thousands of memory banks and wires.

She got some help from her dad.

The machine enables her to see what would have happened if things had been different. She just points a special camera at something that happens, then, when she is in her laboratory, she programmes in the change and it shows her what *would have happened* on a video screen. Saheela and her dad call their machine 'The Otherwise Machine'.

She wonders if small changes would make as much of a difference as big changes. She thinks that they might, but her dad doesn't think so. To decide, Saheela makes a bet with her dad. One morning her brother leaves for school wearing a blue sweater. She says, 'I bet that a small change like the colour of his sweater will make a big difference to his day.' But her dad replies, 'He would just have a red sweater on instead of a blue one. Everything else would have been the same.'

Start Question 1   Do you agree with Saheela or with her dad?

Questions to take you further

❖   Do small changes matter?

❖   Do big changes matter?

❖   Would everything have been the same, as her dad suggested?

❖   Would it be a small change or a big change if his favourite colour was blue?

❖   What sort of effect do you think you have on the world?

❖   Do the things you do matter?

❖   Is it possible to know what might have happened?

Next morning her brother gets up and puts on his usual blue sweater again and sets off for school, but this time Saheela had secretly pointed her special camera at him when he put on his sweater. That night, after dinner, she and her dad go into their secret workshop under the house and programme in the change. She types, 'My brother puts on a red sweater instead of the blue one'. Then she presses 'return'.

Activity   Can you construct a story of what could happen?

Questions to take you even further

❖   What do you think the machine will show?

❖   Do you think her brother's day will be different just because he has a different coloured sweater on?

Meanwhile, when her brother had got up and put on his usual blue sweater here's what happened:

He had been selected for the blue-sweater team in a class football match. 'The blues' had won. Having been in the winning team he had come home full of confidence and happiness. This had resulted in her brother being in a good mood so he completed his homework. Because he had completed his homework his teacher gave him a commendation. He went home in a good mood again and continued to complete his homework all week …

Start Question 2   If he had worn the red sweater, do you think anything would have happened differently?

Questions to take you further

❖ How much of his future could these changes affect?

❖ What will happen differently?

❖ Could he still win the football match?

Works well with

✓ Other entries in the 'Freedom' section

✓ Nick of Time

✓ The Butterfly Effect

✓ The Wicked Which

✓ Charlie's Choice

✓ What Zeus Does When He's Bored

✓ *Thoughtings*: Are You Free?

✓ *The If Machine*: The Happy Prisoner, The Frog and the Scorpion, The Little Old Shop of Curiosities, Billy Bash, The Robbery

Philosophy: Contingency and causation.

What Zeus Does When He's Bored
Peter Worley

Starting age: 10 years   Advanced

The gods of Mount Olympus are able to watch the world from their stage, high up above everything, outside of the world, separate from it.

One day, whilst entertaining himself by lining up thousands of dominos and then watching them cascade down again upon flicking the first one over, Zeus – king of the gods of Olympus – begins to wonder to himself. He wonders if yesterday were to happen again whether it would happen differently or exactly the same. *Well, seeing as I'm a god,* he thinks to himself, *why don't I find out?* So, Zeus, being extremely powerful, makes everything in the world go back to yesterday morning. All the people of the world start to move quickly but in reverse like a film being rewound until they reach yesterday morning again. Then Zeus makes them all stop, frozen where they stand.

Start Question 1   Before Zeus clicks his fingers to let yesterday play out again, do you think it will happen differently or exactly the same as it did the first time yesterday happened?

Questions to take you further

❖   For instance, if the wind blew a tree over the first time would that happen again?

❖   If a boy just missed a bus, and was late for school as a result, would that happen again?

❖   If a girl chose to stay in and watch TV instead of going out to play with her friends would that happen again?

❖   If a boy chose to do something naughty for which he got into terrible trouble would he be able to choose not to do it if yesterday happened again?

❖   Could people choose different things if yesterday happened again or would they just choose the same things?

❖   If you knew that this was the second time today was happening would you do things differently?

❖   If you knew what you did the first time would you do things differently?

❖   If you didn't know it was the second time today was happening do you think you would do things differently or the same?

Advanced extension activity:

Think back to the last time you made a choice, such as choosing which cereal to eat or what TV channel to watch. Now imagine that Zeus has 'rewound reality' to *just before* you made the choice.

Start Question 2   Is it possible that you would choose something other than what you chose when you first made the choice?

❖   What if you knew what you did the first time and you knew that reality had been 'rewound'? Would you choose differently?

❖   What if you didn't know what you did the first time and you also didn't know that reality had been 'rewound'? Would you choose differently?

Questions to take you even further (for older participants)

❖   What does your answer tell you about choices?

❖   Some philosophers think that for your choices to be genuine choices (for us to have a genuine *free will*) then it must be possible for you to have been able *to do something other than you did* at any given moment in time. What do you think about this?

❖   Do you think you could have done other than you did the last time you made a choice?

❖   If not, then you may be a *determinist* (someone who doesn't believe in free will).

❖   If so, then you may be a *metaphysical libertarian* (someone who believes in free will).

❖   Could you be both a determinist and a metaphysical libertarian?

Your Questions

❖

❖

❖

Works well with

✓   The Queen of Limbs

✓   Are There Cogs Beneath the Wind?

✓   The Clockwork Toymaker

✓   *The If Machine:* The Happy Prisoner, The Little Old Shop of Curiosities, The Frog and the Scorpion

✓   *Thoughtings:* Are You Free?

Source and Philosophy: Necessity and contingency and the problem of free will and determinism; Spinoza, Hume, Schopenhauer and Kant on free will and determinism; Simone de Beauvoir on 'situated freedom'.

Metaphysics: Personal Identity

Identity Parade
Andrew Routledge

Starting age: 12 years

The six entries included in Identity Parade can be run as discussions in the same way as the other entries in the book; however, below, the author offers a more involved – and fun – way for classes and groups to think about the issues involved.

Identity Parade activity

Starting

One pupil is to be selected randomly as 'the prisoner'. This can be done in any number of ways but it can serve as a useful icebreaker. One way of choosing the prisoner is to use a raffle: unbeknown to the participants when they first sit down, each chair in the room has a raffle ticket taped to the bottom of the chair. A number is then drawn and read out.

Having been chosen, the prisoner is given a 'scenario-card' (see the various entries in Identity Parade) and they must then sit in 'the cage' until a verdict is reached (the 'cage' could be a chair). The scenario-card should be read out by the workshop leader, who acts as a judge. The rest of the group should be split into 'prosecution lawyers' (who will argue that the prisoner is the same person as the criminal), 'defence lawyers' (who will work with and help the prisoner argue that they are not the same person and so should be freed) and – finally – a small panel of 'jurors' who will, at the end of the trial, weigh up the arguments and record a 'guilty' or 'not-guilty' verdict.

The exact numbers for each of these will depend on the number of the group. Again, there is flexibility here with only a small number essential for each. For very small groups, you need not have both lawyers and separate jurors. Rather, the whole group can argue the case and then vote at the end.

Acting as a judge, the role of the workshop leader should be limited but it will allow them, within the terms of the game, to keep the debate on track and steer it along by asking the lawyers particular questions or suggesting that the jurors consider certain evidence.

Ten minute debate

During this time the group should consider the scenario they have been presented with. For example, it could be the case of a criminal mastermind responsible for a robbery at an art gallery. Having carried out the crime they take a drug that wipes all of their memories and changes their personality forever. However, police find one of the priceless paintings hidden at their house. The person no longer remembers the robbery – or anything else from the past – and cannot believe that they would have done such a thing. Is the person the same person as the one who robbed the art gallery? Should they be punished? How crucial are memories to making us who we are? Is personality important for personal identity? These are some of the questions that this scenario raises.

Issues about the purpose of punishment may arise during the course of these discussions. Should the legal system be about retribution, reforming the offender or deterring future offenders and so on. Don't feel the need to stifle this. It is independently interesting and an important philosophical issue in itself. Nurturing their philosophical curiosity is the main priority.

Five minute conclusion

During this time the jury should consider the evidence and privately pass their guilty/not-guilty verdicts in an envelope to the judge. With a suitably dramatic pause the judge should announce the verdict. The remaining time should be spent making explicit the philosophical ideas covered in the discussion. Briefly review and go over some of the thoughts/arguments that have been given and link the questions to the areas of philosophy that they come from. Finally, the workshop leader can point participants to resources available for wider reading.

Note: A selection of scenarios is presented in what follows. For longer sessions there is the further option of allowing participants to go on to write their own scenarios. This is very good practice for philosophy, helping them understand how to put together thought experiments – a core tool of philosophy. In order to design a scenario, participants need to come up with (a) a name for the offender, (b) a crime and (c) spell out exactly how the person has changed. The same question will then be asked: *Are they still the same person?* For anyone struggling to come up with something, remember the scenario doesn't have to be completely new and different to those already discussed. In fact, philosophy often proceeds by just tinkering with existing scenarios, changing X but keeping Y the same. And then asking: Does this make a difference? By doing this, it allows you to get a closer grip on exactly what it is that really matters. For example, you might have a slightly revised scenario in which somebody's personality drastically changes but they still have most of the same memories.

Philosophy: Personal identity, the persistence of the self through time, materialism, selfhood.

Identity Parade (1): Memory
Andrew Routledge

Starting age: 12 years

A mastermind criminal robs an art gallery and gets away with millions of pounds worth of famous paintings. They are set to be rich for life. To make sure they never give themselves away or get tempted to carry out another robbery, they take a drug that wipes all of their memories and changes their personality. The way that they think and behave is completely different – they become a good person dedicated to helping others. However, police find a painting hidden at their house after a tip-off. They arrest the person and find traces of the drug still in their body, but because of the drug the person no longer remembers the robbery – or anything from the past – and they cannot believe that they would have done such a thing. The thought of robbing a place horrifies them.

This person is now sat in the cage in front of us today. What we need to decide is this:

Start Question   Are they still the *same person* as the one who robbed the art gallery? Should they be punished?

Questions to take you further

- ❖   How important are *memories* in making us who we are?

- ❖   And how much does our *personality* matter?

- ❖   Is taking this drug the same as dying?

- ❖   How would *you* feel if you were the person in the cage? Would you think you should be punished?

Your Questions

- ❖
- ❖
- ❖

Works well with

- ✓ Other entries in the 'Personal Identity' section (particularly Identity Parade: Body, Body Copy, Brains, Cloning, Change, All That Glitters …)
- ✓ Trying to Forget
- ✓ Jemima or James
- ✓ *Thoughtings:* You, Me, Aliens and Others
- ✓ *The If Machine:* The Ceebie Stories, The Ship of Theseus, Yous On Another Planet, Where Are You?

Identity Parade (2): Body

Andrew Routledge

Starting age: 12 years

Somebody has been flooding the country with fake banknotes. Police raid an abandoned factory and find a gang with several briefcases full of notes. The leader of the gang is nowhere to be seen but the police know who it is: they have been in prison before and they know what the person looks like, their height, weight, build and so on. A nationwide hunt begins.

Seeing the story in the news, the gang leader realises that drastic action is needed. They get in touch with two old contacts. One of them works for a company that finds organ donors and the other is a corrupt surgeon in a hospital. The surgery they're involved in is dangerous and expensive but the gang leader is desperate to avoid capture. In the first few weeks the surgeon removes the person's legs and feet, replacing them with the legs and feet of another individual. When they recover from the operation the surgeon begins to swap their arms and hands and eventually moves on to their internal organs such as their lungs and heart. Almost a year later, the person is unrecognisable. The surgeon puts the finishing touches to them by performing a brain transplant.

The person that eventually walks out of the surgery has no body parts or organs that are the same. Every part of the body has been gradually replaced over the weeks and months. But despite their best efforts, the person is caught. After investigating a series of organ thefts, police find financial records of the person and track them down. Their unusual number of body scars gives the game away immediately.

This person is now sat in the cage in front of us today. What we need to decide is this:

Start Question   Are they still the *same person* as the gang leader who forged the banknotes? Should they be punished?

Questions to take you further

❖   How important is our *body* to making us who we are?

❖   What kinds of changes can it undergo before it just becomes a different person?

❖   How much of you would you let a surgeon replace?

❖   Does it matter how *gradually* these changes happen?

Your Questions

❖

❖

❖

Works well with

✓   Other entries in the 'Personal Identity' section (particularly Identity Parade: Memory, Body Copy, Brains, Cloning, Change)

✓   Revelation

✓   Pinka and Arwin Go Forth (1): Of Macs and Men

✓   Pinka and Arwin Go Forth (3): Making Up Their Minds

✓   Bobby the Punching Bag

✓   Jemima or James

✓   *Thoughtings:* You, Me, Aliens and Others

✓   *The If Machine:* The Ceebie Stories, The Ship of Theseus, Yous On Another Planet, Where Are You?

Philosophy: Thomas Hobbes and materialism, John Locke and identity through time.

Identity Parade (3): Body Copy
Andrew Routledge

Starting age: 12 years

A number of government computers have been hacked into. Somebody has got access to highly sensitive information. Police believe that the information has been sold on and think they know who was involved. But the person responsible had an escape plan ready. Whereas in the past criminals might have used a getaway car, in this day and age (in the future from now) some criminals are able to afford *getaway machines*. When a person steps into one of these machines, it scans their entire body and sends the information about what it is like to a machine on the other side of the world via satellite. Following this blueprint, the second machine then builds an exact copy of the person out of some new chemicals. They have an identical body and an identical brain. They look the same and behave the same, believe all the same things and want all the same things. Then, at the exact moment that the second machine builds this copy, the body in the first machine is zapped and destroyed so that there is only one of them. Unfortunately for the person who stepped out of this machine, Interpol had been tracking the sale of these new pieces of technology and arrested the person within an hour.

This person is now sat in the cage in front of us today. What we need to decide is this:

Start Question   Are they still the *same person* as the hacker? Should they be punished?

Questions to take you further

❖   How important is our *body* to making us who we are?

- ❖ What is it about our body that is most important?

- ❖ Does it matter which stuff it is made of or just how it is put together or arranged?

- ❖ Would *you* step into a getaway machine if you were on the run?

Your Questions

- ❖

- ❖

- ❖

Works well with

- ✓ Other entries in the 'Personal Identity' section (particularly Identity Parade: Memory, Body, Brains, Cloning, Change, The Copying Machine)

- ✓ Pencil Person Meets Pencil Person!

- ✓ The 2 Square

- ✓ *Thoughtings:* You, Me, Aliens and Others

- ✓ *The If Machine:* The Ceebie Stories, The Ship of Theseus, Yous On Another Planet, Where Are You?

Philosophy: Derek Parfit's *Reasons and Persons*.

Identity Parade (4): Brains
Andrew Routledge

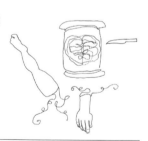

Starting age: 12 years

A daring criminal has managed to escape with the Crown Jewels. Everybody in the country has seen the dramatic CCTV footage of their escape and has been urged by the police to keep a look out for the person. The criminal goes into hiding, while a small group of accomplices arrange for a state-of-the-art brain transplant. Their brain is taken out of their body and hooked up to another body. Their old body is buried, secretly. The person now looks completely different and only has the same brain as before. Unfortunately for them, they try to sell the stolen Crown Jewels to the wrong person and are double-crossed. When they go to pick up the money, armed police are waiting for them.

This person is now sat in the cage in front of us today. What we need to decide is this:

Start Question   Are they still the *same person* as the thief? Should they be punished?

Questions to take you further

❖   If your brain was put into another body, where would you be: where your old body is or where you brain now is?

❖   What is more important to who we are: our body or our personality?

❖   If your brain was put into another body do you think you would have the same personality?

❖   If you had to choose, would you rather keep your brain or the rest of your body?

❖   Would your memories be the same? What about your personality?

Your Questions

❖

❖

❖

Works well with

✓   Other entries in the 'Personal Identity' section (particularly Identity Parade: Memory, Body, Body Copy, Cloning, Change)

✓   Mind the Planet

✓   Pinka and Arwin Go Forth (2): Making Up Their Minds

✓   *Thoughtings:* You, Me, Aliens and Others

✓   *The If Machine:* The Ceebie Stories, The Ship of Theseus, Yous On Another Planet, Where Are You?

Identity Parade (5): Cloning
Andrew Routledge

Starting age: 12 years

A rich Hollywood actor is being blackmailed. The blackmailers want one hundred million dollars to guarantee the safe return of his wife. Police manage to trace the letters and raid the garage where the woman is being held captive. Although they manage to free the actor's wife, the criminal already has an elaborate escape plan in place. Whereas in the past criminals might have used a getaway car, in this day and age (in the future from now) some criminals are able to afford *getaway machines*. When a person steps into one of these machines, it scans their entire body and sends the information about what it is like to a machine on the other side of the world via satellite. Following this blueprint, the second machine then builds an exact copy of the person out of some new chemicals. They have an identical body and an identical brain. They look the same and behave the same, believe all the same things and want all the same things. Then, at the exact moment that the second machine builds this copy, the body in the first machine is zapped and destroyed. Unfortunately, in this case the machine malfunctions when the criminal steps into it. It starts making funny noises and smoke begins to pour out of the side. Instead of making just one copy of the person, it makes three. All of them are exactly the same as the original that has now been destroyed. Each of them remembers stepping into the machine! They are later tracked down by Interpol and put on trial separately.

One of the three is now sat in the cage in front of us today. What we need to decide is this:

Start Question   Are they still the *same person* as the blackmailer? Should they be punished?

Questions to take you further

❖   If there are now three different people, how can we decide which of them is the same as the original?

❖   Does the malfunction mean that none of them are the same?

❖   Has the machine killed the blackmailer?

❖ What if the machine had malfunctioned and failed to destroy the original blackmailer. Which one of the four should then be punished? Or should it be all of them?

Your Questions

❖

❖

❖

Works well with

✓ Other entries in the 'Personal Identity' section (particularly Identity Parade: Memory, Body, Body Copy, Brains, Change)

✓ Pencil Person Meets Pencil Person!

✓ How Many Dogs?

✓ The 2 Square

✓ *Thoughtings:* You, Me, Aliens and Others

✓ *The If Machine:* The Ceebie Stories, The Ship of Theseus, Yous On Another Planet, Where Are You?

Identity Parade (6): Change
Andrew Routledge

Starting age: 12 years

During a war many years ago, a certain individual was responsible for killing and torturing many innocent people. When the war ended they fled the country, fearing punishment for their crimes. They made their way to Latin America and settled there, in hiding. Years and years passed and the person began to grow older. They no longer remembered what happened all that time ago and they would no longer behave that way if they were in a similar circumstance now. The way that they think about the world is very different. Their personality has completely changed. Their body has also aged and looks drastically different. Almost every cell in their body has died and been replaced by a different cell. Campaigners for justice are tipped off by locals, however, that this person may be a war criminal. The person is arrested.

This person is now sat in the cage in front of us today. What we need to decide is this:

Start Question   Are they still the *same person* as the war criminal? Should they be punished?

Questions to take you further

❖   What matters about the way that we change?

❖   Are some ways of changing more natural than others? If so, why?

❖   Why is it that we can survive changes of one kind but not another?

❖   Does how *slowly* or *gradually* we change matter?

Your Questions

❖

❖

❖

Works well with

✓   Other entries in the 'Personal Identity' section (particularly Identity Parade: Memory, Body, Body Copy, Brains, Cloning, All That Glistens …)

✓   *Thoughtings:* You, Me, Aliens and Others

✓   *The If Machine:* The Ceebie Stories, The Ship of Theseus, Yous On Another Planet, Where Are You?

Backtracking
Peter Worley

Starting age: 9 years

Make yourself comfortable and try the following thought experiment. Give yourself a moment to think between each numbered part of the exercise:

1. Think back to where you were ten minutes ago.

2. Now think back to where you were one hour ago.

3. Where were you a day ago?

4. What about a year ago?

5. Now think back to where you were five years ago.

6. Ten years ago.

7. Where were you one hundred years ago?

8. What about one thousand years ago?

9. And one million years ago?

10. What about ten million years ago?

11. And one billion?

Start Question   *What* were you and *where* were you before you were born?

Questions to take you further

❖ Does it make sense to think of yourself at a time before you were born? Was there a 'you' before you were born?

❖ Did you exist before you were born?

❖ Did you exist genetically (or in your ancestors) before you were born?

❖ Did the chemicals that make you up exist before you were born? (You may want to try to find out what chemicals you are made of!)

❖ Do you think you had a soul before you were born? If so, where was it?

❖ Is there something that all things are made of?

Your Questions

❖

❖

❖

Works well with

✓ Other entries in the 'Personal Identity' section (particularly Who Do You Think You Are?)

✓ Mind the Planet

✓ *Thoughtings:* You, Me, Aliens and Others

Source: Carl Sandburg's poem 'Who Do You Think You Are?'

Philosophy: The philosophy of the soul and the self, the fallacy of composition.

Who Do You Think You Are?
Nolen Gertz

Starting age: 14 years

John is a student who recently moved and is starting at a new school. On his first day John is greeted by his new tutor, Paul, who takes him to meet the other students. When they arrive in the classroom Paul asks John, 'Can you tell everyone a little bit about yourself?' John nods and says, 'Hi, everyone, I'm John. I used to live in Brighton, but my family recently moved here to London and I look forward to studying here with all of you.' Paul, looking confused, turns to John and says, 'Thank you for that information, but what I meant was: can you tell us about *who you are?*' John chuckles and tries again. John says, 'Ah, sorry, well I have an older sister, Simone, and a cat named Albert …' Before John can continue, Paul interrupts, 'John, sorry, but that's just more *information*. Please tell us about *you*.' John apologises and tries again, but just as he starts talking about his parents and his favourite games, Paul again interrupts and again asks John to tell everyone 'who he *is*'. John, now very confused, says, 'Okay, well I thought I was.' Paul, trying to help, explains, 'John, we don't want to hear details about your past, about your home, about your family, or about your interests. We only want to hear about you, and *who you are*.' Unable to think of anything else, John simply blurts out, 'Well I'm *me*!'

Start Question   Who are you?

Note: If you feel a certain frustration similar to that of John, that's fine. Can you say why you feel that frustration?

Questions to take you further

❖   Can you answer this question without simply listing information about yourself?

❖   Is John's reply, 'Well I'm *me*!', the only way to answer Paul's question?

❖   Is 'Well I'm *me*!' an answer to the question 'Who are you?' If so, is it a good answer?

❖   How do you typically introduce yourself to other people? How do other people introduce themselves to you?

❖   What do you think Paul wanted John to say? Can you come up with a better answer to Paul's questions?

❖   Is there a difference between 'information about you' and 'who you are'? If so, what is the difference?

Your Questions

❖

❖

❖

Works well with

✓   Other entries in the 'Personal Identity' section (particularly Backtracking)

✓   Revelation

✓   Only Human

✓   Can I Think?

✓   *Thoughtings:* You, Me, Aliens and Others

Philosophy: Heidegger, Sartre, existentialism, existential anxiety, selfhood.

All That Glistens …
Emma Worley

Starting age: 9 years

Natasha was 9 and her heart was pounding as she reached up to the shelf to grab the liquorice. It glistened in front of her and she just couldn't resist it. She ran out of the shop as quickly as she could. But not quick enough – the shopkeeper caught her and took her home, where she was punished.

33 years later …

Natasha was 42 and her heart skipped as she reached forward to pick up her autobiography. Her name glistened on the cover. She opened the book to read the first few words which she knew by heart. She put the book down and walked out of the shop. A smile crept over her face as she remembered stealing the liquorice all those years ago, a story she tells in the book.

40 years later …

Natasha was 82 and her heart beat gently as she read different stories of her life to her 7-year-old grandson. Kwami's eyes glistened as he listened to the adventures of his nana. After reading the chapter that tells of Natasha's punishment after stealing the liquorice, Kwami exclaims: 'Nana! I didn't know you were a thief!' Natasha looks at her grandson, and with complete honesty says, 'Neither did I, Kwami. I had completely forgotten about that moment in my life.'

Start Question 1 Is Natasha a thief?

Questions to take you further

* Are we responsible as adults for things we did as children?

* Can we be held responsible for something we did that we have no memory of having done?

The 80-year-old Natasha remembers her autobiography being published when she was 40.

The 40-year-old Natasha remembers stealing the liquorice as a 9-year-old.

But the 80-year-old Natasha does not remember stealing the liquorice.

Start Question 2   Are they the same person?

Questions to take you even further

❖   If so, what makes them the same person if they don't share the same memories?

❖   Is the 7-year-old Natasha responsible for her actions as a 9-year-old? Can we be held responsible for things we will do but haven't yet done? And is it the same as being held responsible for something we can't remember having done?

❖   How important are our memories in making us the people we are?

❖   What connects us to our past?

❖   What makes us the same person tomorrow or five years from now?

❖   Are we the same person at different times in our lives?

❖   If we need to remember our past in order to be the same person, what about people who have memory loss?

❖   If memory isn't what makes us the same person through time, what is?

Your Questions

❖

❖

❖

Works well with

✓   Identity Parade (1): Memory

✓   Nick of Time

✓   Whose Bump?

✓   Not Half the Man He Used To Be

✓   *Thoughtings:* You, Me, Aliens and Others

✓   *The If Machine:* The Rebuild

Source: Thomas Reid's 'the flogged boy and the general'.

Philosophy: John Locke's continued consciousness, personal identity, memory, responsibility.

Whose Bump?

Peter Worley

Starting age: 7 years

When Byron arrived at school this morning everyone called him 'Brian'. He was most annoyed because his name was Byron. When the register was taken no 'Byron' was mentioned, just 'Brian'. But Byron did not respond to the name 'Brian'. The other children insisted that his name was Brian. They said that it had always been Brian. His teacher said that his name was Brian and that she could prove it: 'It's here,' she said, 'in the register.' Brian was still confused because he had no memory of anything before breakfast.

Start Question 1   How can Byron (or Brian) find out about himself if he has no memory of who he was before breakfast?

Questions to take you further

❖   How do we know who we are?

❖   Without memory, how would you know who you are?

❖   Can we know ourselves by what others tell us?

❖   Do other people know us? If so, how well do other people know us?

Here's what had happened: that morning, before breakfast, Byron was Brian. But Brian had bumped his head quite severely. When he had come to, he had lost all his memories of his life before the bump. He thought his name was Byron and could only remember what had happened to him since the bump. His mum took him to school anyway. She thought it might do him good and help to bring back his memories.

Start Question 2   Is Byron the same person as Brian?

Questions to take you further

❖　Is the person after the bump the same person as the person before the bump?

❖　If he regains the memories of before the bump then would he be the same person or not?

❖　If he never regains the memories of before the bump would he be the same person or not?

While at school he bumps his head again but this time the bump restores all his memories. His teacher and classmates are happy to see Brian again. But where's Byron gone?

Question to finish with　　What has happened to Byron?

Your Questions

❖

❖

❖

Works well with

✓　This pairs well with, and as a follow-up to, All That Glistens …

✓　Identity Parade (1): Memory

✓　Not Half the Man He Used To Be

✓　Trying to Forget

✓　*Thoughtings:* You, Me, Aliens and Others

✓　*The If Machine:* The Rebuild

Source: Thanks to David Birch for the question, 'If you forget who you are then how would you find out?'

Philosophy: Body, memory and personal identity; John Locke; Thomas Reid.

The Copying Machine
Peter Worley

Starting age: 7 years

The copying machine does not photocopy pictures and writing; it is much more interesting than that. It copies people. But it doesn't just make picture copies; it makes another physical copy of a person. Everything down to the number of hairs and the placement of freckles is identical.

There are two booths: booth number 1 and booth number 2. When a person or thing is placed into booth number 1 and the 'copy' button is pressed by an operator, a perfect copy of the person or thing is made in booth number 2.

Imagine that *you* step into booth number 1. The 'copy' button is pressed. You step out of booth number 1 whilst your exact double steps out of booth number 2.

Start Question 1   What would it be like to meet yourself?

Questions to take you further

❖   What would you talk about?

❖   Would you have much to say?

❖   Would there be any point to a conversation?

❖   Would you know everything about each other?

❖   Would there be anything you didn't know about each other?

Start Question 2   Which one is you? Are they both you?

Questions to take you further

❖   What is it that makes you *you*?

❖   **What is *you*?**

A week later one of the yous is involved in an accident and breaks an arm. It's very painful.

Start Question 3   Does that mean that *you* broke your arm?

Questions to take you even further

❖ In order to avoid feeling the pain of breaking your arm does it matter which one of the *yous* it was that broke their arm? To help think about this, consider the following questions:

❖ If the *you* that broke their arm was the one in booth number 1 (i.e. the original) does that mean that you broke your arm?

❖ If the *you* that broke their arm was the one in booth number 2 (i.e. the copy) does that mean that you broke your arm?

Your Questions

❖

❖

❖

Works well with

✓ Other entries in the 'Personal Identity' section (particularly Identity Parade: Memory, Body, Brains, Cloning, Change)

✓ Pencil Person Meets Pencil Person!

✓ BURIDAN's Asteroid

✓ The 2 Square

✓ *Thoughtings:* You, Me, Aliens and Others

✓ *The If Machine:* The Ceebie Stories, The Ship of Theseus, Yous On Another Planet, Where Are You?

Source: The film *The Prestige* directed by Christopher Nolan.

Philosophy: The philosophy of the self, selfhood, personal identity, Leibniz's Law (identity of indiscernibles).

Not Half the Man He Used To Be

Peter Worley

Starting age: 8 years

Methusela, or Metty, wants to live for as long as possible but he is getting old. Today, Metty's not half the man he used to be. His knees aren't working as well as they once did. However, because this story takes place in the future, he is able to replace his parts when they stop working with mechanical parts made from plastic and metal. Even these days we are able to replace our knees but in Metty's time he is able to replace not just his knees but every part of his body with new, perfectly working parts.

First he replaces his knees and then, when his eyesight begins to deteriorate, he has some new, special camera-eyes put in. They work even better than his eyes when they were healthy. Metty is very happy with his new eyes. He carries on in this way: every time a part of him stops working so well he has it replaced.

Start Question 1   How long can he go on replacing things before he becomes a different person?

Questions to take you further

❖   Is it after the first replacement?

❖   After the last replacement?

❖   Or somewhere in-between?

Eventually, another one hundred years later, he has replaced every part of his body with new, perfectly working, plastic and metal parts; every part that is, except for his brain. Metty has noticed, however, that it isn't working as well as it used to – his memory in particular is not half of what it used to be. He has been thinking about having a new computer-brain put in to replace his old brain. He has been told that it will work much better than his original ever did. He will be super-clever and have a phenomenal memory and, what's more, he'll be able to have all the memories from his own brain transferred into the new, computer-brain. It will also last for another two hundred years at least. His old brain, however, will die very soon if it is not replaced. He wonders: should he have his old brain replaced with a new computer-brain?

Start Question 2   If he does replace his brain with the new computer-brain will he be the same person or a different person?

Questions to take you even further

❖   If he didn't have his memories transferred then would he be the same person or a different person?

❖   Once he replaces his brain there will be no parts of the original Metty left. Does that matter if he still has the memories of the old Metty?

❖   If he replaces his brain will the old Metty be dead or alive?

Your Questions

❖

❖

❖

Works well with

✓   Other entries in the 'Person Identity' section (particularly All That Glistens …, Backtracking, Who Do You Think You Are?)

✓   Revelation

✓   Only Human

✓   *Thoughtings:* You, Me, Aliens and Others

✓   *The If Machine:* The Ceebie Stories, The Ship of Theseus, Where Are You?

Source: Plutarch's the Ship of Theseus (see Thomas Hobbes).

Philosophy: John Locke and Thomas Hobbes on identity.

Metaphysics: Philosophy of Mind

Pinka and Arwin Go Forth (1): Of Macs and Men
David Birch

Starting age: 7 years

Two curious aliens from a distant galaxy arrived on Earth to find out what it was like. They were fascinated by what they found. This tiny out-of-the-way planet was a very interesting place indeed. They decided to write about everything they saw so they could tell the aliens back home all about it. The two aliens started making lists of all they encountered.

Flowers: roses, irises, daffodils …

Oceans: the Atlantic, the Pacific, the Indian …

Food: rice, chips, jam …

The two aliens, however, got into a fierce disagreement over where they should place humans on their lists. Alien number 1 – named Arwin – thought that humans should go in the *Animals* list with the ducks and whales and so on. But Alien number 2 – named Pinka – believed humans should be listed with the *Machines*, with the computers and phones and so on.

Start Question 1   Should humans go on the 'Animals' list or the 'Machines' list?

Questions to take you further

❖   What reasons do you think Arwin and Pinka might give for putting humans on (a) the 'Animal' list (Arwin) and (b) the 'Machine' list (Pinka)? Try to think of at least two reasons for each. Compare your reasons to the ones Arwin and Pinka come up with.

(*Their conversation is here translated for us to understand.*)

'Humans are more like animals because they sleep, just as animals do,' Arwin said confidently.

'But humans can do maths and so can computers. Animals can't do maths,' Pinka replied.

'That may be so,' said Arwin, 'but computers don't eat, do they? Yet humans do, and so too do animals.'

'Can an animal play chess? Could a duck play chess?' Pinka asked, thinking the answer obvious.

'It might be able to,' Arwin answered stubbornly. 'I've never tried to play chess with a duck. Anyway, even if they can't, humans grow older like animals do. Computers don't grow old.'

'But humans can problem-solve. They can figure things out, just like machines. Humans belong in the *Machine* list,' said Pinka exasperated, his face flashing purple and green.

The argument went on deep into the night.

Start Question 2   Are humans more like computers/machines or animals?

Questions to take you even further

❖   **What is an animal?**

❖   **What is a machine?**

❖   Can machines be alive?

❖   Do machines have to have electricity to work?

❖   What does 'alive' mean?

Days later the two aliens were still arguing. They looked terribly tired and having not brushed their gums (they don't have teeth) for days, their breath was ferocious. Still, neither of them would accept what the other said. Arwin still insisted that humans were more like animals, and Pinka maintained they most certainly were not, they were more like computers.

'Look,' Pinka begged, 'humans *know* so much. They *understand* so much. Like computers, they just gain more and more knowledge. Right?'

'Humans don't understand all that much. They're not so special,' Arwin replied sleepily.

'Yes they are. They are. Think about ducks; humans understand so much more about the world than ducks.'

Arwin paused for a moment. Pinka held his breath, hoping Arwin was finally about to agree with him.

'Nah,' chirped Arwin. 'A duck knows what it's like at the bottom of a pond. It knows all sorts of things humans don't know.'

Pinka could argue no longer. Something inside him had cracked. He collapsed to the floor in a heap and wept blobby alien tears.

Start Question 3   Do humans understand the world any more than ducks?

Questions to take you even further

❖   What is it to understand something?

❖   Can ducks *understand*?

❖   **What is understanding?**

Your Questions

❖

❖

❖

Works well with

✓   Other Pinka and Arwin Go Forth entries

✓   The Questioning Question

✓   Bat-Girl

✓   The Clockwork Toymaker

✓   Can I Think?

✓   *The If Machine:* The Ceebie Stories

✓   *Thoughtings:* Minds and Brains

Source and Philosophy: The philosophy of cognitive science, Wittgenstein and 'forms of life', J. M. Coetzee's *The Lives of Animals*.

Pinka and Arwin Go Forth (2): Making Up Their Minds

David Birch

Starting age: 7 years

'Pinka, what about our lists?'

The sobbing alien was curled up on the floor.

'Pinka. Our lists,' prodded Arwin.

'All right,' murmured Pinka. 'What now?'

'The bits inside humans,' said Arwin.

Pinka got up and changed eyeballs, putting x-ray ones in. He squinted at a passing human, listing what he saw: 'Kidneys, lungs, liver, bones, blood, ear wax, heart, veins, brain, intestines, snot ... *eww!* This human is *bursting* with snot!' observed Pinka scientifically.

Arwin read over the list. 'You forgot the mind,' he said.

'No, I didn't.'

'Yes, you did.'

'No, I didn't. Gimme.' Arwin handed Pinka the gizmo. 'See, right there: "brain",' said Pinka.

'The brain isn't the mind,' said Arwin.

Start Question 1   Is the mind the same thing as the brain?

Questions to take you further

❖   Is there anything the mind might have that the brain doesn't have?

❖   Is there anything the brain might have that the mind doesn't have?

'Put your x-ray eyeballs in if you don't believe me. There's nothing else. Just that big, grey raisin in their head,' Pinka pointed out.

'You can't see the mind, Pinka.'

'If you can't see it, how do you know it's there?'

Arwin puzzled. 'Well, you can't see thoughts. But we know humans have those.'

'I can see your thoughts,' said Pinka. 'They look like a wrinkly forehead.'

'You can't see thoughts in the brain though,' said Arwin, feeling his wrinkles.

'Look, Arwin,' said Pinka pointing at the snotty human. 'You see all those little flashes in the brain? Those are thoughts. The brain is like a machine and thinking is like machine-work, and thinking happens in the mind, so the mind is the brain.'

'The mind isn't the brain,' replied Arwin. 'It's not a machine. Don't you remember? We agreed that humans are animals, not machines?'

'No we never! Humans are machines – *that's* what we agreed.'

'Animals.'

'Machines.'

'Animals.'

'Machines.'

'Animals.'

'Machines.'

'Animals.'

…

Eternity loomed.

Pinka surveyed his options: he could carry on arguing or he could collapse to the floor kicking and screaming and crying.

The floor looked inviting. Pinka paused a moment and collected his energy.

A tantrum was brewing.

Start Question 2   Should the mind and brain be listed as separate things?

Questions to take you even further

❖   Whose ideas do you agree with more, Arwin's or Pinka's?

❖   Have you any ideas of your own to add to the argument? Do they support Arwin or Pinka?

Your Questions

❖

❖

❖

Works well with

✓   Other Pinka and Arwin Go Forth entries

✓   BURIDAN's Asteroid

✓   The 2 Square

✓   Gun

✓   Pencil Person Meets Pencil Person!

✓   The Clockwork Toymaker

✓   *The If Machine:* The Ceebie Stories

✓   *Thoughtings:* Minds and Brains

Philosophy: Philosophy of mind, Descartes and dualism, identity theory, Gilbert Ryle and behaviourism.

Thoughting: Can I Think?
Peter Worley

Starting age: 7 years

In the future an artificial human has been built in Japan using metal and plastic and it has a computer for a brain. It is called the AH1000 but is known as 'Aitchey'. When asked the following question, 'Aitchey, can you think?' the AH1000 replied:

> Can I think?
> My human friends
> Don't think I can
>
> But I think:
> I think I can think.
>
> Okay, so I'm just
> Nuts and bolts
> And made to work
> With wires and volts

But I think:

I think I can think.

But if I'm wrong

And really I can't,

I only *think* I think I can think?

Start Question   Does Aitchey think that he/she can think?

Questions to take you further

❖   Can a computer think?

❖   **What is thinking?** (Can you say what thinking is without saying the word 'thinking' in your answer?)

❖   Do you think the robot that wrote this poem can think? Why?

❖   What does 'I think: I think I can think' mean? Does it make sense?

❖   Do you think robots will be able to think in the future?

❖   What does a robot or computer need to be able to think?

❖   If a computer says that it 'thinks it can think' can it be wrong?

❖   Does the fact that Aitchey wrote a poem mean that it can think?

❖   Does the fact that Aitchey says 'I' throughout the poem mean that it can think?

❖   If these are Aitchey's words then is it a poem?

❖   Is Aitchey a *he* or a *she*, or neither?

Your Questions

❖

❖

❖

Works well with

✓   Other entries in the 'Philosophy of Mind' section

✓   Who Do You Think You Are?

✓   Pinka and Arwin Go Forth (1) and (3)

✓   I'm Glad I'm Not Real

✓   Jack's Parrot and Wind-Spell

✓   A Random Appetizer

✓   Jemima or James

✓   *Thoughtings:* Minds and Brains

✓   *The If Machine:* The Ceebie Stories

Source: Philip K. Dick, *Do Androids Dream of Electric Sheep?* (filmed as *Blade Runner* by Ridley Scott).

Philosophy: The philosophy of artificial intelligence (AI); John Searle and 'the Chinese Room'.

Trying to Forget and Not Bothering to Remember

Trying to Forget
Robert Torrington and Peter Worley

Starting age: 8 years

A magician had entered into a bet with a magistrate. The magician had lost the bet and that meant, according to the terms of their agreement, that he would have to create a magic spell that would make his opponent 'endlessly wealthy'. But the magician was mean and he didn't want his opponent to get anything so he came up with a devious way to fulfil his side of the bargain but not make the magistrate rich. He told his smiling opponent that if he took a magic stone – which the magician then gave to him – and he placed it over a roaring fire and then performed the incantation – which the magician also taught him – then he would be endlessly wealthy. But there was a catch: 'The spell will only work,' said the magician to the magistrate, 'if you are able *to forget that this bet ever took place*. Ha, ha, ha!' And with that the magician left, having wiped the smile from the magistrate's face.

Start Question 1   Will the magistrate be able to forget that the bet ever took place in order to become wealthy?

Questions to take you further

❖   Can you try to forget something?

❖   **What is forgetting?**

❖   Is it possible to not think of *pink elephants*?

Not Bothering to Remember

Try as he might, each time the magistrate said the incantation, he remembered *why* he was trying to forget. He tried to forget by saying to himself, 'I must forget the bet, *I must forget the bet!*' But the more he tried, the clearer he remembered the words of the magician. 'Curse him! There's no way I can forget those words whilst concentrating so much on forgetting … Unless …' And the magistrate had an idea. He would stop *trying to forget*, and just *not bother to remember* instead. He spent days not bothering, but not *trying*, to remember the bet at all.

Start Question 2   Will not bothering to remember work?

Questions to take you even further

❖   Is there a difference between 'not bothering to remember' and 'trying to forget'?

❖   What is the difference between 'forgetting' and 'not bothering to remember'?

❖   Can you fail to remember something?

❖   How does forgetting happen?

❖   Why do we remember things?

❖   Why do we forget things?

❖   Imagine that there was someone who never forgot anything. What would it be like for them? Would the world be a different place?

Your Questions

❖

❖

❖

Works well with

✓   Whose Bump?

✓   All That Glistens …

✓   Identity Parade (1): Memory

✓   *Thoughtings:* You, Me, Aliens and Others

✓   *The If Machine:* The Ceebie Stories, The Ship of Theseus, Yous On Another Planet, Where Are You?

Philosophy: Franz Brentano, intentionality, intentional forgetting.

Mind the Planet
Peter Worley

Starting age: 11 years   Advanced

... And eventually Planet Earth became *conscious*. Over time it had become aware of itself just like a human mind. But how had this happened? Here's Earth's own account in translation:

> Consciousness first occurred on me only in the bacteria – known as *humanity* – that lives on my skin. The bacteria went on to create infrastructures such as cities and societies. These were all connected up by roads and rivers and then eventually by air and electricity. Communication between the infrastructures became more and more sophisticated and quicker and quicker until eventually the complete globalised system functioned like a single, giant brain. Consciousness began to spread from the individual bacterium to cities and nations. And as information became more and more connected and interactive with the advent of the Internet and the World Wide Web 'the brain' – that

is the Earth – started to become self-aware. Consciousness of an entirely different kind – *planetary* consciousness – had been born. *I* was born.

But I am lonely in this solar system. The others are either dead or non-conscious. And I am ill. The sad part is that the very thing that gave me my mind – the parasite that lives off me – is also killing me. I am not sure how much more time I have left and I wonder if consciousness has been a blessing or a curse.

Start Question   Can a city or a planet become conscious?

Questions to take you further

❖   **What is consciousness?**

❖   What is needed to instantiate consciousness?

❖   Could consciousness occur in places other than the brain?

❖   Is humanity a parasite or a kind of bacteria?

❖   Is consciousness a blessing or a curse?

❖   Is humanity a good for Earth:

    a.   In this story?

    b.   In reality?

Your Questions

❖

❖

❖

Works well with

✓   Other entries in the 'Philosophy of Mind' section (particularly Can I Think?, Revelation)

✓   Bat-Girl

✓   Jack's Parrot and Wind-Spell

✓   Bobby the Punching Bag

Source: Ned Block and 'the conscious nation'.

Philosophy: The philosophy of consciousness, supervenience, environmental ethics.

Revelation

Dan Sumners

Starting age: 11 years *Advanced*

Stephen is taking a quiet stroll alone, walking along next to a river and enjoying the sun. He is distracted because he is thinking about a story he has been writing.

He wanders a little too close to the river, and suddenly he slips and falls. He has seriously injured himself and he realises that this is the first time he can remember having done so.

He looks down and sees that a piece of rusty metal sticking out of the riverbank has made a long, wide cut on his shin. To his surprise, where he expected to see bone and muscle beneath the skin, he sees shiny metal and clusters of delicate wires.

After he has pulled himself out of the river, Stephen goes to see his friend of many years, Natalie, who is a robotics expert. When Stephen shows Natalie what the gash in his leg has revealed, she becomes very excited.

Natalie takes Stephen to her private laboratory and scans his entire body. It reveals that he is a robot covered with a living skin.

'All this time I've known you,' says Natalie excitedly, 'I had no idea you were a robot! I never doubted you were a person.'

'*I am* a person!' replied Stephen indignantly. 'I may not be a human being, but I'm still a person, just like you.'

Start Question 1 Is Stephen a person?

Questions to take you further

❖ Is there a difference between being a human and being a person?

❖ **What is a person?**

❖ Can other animals be 'a person'? Dolphins, for example, or higher primates?

❖ Can an inanimate object be 'a person'?

❖ Could an alien be considered 'a person'?

Start Question 2 Is it possible to be an android and not know?

Questions to take you further

❖   Could *you* be a robot/computer and not know?

❖   If it turned out that you were a robot/computer what would that mean?

❖   Can you think you are alive but be wrong?

❖   Can a robot/computer be alive?

❖   Can a robot/computer have thoughts/feelings?

❖   Does the protagonist in the story have thoughts/feelings? If so, what does this mean?

Your Questions

❖

❖

❖

Works well with

✓   Only Human

✓   Can I Think?

✓   Not Half the Man He Used To Be.

✓   Who Do You Think You Are?

✓   *Thoughtings:* Minds and Brains

✓   *The If Machine:* The Ceebie Stories (particularly Friends)

Source: Adapted from 'Revelation', a short story by Dan Sumners.

Philosophy: The philosophy of artificial intelligence (AI), consciousness, qualia, the concept of a person.

Only Human

Peter Worley

Starting age: 14 years   Advanced

A: Hi, I'm sorry I'm late. Something happened on the Underground that held me up.

B: That's okay. What happened?

A: There was somebody who needed my help. Though I don't like to be late to a date I thought this counted as a good reason to break that rule.

B: That's impressive. Not everyone would have stopped to help.

A: Maybe. But I believe *most* would.

B: You have a better view of human nature than I. *(pause)* Where shall we eat?

A: I know a good place near here: a good Chinese restaurant.

B: Is it greasy food? Grease doesn't agree with me – it clogs up my insides!

A: Yeah, I know what you mean. But it's very *good* Chinese food – it's not takeaway.

B: Sounds good! Let's go there.

They walk together in silence for a few moments.

B: Can we go back to this event on the tube? I don't often go on dates where I learn something morally impressive about my date in the first conversation. I would like to know more about it. Do you mind?

A: I didn't mean to draw attention to myself … now I feel a little embarrassed.

B: Look, *I* asked. You weren't going to say anything until I asked.

A: For humility's sake I probably should have lied to throw you off the scent, but I find it very difficult to tell a lie – I don't know why that is, I just seem to find it impossible.

B: Hey, as far as this date goes, it's a great start. As a quid pro quo: I sometimes don't think I am *able* to be concerned for others. I don't seem to feel anything. I would barely have noticed that someone needed help, so I am very interested in someone who thinks differently. I would like to learn.

A: The fact that you *want* to learn is 'morally impressive' …

***

It was almost five years before I discovered I had fallen in love with an android. We had met like you might meet anyone: an online dating agency. He had impressed me with his thoughtfulness and moral concern. I enjoyed the fact that he was clearly more intelligent than I, though not boastful or unpleasant. He seemed to me a rare specimen indeed – not like other men.

Looking back, there was nothing other than his 'perfectness' that indicated anything out of the ordinary. He did not speak or move like a robot; he was human in all but faults. I should have known it was too good to be true.

Someone once said that significant intelligence could be demonstrated in a machine if a human being in conversation with an unseen computer couldn't tell that the synthetic interlocutor was not human. What about an observer to our first conversation – would they be able to spot what I did not? Could true love be demonstrated similarly? It seems so.

I spent five years in ignorance, and therefore five years in true love. He was a perfect imitation of a human but a great improvement on a man. When I found out what he was, I was naturally angry and I experienced something like grief. But to my rational mind it made no sense to be either angry or to grieve. There was no one to be angry with and no one had ever existed to grieve for. But angry I was; and grieve I did.

Human beings are psychological simpletons: what we do often has little to do with what we know to be true. I know that when I watch a film I'm viewing something that did not happen, that's not really happening on the screen – and yet I cry or feel uplifted. We can suspend our disbelief in all sorts of other contexts too, and I suspended my disbelief with Michael.

I had cultivated the habit of loving him and, once I had got over the initial shock of the android revelation, I continued to love him. I thought: Well, nothing has changed. I could've continued as before, none the wiser, so why can't I continue now? I don't even know for sure whether my own mother is truly alive, except by how she appears to me, so in that sense there's no real difference to me between Michael and any other human being other than myself. I don't know for certain if *anyone* has experiences like me, other than because they *behave* like they have; and Michael certainly behaves like he has.

But there must have been some discrepancy – some indication that might have given you cause for concern, something un-human, you might protest. But my mother often used to complain that my father was 'slightly autistic' and 'socially inept' because he did not display 'a normal human ability to read between the lines' or assess a social situation well, as she claimed. I never thought he might be a robot. But maybe I should have …

So I concluded that I could love Michael, and I had no real reason to doubt that he was alive and self-aware. If I asked him he would say, 'Of course I'm alive. I certainly feel alive.' How could I then say, 'You may *think* you're alive, but you aren't really – you're just programmed to respond that way'? After all, many of the things human beings do and believe are hardwired into them, recalling ancient rites performed by their ancestors. We're just programmed to respond that way.

***

Now I have reached my seventy-ninth year. I am still with Michael, and I still love him, but I have grown older. I have become frail and decrepit. I look at his ever-beautiful body and the crystalline youth Michael still possesses, and I am saddened. When his body wears out he simply has his data transferred to a new and identical body. His memories, personality, thoughts and characteristics – should I say his *soul*? – are all downloaded onto a computer hard-drive and then transferred swiftly and silently into the new body. The hardware is replaceable and the software transferable.

The human machine is very different. Even if in principle it's the same, there is a much stronger correlation, a more intimate and overwhelming connection, between the body and the mind and we have not yet been able to separate the two in the way we can with Michael. Not yet: the death of the biological body seems to bring about the death of the mind. And because of the human intimacy between the mind and the body, to transfer the mental data of one human into the body of another would seem to mean the death of one person and the creation of another, albeit intellectually continuous with the first. So why is this not the case with Michael? Or *is* it the case, but I am not able to think of it in the same way? Perhaps, if an android can be alive, then he has died many times. But I grieved only once.

Of course, not being subject to human vagaries Michael has continued to love me, although I have aged and he has not. Is this the final proof that he has never *really* loved me? This is a question I choose not to answer. After all, I am only human.

Start Question   Is it possible for a human to love a machine?

Questions to take you further

❖   Is it possible for a machine to love a human being?

❖   Is a human a kind of machine?

❖   **What is love?**

❖   Are there different kinds of love?

❖ What kinds of things can love each other?

❖ In the first section, who is A and who is B?

❖ Is the narrator male or female? How can you tell? Does it matter?

❖ Would you make the narrator's choice to not answer the final question? Why or why not?

Your Questions

❖

❖

❖

Works well with

✓ Other entries in 'Philosophy of Mind' section (particularly Revelation)

✓ The Ticklish Grump

✓ The Grumpiest Poet in the World

✓ The Tadpole and the Pike

✓ *Thoughtings:* Love, Goodness and Happiness

✓ *The If Machine:* The Ceebie Stories (particularly Friends)

Source: Inspired by the *Robot* stories of Isaac Asimov. 'Only Human' by Peter Worley was first published in *Philosophy Now* magazine, issue 69, September/October 2008.

Philosophy: The philosophy of artificial intelligence (AI), John Searle, the philosophy of love.

Metaphysics: Fiction

Wondering About Wonderland
A. C. Grayling

Starting age: 10 years   Advanced

Narrator: David enjoyed reading *Alice in Wonderland* very much, and thought that Alice was a brave and clever girl because of all that she said and did during her adventures down the rabbit hole. He told his friend Paul that he thought Alice was brave.

Paul: She wasn't brave, because she didn't exist. She is only a character in a story. How could she be brave? You have to really exist to be brave – or cowardly, or silly, or clever, or anything else for that matter.

Start Question 1   Was Alice brave?

Questions to take you further

❖   Can a fictional character be brave?

❖   Can statements about fictional characters be true or false?

❖   Is it true that Alice was brave?

❖   Do true sentences need a thing that makes them true?

❖   Do fictional characters exist?

David: But if I said, 'Alice in the story *Alice in Wonderland* fell down a rabbit hole', what I say would be true. In that story, did she or didn't she fall down a rabbit hole? Yes, she did. So the statement 'Alice fell down a rabbit hole' is true. And if we can say true things about people, even if they only exist in stories, why can't these true statements include ones like 'Alice was brave', 'Alice was clever' and so on?

Paul: If a story is fictional, everything in it is a fiction, and fictions by definition are not true. So there cannot be any true statements in a story.

David: What if there were a fictional story in which the statement occurs that 'Water is wet'. Isn't that a true statement, even though it is in a fictional work?

Paul: That's not the same thing, and that's not what I meant. I meant such statements as 'Alice is brave' and 'Alice fell down the rabbit hole'. After all, people don't fall down rabbit holes, do they! That only happens in stories. And fictional stories are just that – fictions.

Start Question 2   Who is right and who is wrong? Why?

Questions to take you even further

❖ Are they both right?

❖ Are they both wrong?

❖ Do either of them give any reasons for what they think?

❖ Whose reasons do you think are best?

❖ Is it true that water is wet?

❖ If it says that water is wet in a fictional story then has the fictional story said something true?

❖ If one of them is right does that mean that he has said something true? But if Paul and David are not real how can either of them say something true?

❖ Is 'fiction' the same thing as 'falsehood'? Is fiction a lie? Does a storyteller tell lies?

❖ If it is, would that make fiction bad?

❖ What's the point of fiction?

❖ **What is fiction?**

❖ Can we learn truths about human nature and character from stories?

Your Questions

❖

❖

❖

Works well with

- ✓ Other entries in the 'Fiction' section
- ✓ Tralse
- ✓ Jack's Parrot and Wind-Spell
- ✓ A Random Appetizer
- ✓ Negative Nelly
- ✓ The Accidental Confession

Philosophy: Truth-value in fiction.

I'm Glad I'm Not Real

Amie L. Thomasson

Starting age: 7 years

There once was a fictional character. And her name was May. May was 4 years old; or, at least that's what the story said. In fact, she had been written quite recently, 'and so in that sense, I am a newborn fictional character,' she liked to say. Especially when she was looking for a good excuse to curl up on the rug like a teeny tiny baby, suck her thumb and bat at things in a homemade play gym.

May was a lovely little fictional character, bouncy, fun, very clever and with an uncanny ability to eat olives. Put as many as you like in front of her, and they'd always be gone by the next page.

But still May was not happy, for although she appreciated her book, she was lonely. 'Why don't I have a mummy or daddy to take care of me?' she asked.

'But you do have a mother. I created you from words and pictures,' her author said.

'That's *not* what I mean.' The little girl sulked, and she slumped down right in the corner of the page, folding one edge over to hide herself.

'Oh, alright then,' the author said. And she made her a mother. A mother who loved her more than anything in the world, who taught her to paint and to laugh at herself, who sat on the floor for hours making zoos and block houses and earthquakes to destroy them. And she made her a father. A father with constant love and gentle patience, who taught her to bake banana bread and to play the piano and to name every bird in the garden. And they were happy together.

They came to live in a book. A real hardcover book, with full colour pictures and shiny pages. And the book came to be on the shelves of a little girl – a 4-year-old girl, as it happens – by the name of Natalie. The various dragons and bears who lived in tatty second-hand paperbacks on lower shelves really quite envied them.

Till one day, just before bedtime, Natalie spotted the book, sticking out slightly between a board book about ducklings and something involving a circus. 'What's this book?' she asked. She had never seen it before. 'I want to read it now! Can't we read it pleeeaaase?' she asked. 'Well, it's a bit late,' her mum said, 'but I guess we could read just this one.' And they all plumped down on Natalie's fluffy red comforter, and her dad began to read.

As they closed the book for the night, Natalie's mum said, 'Well, I'm glad little May got some parents and isn't lonely any more.'

'But muuuummmy,' Natalie protested, 'she's not *real*!'

'Oh yes,' admitted her mum, closing the book gently and turning out the light.

'I'm glad I'm real and not just in a book,' said Natalie quietly as she curled up with her blanket.

'So am I, sweetheart,' her mummy agreed as she kissed her soft cheek goodnight.

Once the book was closed little May began to cry. 'What does she *mean* I'm not real?' asked May who, like most children, had forgotten those muddled early days after she was first made, those days when she was lonely.

'Well,' her mother explained, 'we are just characters in a book. We do what our author writes, there's no more to us than she's given us, and we stay in the world of these pages.'

'But I want to get out of here!' May protested. 'I want to be really *real*. I want to have toes' (for these had never been seen in the pages). 'I want to know what happened when I was just 2' (for this had never been spoken of). 'And I want to go wherever I want to go, not where some author puts me!' she railed. And she wept and she struggled and she stewed. Her mother cried a bit too, to see her daughter realising these sad truths, but her daddy just held her hand.

'You know,' he said, 'since we're not real, we'll never get sick' (no sickness is ever mentioned). 'We'll never bump too hard off a slide. Or get bitten by mosquitoes.'

'And will no one ever steal the olives out of my lunch box?' May wanted to know.

'Nope, no one will ever steal the olives out of your lunch box. Or your vanilla cookies either. And best of all, none of us will ever die – we can stay here together for always, loving each other in this book.'

'I'm glad we're not real,' May decided. And she curled up in a corner of the page, sucking her thumb quietly, and went to sleep.

Start Question   Is May real?

Questions to take you further

❖   Is Natalie real?

❖   Is the author of the book May is in real?

❖   Is the author of the story 'I'm Glad I'm Not Real' real?

❖   **What is 'real'?**

❖   Could *we* be characters in a book?

❖   Does May have toes? Does Natalie have toes? Does the author of the book have toes? Does the author of the story have toes?

❖   If May walks off the edge of the page does she still exist?

Questions to take you even further

❖   Do authors create fictional characters? If a fictional character has parents (as May does eventually), who really creates her: the author or the parents?

❖   Could a fictional character get out of a book and become real? If they could then would they be the same person?

❖   Do fictional characters (once created) survive forever? If not, when do they cease to exist? Are they killed off when they die in the book? Or when copies of the books about them are destroyed? Or when no one remembers them?

❖   Is it better to be real, to often be sick, to die and watch our loved ones die; or would it be better to be more like a fictional character whose story is laid out by someone else, and is safe from any bad events happening, from sickness and death, but without having control of one's life?

❖   For older students, watch the Woody Allen film *The Purple Rose of Cairo* to discuss the relation between fictional characters and real people.

❖   Read 'An Enchanted Place' in *The House at Pooh Corner* by A. A. Milne and/or the final section of C.S. Lewis' *The Last Battle*. What do you think these chapters are saying? Are they suggesting that fiction can have its own reality? If so, how?

❖   For younger ones read, *Wolves* by Emily Garrett to discuss a book-within-a-book that refers to itself. Ask them: What do you think is in the book that the rabbit is reading?

Your Questions

❖

❖

❖

Works well with

✓ Other entries in the 'Fiction' section

✓ Itselfish

✓ The Questioning Question

✓ Can I Think?

✓ Mind the Planet

✓ Who Do You Think You Are?

✓ *Thoughtings*: Where's Mr Nobody?

Philosophy: The ontology of fictional entities.

Fictional Feelings
Berys Gaut and Morag Gaut

Starting age: 7 years

Best friends Mary and Jane are having a fictional story read to them by Mary's mother in which the hero is badly injured after he bravely risks his own life to save another. 'I feel so sad for him,' Mary cries, and bursts into tears. Jane says, 'Don't be silly, it's only a story, so he didn't really get hurt.'

'But you're crying too!' objects Mary.

'No, I'm not,' replies Jane sharply, but she won't look at Mary because tears are starting to spill out from her eyes too, no matter how hard she tries to hold them back. 'It's *just a story*!' she insists, as much to herself as to Mary.

Start Question   Do we really feel sad for people in fictional stories, or is this just pretend sadness?

Questions to take you further

- ❖   If we really do feel sad, is it reasonable for us to feel this?

- ❖   Is it good for us to feel sad at fictional stories?

- ❖   Can we feel grief, anger, fear, pity and so on for people in fictional stories?

- ❖   Would Mary's response be reasonable if she was reading an account of something that had really happened?

- ❖   Why is Jane crying when she clearly seems to believe that the story is not true? And why can't she stop herself from crying if she's knows it's not true?

- ❖   Does she believe that the story is not true?

Your Questions

- ❖

- ❖

- ❖

Works well with

- ✓   Other entries in the 'Fiction' section (particularly Feelings About Fiction)

- ✓   Bobby the Punching Bag

Philosophy: The paradox of fiction, Plato and the emotions, Kendall Walton.

Feelings About Fiction
Anja Steinbauer

Starting age: 7 years

[*Feelings About Fiction should be done as a follow-up session to Fictional Feelings. Make sure you read Fictional Feelings first, before reading this one.*]

On their way to school, Conrad, one of Mary's other friends, tells Mary about his puppy that was run over by a car. 'He's alive but his paw is badly hurt, and he'll never be able to run properly any more.' Mary, close to tears at the thought of the little dog in pain and distress says, 'That's terrible.' Conrad starts laughing, 'You're so gullible; I don't even have a puppy!'

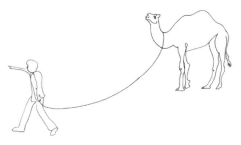

Start Question 1   Is what Conrad told Mary fiction or lies?

Questions to take you further

❖ Is fiction the same as lying? If not, what's the difference?

❖ How might she feel after he tells her that he just made the puppy up? Will she still be sad? Why or why not?

❖ What's the difference between the story Mary's mother was reading to them and the fib Conrad told Mary? Is there a difference?

❖ Some people say that stories are 'permitted lies'. Do you agree?

Question to take you even further

❖ Find out about the 'suspension of disbelief'. Is the suspension of disbelief the same as believing something?

Later that week Conrad says to Mary, 'My mum got me a puppy at the weekend but it got run over by a car. It's still alive but his paw is badly hurt, and he'll never be able to run properly any more. You probably won't believe me, but *honestly*, it's true!' Mary looks at Conrad in disbelief. She feels no sadness towards the dog in Conrad's story but she does feel angry towards Conrad. 'Don't tell lies!' she shouts at him and then she stamps off.

Start Question 2   Mary felt sad when her mother told her a fictional story even though it wasn't true. Why didn't she feel sad when Conrad told her about the puppy he said his mum had got him at the weekend?

Questions to take you further

❖   If Conrad's account is true should Mary feel sad?

❖   If it's not true should she feel sad?

❖   Is Conrad's account a story?

❖   Why do we respond differently to different accounts of things that aren't true?

Your Questions

❖

❖

❖

Works well with

✓   Other entries in the 'Fiction' section (particularly Fictional Feelings)

✓   A Bad Picture

✓   What We Talk About When We Talk About Words

✓   *The If Machine:* The Lie

Philosophy: The paradox of fiction, Kendall Walton, aesthetics, the emotions, the suspension of disbelief, Colin Radford.

Phil and Soph and the Stories
Philip Cowell

Starting age: 5 years

Phil and Soph are doing some creative writing. Phil is writing a story about Soph and it starts, 'One day Soph woke up and the sun was shining and she thought she would get out of bed and make some breakfast …' Soph's story is about monsters from another planet and her story starts, 'The Klopotron Monopod zoomed in to Yopox II, shooting into the Galactic Bopplesphere …'

Start Question   Are Phil and Soph writing fiction?

Questions to take you further

❖   Is it Phil who is writing fiction or is it Soph? Are neither of them writing fiction or are they both writing fiction?

❖   **What is fiction?**

❖   What is not fiction?

❖   What is non-fiction?

❖   Are both of their stories about something?

❖   What does the word 'Soph' refer to in Phil's story?

❖   What does the word 'Bobblesphere' refer to in Soph's story? Anything?

❖   Does Soph's story make sense?

❖   Given that Phil and Soph are themselves in a story, is either of them writing anything?

❖   If aliens exist does that mean that Soph's story is true or not?

❖   If aliens don't exist does that mean that Soph's story is true or not?

Your Questions

❖

❖

❖

Works well with

✓   Other entries in the 'Fiction' section (particularly Feelings About Fiction and Wondering About Wonderland)

✓   Other Phil and Soph stories

Philosophy: The philosophy of literature, truth and falsehood, truthfulness, sense and reference, creative writing.

The Shop Part II

Epistemology or What Can Be Known About What There Is

Epistemology: Knowledge

Pinka and Arwin Go Forth (3): Different Animals?
David Birch

Starting age: 10 years

Pinka had a talent for tears. He cried long and hard. He cried till he had no more blobs in him left to shed. He gathered himself together, wiped his nose and told Arwin that he wanted to go home.

'Not yet,' said Arwin. 'We haven't finished our lists.'

'Whatever,' sniffed Pinka. 'Do what you want, put humans in the *Animals* list, see if I care. I just want to go home.'

'Very well, humans in the *Animals* list,' said Arwin, noting it down in his gizmo. 'And that's about it. I'm ready when you are.'

'You'd better put those short-haired creatures on the list too,' suggested Pinka.

'What short-haired creatures?'

'You know, the ones that look sort of like the humans, but they don't give birth.'

'The men and boys?'

'Yes, the men and boys,' replied Pinka. 'If you're putting the humans on the *Animals* list, they may as well go on there too.'

'Pinka, you dope, they're already on the list, as "humans",' tutted Arwin.

'Oh, I thought "humans" meant the birth-giving ones, the women and girls. Okay, well make sure the women and girls are on the *Animals* list along with the humans,' instructed Pinka.

'What planet are you on? They are humans! Boys and girls, men and women, they're all human. They're the same animal.'

'Don't be silly, no they're not.'

'Yes, they are.'

'No, they're not.'

'Yes, they are.'

'No, they're not. They're so different to each other.'

'How? How are they?' barked Arwin.

'You know, the girls are all like "woo", and the boys are like "yeah" and so, you know – they're different,' shrugged Pinka.

'Well, that was well explained,' said Arwin sarcastically.

'Don't be cruel, I'm tired. You're always cruel to me. I want to leave. Just put the boys on the list along with the humans and let's please go.'

'Boys *are* humans! So *are* girls! They're the *same* animal.'

'But they're so different.'

'No, they're not.'

'Yes, they are.'

'No, they're – oh, this is ridiculous,' hissed Arwin. 'This is the last time I go on holiday with you.'

'You're being mean again,' sobbed Pinka, as fresh blobs began to fall.

'And you're being a complete and total …'

Suffice it to say that Arwin and Pinka never were able to reach an agreement. And to the great benefit of their health, and their lives in general, they never did go on holiday together again.

Start Question   Should boys and girls (men and women) be listed as separate animals?

Questions to take you further

❖   Are there differences between the sexes? Why?

❖   Are we born with these differences or are they given to us?

❖   Can we choose which sex we are?

❖   What would a third sex be like?

❖   Is there a difference between a 'sex' and a 'gender'? If so, what?

Your Questions

❖

❖

❖

Works well with

✓ Pinka and Arwin Go Forth (1) and (3)

✓ Teenage Angst

✓ Jemima or James

✓ Perfect People

✓ C'est de l'or

Philosophy: Queer theory, difference feminism.

Tina's Ghost
Philip Gaydon

Starting age: 7 years

Tina tells Laura that she saw a ghost last night. Laura doesn't believe Tina because she doesn't believe in ghosts. Laura tells Tina that she must have been dreaming. Tina says she knows she was awake because it felt so real and everything in her room was exactly the same as any other time she had woken up in the night – except for the ghost. Laura still doesn't believe Tina and tells her she shouldn't tell lies otherwise she could get into trouble. Tina is very upset because she has never told Laura a lie and doesn't like that her best-friend won't believe her.

Start Question   Given that Tina is not lying, is Laura right not to believe Tina?

Questions to take you further

❖ Why doesn't Laura believe Tina?

❖ If Tina is telling the truth does that mean she saw a ghost?

❖ Is Tina right to be upset?

❖ Would you believe your best friend if they told you they had seen a ghost?

❖ What would change your mind?

❖ If you saw a ghost would you be worried about telling people in case they didn't believe you?

❖ How do you think you could convince them you had seen a ghost if they didn't believe you?

❖ **What is belief?**

Your Questions

❖

❖

❖

Works well with

✓ The Confession makes a good follow-up to this one

✓ The Traffic Light Boy (3)

✓ Knowing Stuff

✓ The Adventures of Poppy the Bear

✓ The Pencil

✓ The Three-Minute-Old Universe

Source: George MacDonald's *The Princess and the Goblin.*

Philosophy: Epistemology, the right to believe, testimony.

The Confession

Peter Worley

Starting age: 9 years

John and Hosper are brothers. When John was 9 years old he heard a knock at his bedroom door in the middle of the night. When he opened the door he found no one there and from that day on he believed that he had been visited by a ghost. For thirty years John told the story of the ghost visitation as a true story. Thirty years after the event his brother Hosper confessed to him that he had been responsible for the knocking John had heard all those years ago. But John still believed he had been visited by a ghost. His brother said, 'No, you don't understand. There was no ghost – it was me!'

'I *was* visited by a ghost that night. I'm certain of it. If it's true that you knocked on my door, that doesn't prove that there wasn't a ghost there. It could have been there *as well as* you.'

Start Question   If it was Hosper who knocked on John's door, is John right to continue with his belief that he was visited by a ghost when he was 9 years old?

(With older students you could add, as John Hosper does – see source below – that John believed that he had been visited by the ghost of *his recently deceased grandmother*, whom he missed greatly.)

Questions to take you further

* Could both accounts be true? In other words, could Hosper be telling the truth and there have been a ghost there that night?

* If you were to accept only one of the accounts, which one would you accept and why?

* Why do you think John won't give up his 'ghost' account?

* John feels certain that it was a ghost, so does that mean that it was a ghost?

* Is feeling certain of something the same as knowing it?

* Should he give up his 'ghost' account?

* Are they both entitled to their opinion?

* If John is wrong would he still be entitled to his opinion?

* Does John have good evidence for his belief that he was visited by a ghost?

❖ Is there good evidence that he wasn't visited by a ghost?

❖ The principle of Occam's razor says that you should always accept the simpler explanation. What do you think this means? Which explanation would the principle of Occam's razor recommend that you accept?

Your Questions

❖

❖

❖

Works well with

✓ As a follow-up to Tina's Ghost

✓ The Adventures of Poppy the Bear

✓ The Traffic Light Boy (3)

✓ The Broken Window

✓ What Goes Up …

Source: John Hospers' *An Introduction to Philosophical Analysis*.

Philosophy: The principle of Occam's razor.

The Adventures of Poppy the Bear
Lisa McNulty

Starting age: 7 years

Katie's favourite toy is a very old bear called Poppy. Katie has had Poppy ever since she can remember. Poppy is worn and battered from being washed so many times. But she has bright black button eyes and a red ribbon around her neck. Katie loves Poppy very much.

Katie loves Poppy so much that one day she thinks: maybe Poppy is alive, like me. I've never heard her speak or seen her walk. But I can't always see her, and I wouldn't always hear her. Every night I go to sleep; maybe when I'm asleep, Poppy wakes up and has all sorts of adventures! Maybe she sneaks down to the kitchen and helps herself to milk and chocolate biscuits. Maybe she rides Doug the dog like a pony! Maybe she walks right out of the house, goes down to the park and plays on the swings all by herself in the moonlight.

Every time Katie thinks about Poppy's adventures she believes in them a little bit more. Those crumbs on Poppy's face might be from eating biscuits. Poppy always has a bit of Doug's fur on her somewhere. The dirt on her paws could be from walking to the park. Anyway, Poppy just *looks* so alive!

One day, Katie tells her brother, Jack, all about Poppy. 'Poppy is alive,' she whispers to Jack. And she tells Jack all about Poppy's adventures.

Jack laughs. 'Poppy is just a teddy bear,' he says. 'Teddy bears aren't alive. She can't move, or talk, or do anything at all. You are just being silly.'

'I am not being silly!' insists Katie.

'Yes you are,' says Jack firmly. 'We haven't seen Poppy move, or speak or ride Doug like a pony. So she doesn't.'

Katie is very cross with her brother for not believing her. She feels cross as she eats her dinner. She feels cross as she has a bath. She won't talk to her brother all evening, because she feels too cross.

When she goes to bed, she picks up Poppy and kisses her on the nose. 'You are alive, aren't you, Poppy? I'm sure you are. Goodnight.' Katie snuggles down to sleep.

Start Question 1a   Does Katie know that Poppy *does* come alive when Katie is asleep?

Start Question 1b   Does Jack know that Poppy *doesn't* come alive when Katie is asleep?

Questions to take you further

❖   Can Katie *prove* to Jack that Poppy does come alive when Katie is sleeping?

❖   Can Jack *prove* to Katie that Poppy doesn't come alive when Katie is asleep?

❖   Poppy has biscuit crumbs on her, which she might have got from eating biscuits. She has Doug's fur on her, which she might have got from riding Doug. And she has dirt on her paws, which she might have got from walking to the park. Are these good reasons to think that Poppy is alive?

❖   What does 'maybe' mean?

❖   **What is proof?**

It's quiet and peaceful in the bedroom, and Katie falls asleep very quickly. But then she hears a noise. It's a soft noise, exactly the noise a teddy bear would make jumping off the bed and landing on the carpet. And then, straining her ears, Katie hears an even softer noise: exactly the noise a teddy bear would make tiptoeing secretly out of a bedroom. So Katie turns on the light, and sure enough, she sees Poppy tiptoeing towards the bedroom door. 'Poppy! I knew you were alive!' she cries excitedly.

Start Question 2   Did Katie know that Poppy was alive *before* she saw her tiptoeing?

Questions to take you further

❖   Does she know now, after seeing Poppy moving about, that Poppy is alive?

❖   When Katie sees Poppy tiptoe out of her bedroom, should she think that Poppy is alive? Or should Katie think that she must be dreaming?

Your Questions

❖

❖

❖

Works well with

✓   Tina's Ghost

✓   The Confession

✓   The Three-Minute-Old Universe

✓   The Traffic Light Boy (1), (2) and (3)

✓   The Pencil

Philosophy: Evidence, belief, knowledge and cognitive bias.

The Pencil
Michael Hand

Starting age: 7 years

Tim goes up to Miss Brent and complains that Gareth has stolen his pencil. Miss Brent asks Tim if he saw Gareth steal it. Tim replies, 'No, Miss, but Gareth lost his pencil this morning and now he's got one exactly like mine, so I know it was him.'

Start Question   Does Tim *know* that Gareth stole his pencil?

Questions to take you further

* What's the difference between knowing and suspecting?

* When are we justified in saying that we know something?

* If a classmate reports that she saw Gareth take the pencil from Tim's pencil-case, would that settle the matter?

* Is borrowing without permission the same as stealing?

* Would it make a difference if Gareth had found the pencil on the floor, rather than taking it from Tim's pencil-case?

* Is it stealing to keep things that others have lost?

* If the pencil is school property, rather than Tim's own property, does it still make sense to say that Gareth stole it?

Your Questions

*

*

*

Works well with

✓   Tina's Ghost

✓   The Confession

✓   Classroom Punishment

✓   The Adventures of Poppy the Bear

✓   The Traffic Light Boy (1), (2) and (3)

✓   Knowing Stuff

✓   The Broken Window

Philosophy: Theories of knowledge, epistemology, inferences.

The Flying Man
Peter Adamson

Starting age: 10 years

Imagine a man who suddenly starts to exist. He's created out of thin air, and actually in thin air – he is floating or flying. But he is in total darkness, and there is no noise, and nothing to taste or smell. His arms and legs are stretched out and he isn't touching anything, even himself; there is no wind for him to feel. So his senses are not telling him anything. And he has only just started to exist, so he cannot remember ever having seen, heard, smelled, tasted or touched anything.

Start Question 1   Would this Flying Man be able to think?

Start Question 2   Would the Flying Man be able to know anything?

Questions to take you further

❖   If he could know anything, then what sorts of things could he know, and how would he know them?

❖   A Muslim philosopher named Ibn Sina (in English he's usually called Avicenna) invented the Flying Man idea. He thought the Flying Man would know at least one thing: that he exists. Was Ibn Sina right about this?

❖   Suppose Ibn Sina was right: the Flying Man would know that he exists. In that case, would the Flying Man know that his body exists?

❖   If he couldn't know his body exists, then how could he know that he exists? Does this mean that he is not his body? For instance, that he is a soul that is different from his body?

Your Questions

❖

❖

❖

Works well with

✓   Become a Sceptic in Three Steps

✓   The Butterfly Dream

✓   Bat-Girl

✓   Pinka and Arwin Go Forth (2): Making Up Their Minds

Source: Ibn Sina (Avicenna).

Philosophy: Philosophy of mind, dualism.

The Traffic Light Boy (1)
Peter Worley

Starting age: 7 years

One day Lisa was walking along a road and she came across a boy who was staring at some traffic lights. The boy was concentrating very hard. Lisa said, 'What are you doing?'

The boy said, 'Shh! I'm concentrating.' He continued to stare at the traffic lights. Every so often the traffic lights would change from green to red and then after a while they would change back to green. After the lights had changed again he turned to her and said, 'I'm able to make the traffic lights change just by staring at them. So that's what I'm doing.' He then turned his attention back to the traffic lights and he started to concentrate again. His face looked like he was trying to go to the toilet, he was concentrating so hard.

Lisa was left wondering: *Is he able to change the traffic lights just by staring at them? He is* staring at them and they *are* changing.

Start Question   Is it true that the boy can change the traffic lights just by staring at them?

Questions to take you further

❖   Is it possible to be able to change traffic lights just by staring at them?

❖   As Lisa had noticed, every time he stared at the traffic lights they changed. So, could it be true that the boy was able to change the traffic lights just by staring at them?

Works well with

✓   The Traffic Light Boy (2) and (3)

✓   Jean-etic

✓   The Broken Window

✓   What Goes Up …

Source: Developed from a thunk in Ian Gilbert's *Little Book of Thunks*®.

Philosophy: Causation, constant conjunction, Hume.

The Traffic Light Boy (2)

Peter Worley

Starting age: 10 years

Unbeknownst to the boy these particular traffic lights have a hidden camera in them and there is a man in a faraway room who can see the boy standing in front of the traffic lights. The man controls the lights from the room with a computer. The man will change the lights from green to red or from red to green *if and only if* the boy is staring at the lights. That means that if the boy does not stare at the lights then the man will not change them, but if the boy does stare at the lights then he will.

While the boy is busy staring at the lights a friend of his sidles up to Lisa and, in a whisper, explains the whole situation to Lisa and explains that the boy doesn't know about the camera and the man. Lisa is still left wondering: *Is the boy able to change the lights just by staring at them?*

Start Question   Is the boy able to change the lights just by staring at them?

Questions to take you further

❖   Is the boy the cause of the lights changing?

❖   **What is a cause?**

❖   What is the cause of the lights changing?

❖   Is there more than one cause of the lights changing?

Works well with

✓   The Traffic Light Boy (1) and (3)

✓   Jean-etic

✓   The Broken Window

✓   What Goes Up …

Source: This thought experiment was developed from an idea thought up by 9-year-old Michael as an extension to Traffic Light Boy (1).

Philosophy: Causation and constant conjunction, equivalence (*if and only if*).

The Traffic Light Boy (3)

Peter Worley

Starting age: 9 years

The boy wants to believe that he can change the traffic lights just by staring at them. He has *decided* that he can change the traffic lights just by staring at them.

Start Question   Is the boy able to choose what he believes?

Questions to take you further

❖   Can we choose what we believe?

❖   Is belief a choice?

- ❖ What is it to believe something?
- ❖ **What is belief?**
- ❖ Can we *trick* ourselves into believing things we do not begin by believing?
- ❖ Can you *choose* to believe:
  - a. In unicorns?
  - b. That you can fly like Superman?
  - c. In God?
  - d. That the chair you are sitting on or the cup you are drinking from and so on is not really there?
  - e. In aliens?
- ❖ If you don't believe something is true (for instance, that the world is flat) can you choose to believe it if you wanted?

Works well with

- ✓ The Traffic Light Boy (1) and (2)
- ✓ Tina's Ghost
- ✓ The Confession
- ✓ The Adventures of Poppy the Bear
- ✓ The Pencil
- ✓ Knowing Stuff
- ✓ What Goes Up …

Source: The Big Question for this one was inspired by a 10-year-old girl who came up with the scenario above.

Philosophy: Belief, the right to believe, autonomy and belief, causes and belief.

Jean-etic
Saray Ayala

Starting age: 11 years

One day, over breakfast, Jean reads the following article in the newspaper:

> The annual report of the Traffic Safety Administration reveals two trends: 80% of car accidents involved people wearing blue jeans, and 60% of car accidents involved people who were drunk. Following the report, the Traffic Safety Administration launched a new campaign with high fines for those who drive after drinking alcohol. Following the implementation of the new measures car accidents have reduced considerably.

After reading the article Jean tells her parents that they must not drink alcohol before driving and she tells them that they must never wear blue jeans when driving either.

Start Question   Is Jean's advice good advice?

Questions to take you further

❖   Is Jean right to think that alcohol *causes* accidents?

❖   Is Jean right to think that wearing blue jeans *causes* accidents?

❖   Do you think that if they prohibit wearing blue jeans car accidents would reduce even more?

❖   Imagine that every time you have gone to see your favourite sports team at their home ground they have lost. Would it be right to think that your presence somehow causes your team to lose when playing at home?

❖   It is said that, statistically, people who do well in life have lots of books in their house. So should you, in order to do well in life, make sure that there are lots of books in your house?

❖   **What does 'cause' mean?**

Your Questions

❖

❖

❖

Works well with

✓ The Broken Window

✓ What Goes Up …

✓ The Confession

✓ Teenage Angst

✓ The Traffic Light Boy (1) and (2)

✓ A Random Appetizer

Philosophy: Correlation-implies-causation fallacy.

Knowing Stuff
Peter Worley

Starting age: 7 years

Scenario 1

Start Question 1a   If you *believe* that something is true, does that mean that you *know* it is true?

Let's see:

Doxa is very little, she's not even 2 years old and she has a belief that she can fly.

Start Question 1b   Does Doxa's belief that she can fly mean that she *knows* that she can fly?

She stands at the top of the stairs and then, quite convinced that she can fly, steps off the top step. The stairs go down for three steps and then there's a platform and the stairs continue at an angle. Doxa takes a step and, as you might expect, she tumbles down the stairs and lands with a bump on the platform. Her mother runs to her aid and picks her up. She's a little dazed but otherwise quite unharmed. That was close! From that moment on Doxa no longer believes that she can fly.

Questions to take you further

❖   **What is belief?**

❖   **What is knowledge?**

❖   Is belief different from knowledge? If so, in what way?

Scenario 2

Start Question 2   If you *believe* something, and *it is true*, does that mean that you *know* it is true?

Let's see:

Verity is asked by her teacher what the answer to the sum 2 + 2 is. She thinks to herself for a moment and then says, 'Yes, I know!' Her teacher asks her what it is and she says, confidently, '4'.

Is Verity right?

The teacher then says, 'Well done, Verity! Why did you answer 4?'

Verity replies, 'Because 4 is my lucky number.'

Verity *believed* that 4 was the correct answer and *it was true* that 4 was the correct answer, so did Verity *know* what the correct answer was to the question the teacher had asked?

Questions to take you further

❖   **What is truth?**

❖   What is the difference between belief, knowledge and truth?

Scenario 3

Start Question 3   If you *believe* something is true, and *it is true*, and you have *good reasons* for thinking that it is true, does that mean that you *know* it is true?

Let's see:

Justine is asked by a passing mother, who is with a girl she guesses is her daughter, whether she knows the way to the school. Justine says that she does know the way to the school because she goes there almost every day, as that's where she goes to school and she has done so for many years. She gives clear directions to the girl and her mother and then they set off for the school. They follow her directions carefully and arrive at the school in plenty of time for their appointment to look around the school that the girl will be attending from next term.

Justine *believed* she knew where the school was; *it was true* that the school was where she thought it was and *she had good reasons* for thinking that the school was where she thought it was – she walked to the school most days and had done so for many years. So, does all this mean that Justine *knows* the way to the school?

Questions to take you further

❖   What is a reason? **What is reason?** Is 'a reason' different from 'reason'?

❖   What is the difference between belief, knowledge, truth and reason?

❖   Did Justine have good reasons for thinking that the girl was the woman's daughter?

❖   Did she know that the girl was the woman's daughter?

❖   If it was true that the girl was the woman's daughter would that mean she did know that the girl was the woman's daughter?

❖   Philosophers call the final account of knowledge (in Scenario 3) the JTB theory of knowledge, which means 'justified true belief'. So, according to this theory, knowledge is when someone has a belief that is true and is justified with good reasons. Is this a satisfactory account of knowledge?

Question to take you much further

❖   Could somebody believe something to be true, it be true and they have good reasons for thinking it is true but still not have knowledge? Can you construct a scenario showing this?

Your Questions

❖

❖

❖

Works well with

✓   As a follow-up to Little Thea's Tricky Questions

✓   Many of the 'Knowledge' section entries because it describes the well-known theory of knowledge which underpins much of the material in this section.

Philosophy: Epistemology, theories of knowledge, Plato's Meno, Plato's Theaetetus, the justified-true-belief theory of knowledge; Edmund Gettier's paper 'Is Justified True Belief Knowledge?'

Phil and Soph and the Meeting
Philip Cowell

Starting age: 5 years

Phil and Soph meet at the weekend in a park. They are sat on a bench having some sandwiches. After lots of lovely chats and a few word games, they both decide to meet again next week. Phil says he's got a bad memory, so he gets out his pad of paper and writes down 'Meet Soph Saturday 3 p.m.'. Soph's got a great memory, so she just says, 'Oh, I'll remember that, no problem.' They have a hug and go their separate ways.

Start Question   Who *knows* when Phil and Soph are next meeting?

Questions to take you further

❖ If you want to know something is it better to write it down or is it better to remember it?

❖ Is memory as good as writing something down?

❖ Is writing something down a form of knowledge?

❖ Is memory a form of knowledge?

❖ **What is knowledge?**

❖ **What is memory?**

❖ If you write something down is it still in your head?

❖ If you forget your birthday for a short time does that mean that, for the short time you have forgotten it, you don't know your birthday?

Your Questions

❖

❖

❖

Works well with

✓ Thoth and Thamus works as a good follow-up to this entry

✓ The Txt Book

✓ The Questioning Question

✓ Green Ideas

✓ It Started in the Library

✓ Phil and Soph and the Numbers

✓ Jack's Parrot and Wind-Spell

✓ C'est de l'or

Philosophy: Plato's Phaedrus, the philosophy of memory, extended mind thesis, epistemology, personal identity, self-knowledge.

The Broken Window

Emma Williams

Starting age: 8 years

One lunchtime, two boys were playing football in the school playground. One of them kicked the ball too hard and it flew into the window of a science classroom. At the moment the ball reached the window it smashed.

A science teacher, who had been inside the classroom at the time, came out angry.

'Your ball just broke my window!' he shouted.

The two boys looked at each other in panic. But then one of them suddenly had an idea. 'How do you know?' he stammered.

'Don't be cheeky,' the teacher said, 'I saw it all. You kicked the ball and then it flew into my window and caused it to smash.'

'But did you actually *see* it cause the window to smash?' the boy continued. 'I mean, how do you know the window didn't smash for some other reason at the same moment the ball hit it?'

'Don't be ridiculous,' replied the teacher, 'that's too much of a coincidence.'

'Perhaps,' said the boy, confident now, 'but *can you be sure* that it didn't happen in that way?'

Start Question   Can the teacher be sure that the ball caused the window to smash?

Task   How many possible explanations for the window smashing can you think of other than the ball causing it to smash?

Questions to take you further

❖   If you think the teacher can be sure then how sure do you think the teacher can be? 100% sure?

❖   Did the teacher actually see the ball hit the window and then the window smash?

❖   Did the teacher actually see the ball *cause* the window to smash?

❖   What other things might have caused the window to smash at the same time? (See task above.)

❖   Of your list of possible explanations, and the explanation that the ball caused the window to smash, which is the most likely explanation?

❖ Are we free to choose whichever explanation we want?

❖ Can we ever definitely know that one event has caused another?

Questions to take you even further

❖ The philosopher David Hume suggested that we could never be sure that one event causes another. This is because we never actually experience causation, all we see is the 'constant conjunction' of two events (in this case, a ball flying into the window and a smashed window). Do you think we ever experience causation?

❖ Suppose Hume is correct, is it reasonable to still believe that the ball did smash the window? Why/why not?

Your Questions

❖

❖

❖

Works well with

✓ What Goes Up …

✓ The Traffic Light Boy (1), (2) and (3)

✓ Jean-etic

✓ The Confession

Philosophy: Causation, Hume's *An Enquiry Concerning Human Understanding*, the problem of induction.

Little Thea's Tricky Questions

Peter Worley

Little Thea's First Tricky Question

Starting age: 5 years

The teacher walked into the classroom and little Thea immediately put up her hand. She didn't put it down all through the register. The teacher, Miss Know-it-all, had noticed Thea's eagerness to ask a question and eventually said, 'What is it, Thea?' with a sigh. Thea was always asking her difficult questions.

'Miss, *how do you know?*' said Thea.

'What do you mean?' said Miss Know-it-all, 'How do I know *what?*'

'Just: how do you know … *stuff?*' Thea beamed eagerly, awaiting Miss Know-it-all's answer.

But, as usual, Miss Know-it-all didn't know how to answer Thea's question.

Start Question 1   Can you answer little Thea's question: How do you know?

Questions to take you further

❖   How do you know stuff?

❖   When we say 'I know', how do we know?

❖   What does 'know' mean?

❖   **What is knowledge?**

Little Thea's Second Tricky Question

Starting age: 7 years

The next day Miss Know-it-all brought in a big encyclopaedia to class and said, 'Thea, I have been thinking about your question from yesterday and I think I know the answer: I "know stuff" because I have read it in here,' she said resting her hand gently on the encyclopaedia.

Thea straight away put up her hand with such enthusiasm that she nearly fell off her chair.

'What is it, Thea?' said Miss Know-it-all, allowing Thea to continue.

'But Miss,' she said, 'How do you *know* that you really know?'

Miss Know-it-all pursed her lips and looked at Thea in silence. She stood in silence because, once again, she had no idea how to answer little Thea.

Start Question 2　　Can you do better? Can you answer little Thea's question: How do you *know* that you know something?

Questions to take you further

❖　　Does this question make sense?

❖　　If you know something then how do you know that you know it?

❖　　Is it the same question as 'How do you know'?

❖　　Is Miss Know-it-all's answer to Thea's question a good answer?

Your Questions

❖

❖

❖

Works well with

✓　　Knowing Stuff works as a good follow-up to this one

✓　　Most of the entries in the 'Knowledge' section

✓　　*Thoughtings:* The Capital of France

Philosophy: Meta-questions, epistemology.

What Goes Up ...

Peter Worley

Starting age: 10 years

Johnny is playing a ball game. He is simply throwing the ball into the air and then catching it. Each time he throws the ball he tries to throw it higher than before. He has found a nice big open space in which to play this game as he doesn't want the ball to get caught in anything. Last time he played this game his ball was lost up a very tall tree. Johnny has called the game 'What goes up must come down!'

He has thrown the ball 50 times and now it's time for go 51. He throws the ball as hard as he can and he's sure that he's never thrown it higher. But then, just as it reaches the apex of the throw, the ball slows and ... just stops. The ball mysteriously seems to be hanging in mid-air.

'But that's impossible!' says Johnny to himself out loud. He thinks it must be some kind of illusion and that the ball is really falling back down so he cups his hands together to catch it. *No! It's still up there, suspended in mid-air!*

'That can't happen!' says Johnny again in astonishment. 'Because everyone knows,' he continues, 'that *what goes up must come down* – it's a kind of law!'

But the ball still hangs in the air. Johnny is left staring up at it trying desperately to think of a reason why the ball has not come down again. He can plainly see that it is not caught on any wires or tree branches; there are no telegraph poles or pylons and there are no trees anywhere near the ball. So, what could be the cause of the mysterious floating ball?

Start Question 1   What could be causing the ball to seem to hover in mid-air?

Questions to take you further

❖   Could something like this really happen?

❖   Is this story impossible, as Johnny says (and he's in it!)?

❖   Is it a law that *what goes up must come down?*

❖   What is a 'law' in the sense that Johnny means (as in 'the laws of physics')?

❖   Are there different meanings of the word 'law'?

- If, every time you have thrown a ball into clear mid-air it has come down again, would it be right to think that this will always happen in the future?

- If something has always happened in the past will it always happen in the future?

- The sun has always risen in the past so does that mean that the sun will always rise in the future?

- Could the laws of physics be different somewhere else in the universe or do the laws of physics have to be the same everywhere?

- Does this story mean that the laws of physics have been broken (in the story) or could there be a perfectly reasonable explanation?

- Is it a law that 'water boils at 100 degrees Celsius'? (Research this!)

Johnny is so amazed and confused that he goes to tell his friend Sarah. He points up at the floating ball – which to his relief is still there – and tells her what happened. Then he says, 'I don't understand what's making it stay there; there doesn't seem to be any reason for it to stay in the air.' He then adds 'But there *has to be a reason!*'

Sarah looks up at the ball as though it was an everyday occurrence and says, 'Some things happen for no reason – they just happen.' Sarah then skips off to find something else to do that's more interesting, leaving Johnny with his mouth wide open in amazement. This time not at the floating ball but at Sarah's indifference to it.

Start Question   Does there have to be a reason or could it just be hovering for no reason?

Questions to take you further

- Might there be more than one reason?

- **What is a reason?**

- Are there different meanings of the word 'reason'? If so, what meaning is Johnny using?

- Does there have to be a reason for the reason?

- How far back do reasons go?

- Would there be a first reason for all the other reasons?

- Can you think of anything that doesn't have a reason?

- Is a reason the same as a cause?

❖   Is this event proof of a miracle?

Your Questions

❖

❖

❖

Works well with

✓   The Broken Window

✓   The Traffic Light Boy (1) and (2)

✓   Jean-etic

✓   The Confession

Philosophy: Hume and the problem of induction, Leibniz and the principle of sufficient reason, Hume on miracles.

The Butterfly Dream
Peter Worley

Starting age: 10 years   Advanced

Chuang Tzu lived in China a long, long time ago and one night he went to sleep and dreamed that he was a butterfly. He dreamt that he was flying around from flower to flower. And while he was dreaming he felt free, blown about by the breeze hither and thither. He was quite sure that he was a butterfly. But when he awoke he realised that he had just been dreaming, and that he was really Chuang Tzu dreaming he was a butterfly. But then Chuang Tzu asked himself the following question: 'Was I Chuang Tzu dreaming I was a butterfly or am I now really a butterfly dreaming that I am Chuang Tzu?' And with that question he poured himself some chai and didn't give it another thought.

Start Question   Was he Chuang Tzu dreaming that he was a butterfly or is he now really a butterfly dreaming that he is Chuang Tzu?

Questions to take you further

❖ How would he be able to tell?

❖ How do we know that we are not dreaming right now?

❖ How do we know that we *know* something?

❖ Is a butterfly free when it is blown about by the wind?

Your Questions

❖

❖

❖

Works well with

✓ Become a Sceptic in Three Steps

✓ The Three-Minute-Old Universe

✓ The Flying Man

✓ Knowing Stuff

✓ The Broken Window

✓ Queen of Limbs

Source: *The Book of Chuang Tzu*

Philosophy: Descartes' *Meditations* (especially 'the dreaming argument' from *Meditation I*), epistemological scepticism, Wittgenstein's 'leaf blown in the wind'.

Bat-Girl

Andy West

Starting age: 11 years

Rachel and Kwesi are best friends; best human friends that is. Rachel's true best friends are bats. She has a pet bat and she adores watching bats on TV. In fact she loves bats so much that one day she says to Kwesi, 'I love bats so much, I think I know what it is like to be a bat.' Kwesi laughs, 'Ha ha, no you don't. Bats sleep upside down. You sleep in a bed.' Rachel agrees but she still wishes that she knew what it was like to be a bat. So that night she went home and slept upside down.

The next morning she said to Kwesi, 'I slept upside down last night and now I do know what it's like to be a bat!' Kwesi looks at her and says, 'No you don't! Bats live in the dark and use echolocation to tell what's going on around them.' Rachel thinks about this for a long time. She decides that Kwesi is right. But that night she goes home, closes her eyes and really listens to the echo in her room.

The next morning she says to Kwesi, 'I learnt how to echolocate last night so I do know what it's like to be a bat!'

'No you don't,' said Kwesi 'Bats fly!' Rachel knew that Kwesi was right and she thought hard. 'I've been hang-gliding,' she said. 'I do know what it's like to fly and so I do know what it's like to be a bat!' Kwesi thinks about it. Rachel can sleep upside down, judge the echo of her room and knows what it's like to fly. He strokes his chin.

Start Question   What should Kwesi say? Does Rachel really know what it is like to be a bat?

Questions to take you further

❖   Is it possible to know what it is like to be a bat?

❖   Would you have to be a bat to know what it is like to be a bat?

❖   Is knowledge a matter of perspective or point of view?

❖   Do animals have minds?

❖   Are humans separate from or part of the natural order?

❖   Are third-person descriptions sufficient for understanding another mind or does knowledge of such a thing require experience?

Questions to take you even further

❖   Can you know what it is like to be your best friend?

❖   Can your best friend ever know what it is like to be you?

❖   If you wrote down everything about you in a book, including all the scientific stuff, and your best friend read it, would they know what it is like to be you?

❖   Is there anything *it is like* to be a rock? (Note: it may not look like it, but this is the correct formulation of this question – take a minute to think about it in order to make sense of it.)

Your Questions

❖

❖

❖

Works well with

✓ Pinka and Arwin Go Forth (2) and (3)

✓ Can I Think?

✓ Revelation

✓ Mind the Planet

Source: Adapted from Thomas Nagel's paper 'What Is It Like To Be a Bat?'

Philosophy: Qualia, Hume on empathy.

Become a Sceptic in Three Steps
Milosh Jeremic

Starting age: 12 years

First step: Can I trust my eyes?

Look at this picture (or look at any optical illusion that produces the appearance of motion or movement on the page):

Figure 1

❖ Are there shapes moving on Figure 1 or not? How do you know?

❖ Do your eyes tell you that there are shapes moving on Figure 1?

❖ Does your mind tell you that there are shapes moving on Figure 1?

❖ Are there really shapes moving on Figure 1? And what does 'real' mean?

❖ When you are watching a film in the cinema you are looking at 25 frames of still pictures per second. All the frames are still, but you see a scene in motion. Your eyes see *motion* but your mind *understands* that there isn't really any motion – it just seems that way.

❖ So, do you prefer to believe your eyes or your mind? Why?

Second step: Can I trust my mind?

Look at Escher's picture *Waterfall*.

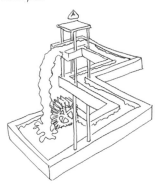

Figure 2

❖ Describe what is presented in the picture (Figure 2). Is it possible in the real world? How do you know?

❖ Can your eyes make sense of the picture (Figure 2)? Can your mind make sense of the picture?

❖ So, should you believe your eyes or your mind? Why?

❖ Can you explain the difference between art and reality?

Third step: Can I trust anybody?

Write a short essay (a few paragraphs) in answer to this question: 'Should you believe your eyes or your mind?' Give it to five of your friends and ask them to make a short interpretation, saying – in their own words – what they think you are saying. Read their interpretations.

* Have they understood your idea?

* Is there any difference between your idea and their interpretations?

* Is it possible to fully understand other people?

Your Questions

*

*

*

Works well with

✓ The Butterfly Dream

✓ The Three-Minute-Old Universe

✓ Zeno's Parting Shot

✓ *Thoughtings:* Socrates' Puzzle

Philosophy: Scepticism, perception, understanding.

The Three-Minute-Old Universe
Peter Worley

Starting age: 11 years

Bertie walked into the room looking at his watch. After a few seconds he smiled and started to sing, 'Happy birth-minute to me, happy birth-minute to me, happy birth-minute to me-hee, happy birth-minute to me!' Still looking at his watch, shortly after he had finished, he smiled again and began to sing again, 'Happy birth-minute to me ...'

'What are you doing?' his sister, Bertrude, asked, beginning to get irritated by her brother's terrible singing.

'I've decided that I'm only two – no, three – minutes old and every new minute that passes I have to sing "Happy Birth-minute" to myself to celebrate.'

'But that's ridiculous!' snapped his sister, 'Of course you're not three minutes old; you're 10 *years* old!'

'But how do you know that the universe and everything in it didn't just pop into existence exactly as it is, complete with all our memories, just three minutes ago?' Bertie replied.

Bertrude thought about it. Then she said, 'That's a good question. But why aren't you singing "Happy Birth-second" instead of "Happy Birth-minute"? I mean, how do *you* know that the universe didn't just pop into existence exactly as it is, complete with all our memories, just three *seconds* ago?'

'That's a good point,' said Bertie, 'I hadn't thought of that …' Then he started singing again, 'Happy birth-second to me – Oh no, I'll have to start again: Happy birth-second to me – this is never going to work, I have to keep starting again every second! No, I'm going to stick with the original theory, it's more practical.' Then he continued, 'Happy Birth-minute to me, Happy Birth-minute to me …' And off he went.

Start Question   Could Bertie's theory – that the universe is only three minutes old – be true?

Questions to take you further

❖   Should Bertie stop believing his theory?

❖   Are there any good reasons for thinking he might be right?

❖   Are there any good reasons for thinking that he is wrong?

❖   Can his theory be proved either right *or* wrong?

❖   If it can't be proved right or wrong is there any good reason for thinking it is true?

❖   Is he free to choose to believe that his theory is true?

❖   Does Bertie have any good reasons for rejecting his sister's 'three-second-old universe' theory in favour of his own theory? What reason does he give? Is it a good reason?

Your Questions

- ❖
- ❖
- ❖

Works well with

- ✓ Tina's Ghost
- ✓ The Confession
- ✓ The Adventures of Poppy the Bear
- ✓ The Traffic Light Boy (3)
- ✓ The Broken Window
- ✓ What Goes Up …

Source: Bertrand Russell.

Philosophy: Solipsism, falsifiability, epistemology, the philosophy of religion.

Epistemology: Perception

How Many Dogs?
Georgina Donati

Starting age: 8 years

Start Question   How many dogs are there here?

Questions to take you further

* Are there any dogs here?

* Is an image of a dog a dog?

* Is the word 'dog' a dog?

* If someone thinks of a dog is it a dog?

* Is a photograph of a dog a dog?

* When you look at a dog do you see a dog or an image of a dog?

Your Questions

❖

❖

❖

Works well with

✓   Other entries in the 'Perception' section (particularly The Duck and Rabbit)

✓   The 2 Square

✓   Just Testing!

✓   Introducing Pencil Person

Philosophy: Frege and sense and reference, perception, sense-data.

Rose-Tinted Speculations
Guy J. Williams

Starting age: 7 years

Prop: Any single-coloured item such as a standard tennis ball.

A philosophical activity:

1.   Take any item that is easily within reach that seems to have a single colour to it.

2.   Place it on the table in front of you.

3.   Now consider the following questions …

Start Question   Does the item have a colour? If so, what is it?

Questions to take you further

❖   Can you devise a way of proving your answer to the question?

❖   How would you prove to someone that the object has a colour to it?

❖   How would you prove to someone what colour it is?

❖ **What is a colour?**

❖ Do colours exist?

❖ Can you 'know' about colours?

❖ If you were arguing about the colour of something, could you win the argument?

❖ Are there any other arguments you can think of that are like arguments about colour?

❖ How do you know that other people see the same colour as you?

❖ Is there a test you could devise to prove that you do see the same colour as other people?

Your Questions

❖

❖

❖

Works well with

✓ Pairs well with More Colour Conundrums

✓ Other entries in the 'Perception' section

✓ Bat-Girl

✓ Phil and Soph and the Ice Cream

✓ Louis' Beauty Detector

✓ 'Music To My Ears!'

Philosophy: John Locke and primary and secondary qualities, sense-data.

More Colour Conundrums

Peter Worley

Starting age: 7 years

The Kingdom of the Blind

Start Question 1 If all the people and all the animals in the world were blind, would things still have colour?

Questions to take you further

❖ Where is colour?

❖ What makes colour colourful?

How Many Rainbows?

Start Question 2 If ten people are looking at the same rainbow then how many rainbows are there?

Questions to take you further

❖ Are rainbows (is colour) in our heads or in the world? Or are they in both?

❖ If rainbows (or colour) are in our heads then how many rainbows would there be?

❖ If rainbows (or colour) are in the world and not in our heads then how many rainbows would there be?

Black and White Thinking

Dogs see in black and white, humans see in colour. Imagine a dog and a human are both looking at the same object, the dog sees it in black and white, the human sees it in colour.

Start Question 3 Of the dog and the human which, if any, sees the correct colour of the object?

Questions to take you further

❖ Do either of them see the correct colour?

❖ If the object is in an entirely darkened room, what colour is it, if any?

❖ If the object is in an entirely darkened room and no one knows about it, what colour is it then?

Your Questions

❖

❖

❖

Works well with

✓ Pairs well with Rose-Tinted Speculations

✓ Other entries in the 'Perception' section

✓ Bat-Girl

✓ Phil and Soph and the Ice Cream

✓ Louis' Beauty Detector

✓ 'Music To My Ears!'

Source: The question for The Kingdom of the Blind was thought-up by 8-year-old Amazon.

Philosophy: John Locke and primary and secondary qualities, sense-data.

The Duck and Rabbit

Harry Adamson

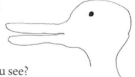

Start Question   Take a look at the picture above. What do you see?

Questions to take you further

❖ Do you see it as a duck or as a rabbit?

❖ If you sometimes see it as one, and sometimes the other, what changes? Does *what you see* change?

❖ If you had never heard of a duck, would you only see it as a rabbit?

- ❖ If you had never heard of a rabbit or a duck, what would you see it as then?

- ❖ Does that mean that *what you see* depends upon what you've heard of, and therefore upon *what you can think?*

- ❖ Does that mean that animals, or very young children, who cannot have the thoughts you have, literally see the world differently?

- ❖ Would people with different thoughts and concepts see it differently too?

- ❖ Does it make sense to speak of the world *as it is in itself*, independently of how we see it?

- ❖ For the world to be real and objective, must it be the way it is independently of how we see it?

- ❖ What, then, does the real world look like?

Your Questions

- ❖

- ❖

- ❖

Works well with

- ✓ Other entries in the 'Perception' section (particularly How Many Dogs?)

- ✓ Become a Sceptic in Three Steps

- ✓ A Knife Idea

- ✓ Green Ideas

Source: Wittgenstein's *Philosophical Investigations*, Kant's *Critique of Pure Reason*.

Philosophy: Perception, thought, concepts and reality.

The Shop Part III

Value or What Matters
In What There Is

Value: Ethics

Teenage Angst
Andrew Day

Starting age: 11 years

Imagine that one day you picked up a newspaper and read the following: 'According to a study, only about 40% of teenagers act like teenagers, and the rest don't'.

Start Question   What would this mean?

Questions to take you further

❖   **What is a teenager?**

❖   How could a study like this be done?

❖   Could the statement be true? Can only a minority of a group resemble the group?

❖   What is it that makes a group of people look or act the same?

❖   Would it be prejudiced to make the statement?

❖   Would it be prejudiced to discuss it?

❖   What is it to be prejudiced?

Your Questions

❖

❖

❖

Works well with

✓   Jean-etic

✓   A Heap of Exercises?

✓   Pinka and Arwin Go Forth (3): Different Animals?

Philosophy: Wittgenstein and 'family resemblances'.

Perfect People
David Birch

Starting age: 11 years

There was once an ambitious and brilliant magician who, one spring morning, decided she wanted to create a perfect person. She thought that by creating a perfect human being everyone else would be able to learn from them and improve themselves. A world of perfect people would be a perfect world, she thought.

Start Question   What do you imagine this human being would be like?

Questions to take you further

❖   Could there be such a thing as a perfect human being?

❖   **What is perfection?**

❖   **What is a human being?**

❖   How might we learn from the perfect people? How might we improve ourselves from their example?

❖   Would a world of perfect people be a perfect world?

Your Questions

❖

❖

❖

Works well with

- ✓ Revelation
- ✓ Only Human
- ✓ Arete and Deon
- ✓ Immy's Interesting Invention
- ✓ The Magician's Misery

Philosophy: Progress and perfectibility, Kant, Hegel, Marx, post-humans and medical ethics.

Thoughting: The Wicked Which
Peter Worley

Starting age: 9 years

Let's play a little game
Just for the next one hour,
Let's imagine that you find a ring,
A ring with a special power.

When you put it on
It does something incredible;
When you put it on
It makes you turn invisible.

You're encircled by a choice now:
To decide just how you'll use it,
Should you pick it up?
Or should you just refuse it?

Which do you think you would do?
With your new-found special power?
Which do you think you *should* do?

Good or bad?

(Just for the next one hour).

Start Question 1a   If you found a ring of invisibility, what *would* you do with it?

Once you've given this due consideration then:

Start Question 1b   If you found a ring of invisibility, what *should* you do with it?

Questions to take you further

❖   What's the difference between these two questions?

❖   If you can't get caught then is it okay to do whatever you choose?

❖   If there's no chance of getting caught is there any reason to do good?

If you or your audience keep sneaking the punitive element back into your answers (for example, 'You should still do good because even with a ring of invisibility you might still get caught because of fingerprints or something.' 10-year-old boy) then here's an extra part to the *Thoughting* to really bring the point home:

This curious ring that you've put on

Has a power of a different sort

That when you do a thing that's wrong

By *magic*, you just *can't be caught!*

Whatever you have dared to do

No one will trace it back to you.

So, if you'll never be suspected

What's to stop you being wicked?

Questions to take you even further

❖   Why should you be good?

❖   Should you only be good to avoid punishment?

❖   **What is good?**

Your Questions

❖

❖

❖

Works well with

✓   Dirty Deeds Done Dirt Cheap

✓   Charlie's Choice

✓   The Salesman

✓   The Magic Crown

✓   Gun

✓   Immy's Interesting Idea

✓   The Otherwise Machine

✓   Prisoner

✓   The Queen of Limbs

Source: Plato's *Republic* (Book II)

Philosophy: Moral motivation.

Bobby the Punching Bag
Philip Gaydon

Starting age: 10 years

There was once a boy who never felt pain and never got hurt. His name was Bobby. He could fall down the stairs and not feel a thing. He could put his hand in the fire and it wouldn't burn a bit. He thought he was very lucky because he could do just about anything without having to worry. One day another boy in Bobby's class punched Bobby. Bobby wanted to know why the boy had done it. 'Because you can't feel anything and I'm having a bad day, so I wanted to punch something,' said the boy. When everyone heard about what had happened they all started punching

Bobby whenever they felt bad. Even people from other classes would come up to Bobby and punch him if they were feeling angry. Some people kicked him, one small girl from Year 1 bit him and a big boy from Year 6 even pushed him down the school steps. Soon Bobby stopped going to school.

Start Question   Given that he couldn't feel anything and was unable to be hurt, were the other children right to punch Bobby?

Questions to take you further

❖   Was the boy wrong to punch Bobby?

❖   Was everyone else wrong to join in?

❖   Why do you think Bobby stopped going to school if he couldn't feel the punches and wasn't hurt?

❖   Are there different kinds of pain?

❖   If Bobby had said it was okay, would it be right for the others to punch him when they felt bad?

❖   When someone hits somebody how important is it that they feel pain?

❖   If Bobby were to do something bad to someone, would it be okay for them to punch him then?

❖   If the boy didn't know Bobby couldn't feel it, would it have been wrong to punch Bobby?

Your Questions

❖

❖

❖

Works well with

✓   Louis' Goodness Detector

✓   Acorn

✓   Gun

✓   Mind the Planet

✓   Fictional Feelings

✓   Identity Parade (2): Body

✓ *Thoughtings:* Big School

✓ *The If Machine:* Billy Bash

Philosophy: Deontology, virtue ethic, consequentialism, the philosophy of respect, Kant and 'the kingdom of ends'.

Not Very Stationary Stationery
A. C. Grayling

Starting age: 8 years

Note to the teacher: If you are doing this session with a class of young children then you could try the following method of presentation to aid their understanding (see Dizzy! on page 269 for more on this):

1. Read it once through.

2. Draw a diagram on the board as you describe it:

3. Invite three children to act it out using a desk and a pencil as props.

4. Read it out sentence by sentence whilst the three children find a way to improvise each stage of the scenario. Give whoever plays Alexander a piece of paper with what he says written on it so that they say it accurately.

5. Ask them to act it out again without you reading it out (prompts may be necessary).

6. You may even get all the children to act out the scene in threes so that they have all done it, though this should not be necessary.

Scene: John saw Peter steal a pencil from Alexander's desk. John was just about to tell Alexander that Peter had stolen his pencil, but at that moment Alexander opened his desk, saw that the pencil had gone, and said, 'Oh, that's lucky; I was just about to throw that pencil away because I didn't want it, but someone has saved me the trouble by taking it.'

So John said nothing; but as soon as Peter had gone out of the room, John went to Peter's desk and took the pencil for himself, and kept it without telling anyone.

Start Question   Given that he took a pencil that Alexander didn't want anyway, did Peter do anything wrong?

Questions to take you further

❖   If what Peter did was wrong, and the pencil wasn't his, did John do anything wrong in taking the pencil from Peter, given that he knew that Alexander didn't want it anyway?

❖   Are there any principles that Peter and John should have obeyed in doing the right things in this case?

❖   If so, what rules or principles should Peter and John have obeyed in doing the right things in this case?

❖   If Peter had known that Alexander didn't want the pencil any more would it have been okay for him to steal it?

❖   Given that Peter had already stolen it, did John steal it? Can you steal something if it's already been stolen?

Your Questions

❖

❖

❖

Works well with

✓   Of Fences

✓   The Pencil

✓   Charlie's Choice

✓   The Wicked Which

✓   Classroom Punishment

✓   Louis' Goodness Detector

✓   Arete and Deon

Philosophy: Deontology, consequentialism, virtue ethics, Kant's moral law and the categorical imperative.

Classroom Punishment
Michael Hand

Starting age: 5 years

Gareth spills paint on the floor at the end of an art lesson. Miss Brent doesn't see him do it and he doesn't own up. She decides to keep the whole class in over break-time to clear up the mess. Dawn says, 'But Miss, it's not fair to punish everyone!'

Start Question   Is Dawn right to say that it's not fair to punish everyone?

Questions to take you further

❖   What's the difference between fair and unfair treatment?

❖   Is it always fair to hold people responsible for their actions?

❖   Is it ever fair to hold people responsible for the actions of others?

❖   Can a group share responsibility for the actions of its members?

❖   Is Dawn correct to say that Miss Brent is *punishing* the whole class?

❖   What's the difference between a punishment and an unpleasant task?

❖   If Miss Brent is not punishing the class, but just keeping them in to clear up the mess, does it cease to be unfair?

Your Questions

❖

❖

❖

Works well with

✓ Not Very Stationary Stationery

✓ Bobby the Punching Bag

✓ Nick of Time

✓ Lucky and Unlucky

✓ Dirty Deeds Done Dirt Cheap

✓ The Good Daleks

✓ Identity Parade

✓ The Pencil

Philosophy: The philosophy of punishment, justice and fairness.

Nick of Time

Peter Worley

Starting age: 11 years

Advanced

Situation 1

Some time in the future the Metropolitan Police department learns to tackle crime in a completely new way. Amazingly, criminals are punished but no one suffers the effects of any crimes. This is because the police department have been using time machines to arrest criminals before they commit their crimes. They use the time machine to travel to a point in time just before the would-be criminal commits the terrible act. For instance, the police arrive while the assailant holds the knife over their victim in a stabbing position but before they actually stab their victim. They have chosen this point in time because the police department believe that it leaves 'absolutely no doubt' that the would-be criminal would have committed the crime had they not intervened, thereby securing, they believe, the assailant's culpability. The would-be criminal is then apprehended before the crime is committed, taken back to the police department's present (the would-be criminal's future) and incarcerated.

Start Question 1   Putting to one side, for now, any time-travel problems you may have spotted in the scenario, are the police department right to arrest these would-be criminals?

Questions to take you further

❖   Can the would-be criminals be held morally responsible for these crimes?

❖   Under what conditions can someone be said to be morally responsible for an act?

❖   Can someone be morally responsible for something they haven't done yet but will do?

Question to take you even further

❖   If the time travel situation is impossible (i.e. it leads to intractable contradictions) is the thought experiment therefore redundant, from the point of view of moral responsibility?

Situation 2

Developments in psychological profile-building have enabled future psychologists to predict with a high degree of certainty (99% certainty) what any one human being will do in the next 24 hours.

Start Question 2   Should criminals who have undergone this test, and where the test has predicted that they will commit a serious crime, be arrested before they have done anything?

Questions to take you further

❖   If we could predict people's behaviour with a 100% degree of certainty should people be arrested and punished for crimes it has only been predicted they will commit?

Your Questions

❖

❖

❖

Works well with

✓   The Queen of Limbs

✓   Prisoner

✓   The Clockwork Toymaker

✓   Immy's Interesting Invention

✓   The Otherwise Machine

✓   Classroom Punishment

✓   Entries in the 'Time' section

✓   Identity Parade (on writing thought experiments)

✓   The Pill of Life (on the nature of thought experiments)

✓   Who's the Philosopher?

Source: The short story (and film of) 'Minority Report' by Philip K. Dick.

Philosophy: Determinism, free will and moral responsibility, the nature of thought experiments.

A Bad Picture
Peter Worley

Starting age: 9 years

A friend shows you a picture they have drawn. They ask you what you think of it and they wait expectantly to find out. You don't think it's very good.

Start Question   Should you tell them what you think or should you say that their picture is good?

Questions to take you further

❖   If you tell them that you think it's good, have you lied?

❖   **What is a lie?**

- If you lie then have you been polite?

- Is being polite compatible with lying?

- If you remain silent then have you lied, have you told the truth or something else?

- What is more important: politeness or truth?

- It is ever wrong to be polite?

- Is it ever right to lie?

- Read What We Talk About When We Talk About Words on page 287. Should Little Dolphin say the truth to sharks or should he do as Big Dolphin suggests and always be polite to sharks?

Your Questions

-

-

-

Works well with

✓ What We Talk About When We Talk About Words

✓ Immy's Interesting Invention

✓ Charlie's Choice

✓ Arete and Deon

✓ *The If Machine:* The Lie

Source: 11-year-old Monica came up with this example.

Philosophy: Kantian morality, the philosophy of lying, truth vs. politeness, Kant and the categorical imperative.

Lucky and Unlucky
Peter Worley

Starting age: 7 years

Consider the following two similar scenarios:

Simon was always being told by his mum to put the broom away after he had finished using it as a witch's broom, or a knight's lance or a light-sabre. 'Someone will trip over it and get hurt!' his mother often warned him.

On Monday he had ignored his mother's admonitions and had left it lying dangerously at the bottom of the stairs. Luckily, no one went up or down the stairs that day.

Start Question 1   Luckily nobody got hurt, so do you think Simon had done a wrong thing by leaving it at the bottom of the stairs or not?

Questions to take you further

❖   Does the fact that no one got hurt make a difference to whether Simon did a wrong thing?

Imagine exactly the same situation as above but with one difference. Simon left the broom in exactly the same place but, this time, his sister came down the stairs without noticing the broom that had been left there by Simon. She tripped on the broom and fell, hurting herself on the floor. She had to be taken to the hospital for some stitches for the cut she had received when she fell.

Start Question 2   Simon did exactly the same thing in both scenarios. Do you think Simon had done more of a wrong thing in either of the two scenarios or not?

Questions to take you even further

❖   Should he receive different levels of punishment for what he did in either of the two scenarios?

❖   If something more serious than a few stitches had been done would that have made Simon's action even more wrong or not?

❖ Does the goodness or badness of doing something depend on luck?

On Friday, Simon's brother, Andrew, is playing in the football team. He is not very good at football but he is in the team because of a shortage of players. They have reached the last few minutes of the game and they are drawing against the other school: the score is 0-0. It is very important that they score or they will be out of the competition for the rest of the season. However, if they win this game they stand a chance of winning the entire tournament. With 30 seconds left of the game Andrew is standing near the opposition's goal not knowing what's going on; he doesn't even know where the ball is. Then, from out of nowhere, the ball hits Andrew on the head and bounces off him and *into the goal*! This wins the game for his team. Andrew is hailed as the unlikely hero of the game. When the team go on to win the tournament a few weeks later Andrew gets a special mention in the assembly for his role in the team's success.

Start Question 3   Does Andrew deserve his hero-status?

Questions to take you further

❖ The team would not have won the tournament were Andrew not where he was at the moment the ball hit his head. Does this mean he deserves his hero-status?

❖ When should you be able to take the credit for something and why?

❖ Can you take the credit for something that was based on luck?

❖ **What is luck?**

Your Questions

❖

❖

❖

Works well with

✓ The Good Daleks

✓ Ooops!

✓ Dirty Deeds Done Dirt Cheap

✓ Classroom Punishment

✓ *The If Machine:* The Lie

Source: An adaptation of Thomas Nagel's 'negligent driver' example from his paper 'Moral Luck'.

Philosophy: The concept of 'moral luck', Thomas Nagel, Immanuel Kant's moral philosophy, Bernard Williams.

Dirty Deeds
Done Dirt Cheap
Peter Worley

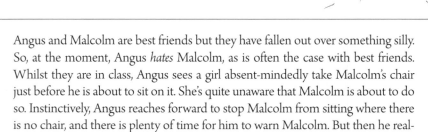

Starting age: 9 years

Angus and Malcolm are best friends but they have fallen out over something silly. So, at the moment, Angus *hates* Malcolm, as is often the case with best friends. Whilst they are in class, Angus sees a girl absent-mindedly take Malcolm's chair just before he is about to sit on it. She's quite unaware that Malcolm is about to do so. Instinctively, Angus reaches forward to stop Malcolm from sitting where there is no chair, and there is plenty of time for him to warn Malcolm. But then he realises that he can use this situation to humiliate Malcolm.

Angus says and does nothing.

Unaware that his chair has been removed from behind him, Malcolm sits back and falls onto his bottom hurting himself considerably, which is nothing compared to the humiliation he feels in front of the class.

Later on, when Angus is summoned to the head's office, the head teacher tells him that he is in big trouble for causing Malcolm harm. Angus protests, 'But I didn't *do* anything!'

Start Question   Did Angus do anything?

Questions to take you further

❖   Can you do something by not doing something?

❖   Can someone be held responsible for doing or saying nothing?

❖ **What is *doing something?***

❖ *Wu wei* is an ancient Chinese, Taoist principle often translated as 'doing without doing'. What could this mean? Is it nonsense or could it be meaningful?

❖ If Angus had deliberately moved the chair from behind Malcolm in order to have him fall on the floor, would he have done anything worse by having removed the chair himself?

❖ Is the girl responsible for Malcolm hurting himself? Should she be the one in trouble?

❖ What is it to harm someone?

❖ **What is harm?**

❖ Did Angus harm Malcolm?

Your Questions

❖

❖

❖

Works well with

✓ Ooops!

✓ The Good Daleks

✓ Lucky and Unlucky

✓ Not Very Stationary Stationery

✓ Charlie's Choice

✓ Louis' Goodness Detector

✓ The Accidental Confession

Philosophy: Acts by omission, the philosophy of action.

Ooops!

Peter Worley

Starting age: 9 years

One day Attilio is walking to the shops. A man comes walking the other way wearing black trousers, a black-and-white stripy top, he has a black mask covering his eyes and he's wearing a black flat cap. He is also carrying an empty bag with the word 'SWAG' written on it. Just then the man stops and asks Attilio, very politely, 'Excuse me! Could you tell me the way to Highdale Place?' Highdale Place is where Attilio lives so he knows exactly how to get there. He also remembers that one of his neighbours, Peter, is having a fancy dress party that very day and he thinks that the man must be on his way to the party. Attilio gives the man clear directions so that he may get there easily. The man thanks Attilio for his help and continues on his way. Attilio carries on to the shops smiling at the fantastic costume the man was wearing.

Later, when Attilio returns from the shops, as he turns into Highdale Place, the man he gave directions to pushes past him and runs off in the opposite direction. Attilio notices that the man's bag is now full. It turns out that his friend Peter has been burgled. With horror he realises that he had given directions to the burglar! This is confirmed when later that week the burglar is caught by the police with a bag of swag full of Peter's things. But by the time he is caught he has already managed to sell many of them.

Start Question   Given that he had provided directions to the burglar, did Attilio do a wrong thing?

Questions to take you further

* Are there different kinds of 'wrong'?
* Is Attilio responsible for the burglary?
* Should he be punished for the burglary?
* Should Peter be angry with Attilio?
* Was Attilio the cause of the burglary?
* Can you be accidentally morally responsible for something?
* Did Attilio intend for Peter to be burgled?

❖ Does the burglary make Attilio a bad person?

❖ What does it mean to say that somebody is responsible for something?

Your Questions

❖

❖

❖

Works well with

✓ Dirty Deeds Done Dirt Cheap

✓ The Good Daleks

✓ Lucky and Unlucky

✓ Classroom Punishment

✓ Nick of Time

✓ *Philosophy*: Unintended consequences, consequentialism, Kant and good will.

The Good Daleks
Peter Worley

Starting age: 9 years

In the long-running British TV show *Doctor Who*, the Daleks are evil and have the single aim to conquer the universe and enslave as many life-forms as they can. They hunger to rule, destroy and enslave. You might think, therefore, that the Daleks only leave destruction in their wake. But you would be wrong.

You see, the Daleks have the following effect: many other warring planets cease their fighting and unite against them; the Daleks create peace among life-forms that would otherwise have been in a state of war. Eventually, the Daleks succeed in *exterminating* war amongst many of the other life-forms in the universe.

Start Question   Does all this mean that the Daleks are good?

Questions to take you further

❖   **What is a good?**

❖   By having this effect, have the Daleks done a good thing in trying to conquer the universe?

❖   Is it possible to produce a good outcome even though you intended to produce an evil one? If so, does it make the original act, or acts (in this case, to conquer, destroy and enslave other life-forms), a good act or acts?

Your Questions

❖

❖

❖

Works well with

✓   Ooops!

✓   Lucky and Unlucky

✓   Dirty Deeds Done Dirt Cheap

✓   The Wicked Which

✓   *The If Machine:* The Lie

Source: *Doctor Who* and *The Genesis of the Daleks* (1975).

Philosophy: Unintended consequences, consequentialism, deontology, Kant and good will.

The Ticklish Grump
David Birch

Starting age: 7 years

Have you ever tried tickling yourself? The grumpiest man in the world has. The grumpiest man in the world likes to be tickled but he dislikes people, so every day he stays at home trying to tickle himself. He runs his fingers all over his feet like a spider and roars with laughter till he realises it isn't at all tickly. He tries stroking his chin with a feather, but that doesn't work either. It's a little gigglier, but not very much. Sometimes he cleans his armpits with a feather-duster; but he doesn't make a peep. He squeezes his waist: nothing. He strokes his ears with his beard: nothing. He tries to tickle himself when he's not expecting it – but he always knows when it's coming …

The grumpiest man in the world knows something he doesn't want to know: he knows that *he can't tickle himself*. If he wants to wriggle with giggles he's going to have to stop being so grumpy and make a friend – preferably one with spindly fingers.

Start Question   Do we need other people to tickle us?

Questions to take you further

❖   Why can't we tickle ourselves?

❖   What would it be like if you were the only person in the world?

❖   Do we need other people?

❖   Do we have friends only because we need them?

❖   Is it okay to use people for our own needs?

❖   Can the grumpiest man in the world live without other people or does he need other people? If so, when would he need others?

❖   What makes people grumpy?

❖   Is it possible to stop grumpy people feeling grumpy?

❖   Why is it fun to be tickled?

❖   Why is it horrible to be tickled?

❖   How can something be both fun and horrible?

Your Questions

❖

❖

❖

Works well with

✓   Bobby the Punching Bag

✓   Only Human

- ✓ The Tadpole and the Pike
- ✓ Philosophical Poetry
- ✓ *Thoughtings:* The Ship of Friends
- ✓ *The If Machine:* Friends

Philosophy: Solipsism, friendship, Kant and 'the kingdom of ends'.

The Grumpiest Poet in The World
Peter Worley

Starting age: 7 years

One day, the grumpiest man in the world wrote the following words:

***Thoughting:* Happy Sad**

I hate happiness
It gets me down.
If people laugh
It makes me frown.

They say that everyone
Wants to be happy,
I disagree, to me
Happy's sappy!

When everyone's happy
It makes me feel bad
Because I'm never happier
Than when I'm sad.

Start Question   Can being sad make you happy?

Questions to take you further

❖ **What is happiness?**

❖ **What is sadness?**

❖ Can happiness in others make you sad?

❖ Can your own happiness make you sad?

❖ Do you think the person in the poem has ever experienced happiness?

❖ Might he change his mind if he experiences happiness?

❖ Does everyone want to be happy?

❖ Do the last two lines, 'I'm never happier | than when I'm sad', make sense?

❖ Can you enjoy being miserable?

Your Questions

❖

❖

❖

Works well with

✓ As a follow-up to The Ticklish Grump

✓ Happiness and Truth

✓ The Magician's Misery

✓ *The If Machine:* The Prince and the Pig, The Happy Prisoner

✓ *Thoughtings:* Love, Goodness and Happiness

Source: *Thoughtings* by Peter Worley and Andrew Day.

Philosophy: The nature of happiness.

The Tadpole and the Pike
David Birch

Starting age: 7 years

Did you ever hear of the tadpole and the pike? It was a most unlikely friendship. They met the day the tadpole got lost – well, loster than usual.

The tadpole was always getting lost. It enjoyed exploring the stream and finding surprising things. Since the tadpole was a tadpole it was very new to the world and the world was very new to it, and when places are new to us they are easy to get lost in. So the tadpole was always getting lost; that's what the tadpole enjoyed. It used to say, 'You need to get lost if you want things to find.'

But one day the tadpole got loster than usual. As night drew near and the stream grew dark, the tadpole was still out swimming, trying to find its way home. The stream became very quiet and still. Most of the fish were now in bed. The tadpole started to feel scared. At that moment a pike swam by.

Now, most pike would certainly enjoy a tadpole as a bedtime snack, so it wasn't at all clever of the tadpole to ask the pike for directions, but that is what it did (after all, the tadpole was young and it hadn't yet learnt what eats what).

The pike's first thoughts when it saw the approaching tadpole were greedy and tummy-minded, but as the tadpole came closer, the pike felt a strange tenderness towards the little lost amphibian.

'How may I help you?' it asked.

'I'm l-lost, I d-don't know m-my way h-home,' the tadpole stuttered.

'Which part of the stream are you from?'

'I l-live by t-the p-purple rock. Do you k-know the p-purple rock?' the tadpole asked, still trembling.

'The purple rock? Yes, I know it well. Follow me, little one,' said the pike kindly.

'Oh thank you, thank you.'

From then on the tadpole and the pike became the best of friends. Every day they would play together in the stream, racing each other, exploring the unexplored, having mud fights, watching rain ripple the water's roof.

It was after one such day of playing when the pair were lying together at the bottom of the stream that the pike turned to the tadpole and said, 'Let's promise to be friends forever. Let's never change.'

The tadpole smiled at the pike and said, 'I promise: friends forever.'

However, the tadpole did change and the two creatures didn't remain friends forever. As it grew older, the tadpole started to turn into a frog. It started to get bigger and grow front legs. Its tail turned into a pair of back legs and soon enough the tadpole had climbed out of the water to discover it wasn't a tadpole any more, it was a frog.

The frog stopped spending all its time in the stream. With its new legs it could spring miraculously through the air, so high it felt it was flying. The frog loved to jump among the plants, to leave the ground for the sky. It loved the thrill of rising higher and higher.

Over time the frog visited the pike and the stream less and less. It made other frog friends. It found playing outside of the stream much more fun. Outside of the stream it could catapult and catch flies. Eventually the frog didn't think much about the pike at all.

But one afternoon, when the frog had gone down to the steam to rest, it saw the pike swimming by.

'Hello!' called the frog, but the pike carried on swimming. 'Hello!' repeated the frog, a little louder this time. But the pike still kept swimming.

The frog followed in pursuit, 'Pike! It's me.'

Suddenly the pike turned round. 'Who?' it snapped.

'It's me. You remember me, don't you?' asked the frog, confused.

'I remember a tadpole who was my friend once,' replied the pike curtly.

'That was a long time ago,' said the frog.

'You promised we'd be friends forever. You promised you'd never change.'

'I like to play outside of the stream now. I have new friends.'

'You promised you'd never change!' boomed the pike.

'But I have changed. I'm not a tadpole any more,' explained the frog.

'You *promised*!'

The frog looked sadly at the pike. It didn't know what else to say.

For a brief moment the pike felt a flicker of the old tenderness towards the frog, it wanted to say something warm, but its heart quickly hardened.

'I should've eaten you when I had the chance,' the pike said, and swam off.

Start Question 1   Was it wrong of the tadpole to break its promise?

Questions to take you further

* Did the pike expect too much of the tadpole?
* Should the frog remain friends with the pike in order to keep its promise?
* Does the frog have a good reason for not being friends with the pike any more?
* Is it bad to change?
* Can change be stopped?
* **What is change?**

Start Question 2   Is a good friend one that lasts forever?

Questions to take you even further

* Does anything last forever?
* What are friends for?
* **What is a friend?**

Your Questions

*
*
*

Works well with

✓ The Ticklish Grump
✓ Only Human
✓ Bobby the Punching Bag
✓ Across the River and Into the Trees
✓ *The If Machine:* The Ship of Theseus

Philosophy: The philosophy of friendship, the philosophy of change, Aristotle, Ralph Waldo Emerson, Simone Weil.

Phil and Soph and the Egg
Philip Cowell

Starting age: 5 years

Soph has been carrying an egg around with her all day. She knows how precious an egg is and only has a few hours left to look after it, without it smashing. Phil comes round and they have chats and giggles. Soph really needs the loo and asks Phil if he will look after the egg for her. Phil says, 'Of course.' Soph says, 'Look after it now – be careful!' Phil goes into the kitchen, holding the egg. He sees an egg box on the side with five eggs – one missing – and realises it must be the one in his hand. Because he's a bit bored, he places the egg Soph gave him back in the box, shuts it and turns it round many times, not realising what he's done. When Soph comes back down, she asks where the egg is, and Phil points to the box, with a puzzled face. Because he's not got a good memory he's forgotten which one it is!

Start Question   Did Phil look after the egg?

Questions to take you further

❖   What does it mean to look after something?

❖   Does not breaking something mean you've looked after it?

❖   If Soph picks any of the eggs, is that okay? Does it matter which egg she picks out?

❖   What are the chances of Soph picking the egg she's been looking after all day?

❖   Is it possible to do an egg wrong?

❖   Is an egg a living thing or not?

❖   Is Soph justified if she feels upset?

Your Questions

❖

❖

❖

Works well with

✓   Other Phil and Soph stories

Philosophy: The ethics of care, identity, responsibility, citizenship, the existence of other minds.

Jemima or James
David Birch

Starting age: 10 years

On Wednesdays James goes to school as Jemima. He dresses in a skirt, puts in earrings, answers to the name 'Jemima' and plays and talks mostly with girls. On Wednesdays, James says that he is a girl.

Any other day of the week, he calls himself James, he doesn't wear earrings or a skirt and he plays and talks mostly with boys. But Wednesdays are different.

A friend of James was curious and confused by this. He asked him, 'Why do you pretend to be a girl when really you're a boy?'

'On Wednesdays I'm not a boy. On Wednesdays I'm a girl,' James replied.

'But you're a boy. You have the body of a boy,' said his friend.

James thought about this and asked, 'What's your favourite thing?'

'Playing the piano,' answered his friend.

'But you have very small hands, far smaller than normal, and you find it hard to play big chords. Some chords you can't even play at all. You don't have a pianist's hands. Does that mean you're not a pianist?'

'No,' replied his friend, hurt by the question. 'I am a pianist. Being a pianist isn't only about how big your hands are; it's also about how you use your hands, how you play and the way you play. Being a pianist is not just about your hands.'

'That's like me,' said James. 'I think being a girl isn't just about your body. And on Wednesdays I like to be a girl. I do it because I want to.'

Start Question   On Wednesdays is James a girl?

Questions to take you further

❖   Is the difference between girls and boys just a difference between their bodies?

❖   If you dress up and play as a boy or girl, does that mean you are one?

❖   What do you think of what James says to his friend about his hands? Is he right?

❖   If being a girl or boy isn't just about how your body is, how do we know which one we are? How do we become one or the other?

❖   **What is a girl?**

❖   **What is a boy?**

Your Questions

❖

❖

❖

Works well with

✓   Pinka and Arwin Go Forth (1), (2) and (3) (particularly Different Animals?)

✓   Identity Parade (2): Body

✓   The Duck and Rabbit

✓   Bat-Girl

✓   C'est de l'or

Philosophy: Biological determinism, Simone de Beauvoir and gender, Judith Butler and performativity, queer theory.

The Pill of Life[1]

Miriam Cohen Christofidis

Starting age: 11 years

Scientists are always working away on medicines to prevent and cure illnesses and ultimately to keep people alive longer. Imagine if they were to discover the ultimate solution to the problem of death: a pill that could be taken to prevent the person from dying, ever! Sally has discovered it and is about to take it but is then a bit concerned about what it will be like. She thinks it will be okay as long as everyone takes it. Is she right?

Start Question   Would the world be better if no one ever died?

Questions to take you further

❖ Would it be better if everyone took this pill or would it be okay for it to be optional?

❖ If the pill was scarce, would it be okay to let some have it? None? And if some, would there be a way of selecting who should/would get it?

❖ If death is bad, who is it bad for?

❖ If death is not bad, why do we try to avoid it?

❖ Should scientists be allowed to discover medicines and technology that can keep us alive forever?

❖ Can we really imagine a life without death? Or would it be too different from the life we live?

❖ Is the thought experiment impossible?

---

1   Approach discussions about death with children carefully and with sensitivity, but don't be afraid to do so.

Your Questions

❖

❖

❖

Works well with

✓   The Magician's Misery

✓   Who Gets What and Why?

✓   The Magic Crown

✓   Perfect People

✓   Not Half the Man He Used To Be

✓   Only Human

✓   Nick of Time (on thought experiments)

✓   Identity Parade (on thought experiments)

✓   Who's the Philosopher?

Philosophy: Values, essences, justice, the nature of thought experiments.

Charlie's Choice
Peter Worley

Starting age: 9 years

Charlie has a problem. His teacher has had her special pen stolen (it was a gift from an old friend) and he knows who did it. It was his best friend Hakim. His teacher has been asking each member of the class if they know anything about it, and it's Charlie's turn to see his teacher. He doesn't know what to do. If he tells the teacher what he knows then he will have broken the rule that 'you mustn't tell on your friends'; but if he doesn't tell the teacher what he knows he will have broken the rule that 'you should always tell the truth'. These rules are very important to

Charlie and he would like, if possible, not to break either of them. Plus the fact: he really likes his teacher and he wants her to get her pen back.

Start Question 1   What should he choose to do? And how should he decide?

Questions to take you further

❖   When you attempt to answer Start Question 1, ask yourself this question: *Does your solution break either of Charlie's rules?*

Rule 1: that you mustn't tell on your friends.

Rule 2: that you must always tell the truth.

❖   If he has to choose between them, is either of Charlie's two rules more important than the other? How can he find out?

❖   What should he do if he decides they are of equal importance?

❖   Are Charlie's rules good rules?

❖   What will bring about the best outcome? Is a good outcome more important than following the rules?

❖   What choice would make him the kind of person he thinks he should be? What kind of person should he want to be?

In the end Charlie decides that the choice is too much for him so, instead, he chooses not to choose at all.

Start Question 2   Is it possible for Charlie not to choose what to do?

Questions to take you even further

❖   When you are faced with a choice is it possible not to choose?

❖   If you don't make a choice, have you still chosen? For instance, if your mum asks you and your friends whether you want to go to the cinema or to go swimming and six out of eight of you choose swimming, but you don't choose either, did you or did you not make a choice?

❖   Are there different types of choices?

❖   **What is a choice?**

Your Questions

- ❖
- ❖
- ❖

Works well with

- ✓ Not Very Stationary Stationery
- ✓ Prisoner
- ✓ The Wicked Which
- ✓ Louis' Goodness Detector
- ✓ Lucky and Unlucky

Source: Based on a real situation that happened to the author. Thanks to Georgina Donati for the question 'Is it possible to choose not to choose?'

Philosophy: Moral dilemmas.

Arete and Deon
Peter Worley

Starting age: 9 years

Arete and Deon are best friends but they are very different kinds of people. Arete has been brought up well and is consequently very helpful and kind; she *likes* being kind and helpful. Deon, on the other hand, was not brought up so well and is consequently much more selfish; she *doesn't like* being kind and helpful.

Deon, however, really admires Arete and wishes that she was more like her. Recently Deon has decided that she should actually *try* to be more like Arete. So, despite her inclinations towards selfishness, she begins to make a concerted effort to act more like Arete. Every time she finds herself in a situation where others need help she overrides her selfish instinct that says, 'It's not my problem!' and instead she musters enough willpower to help other people when she can, even though she doesn't particularly enjoy doing it.

Last year the school began issuing a prize for 'the model pupil' and Arete won the prize that year. This year the judges are trying to decide between Deon and Arete.

Start Question 1   Who, out of Deon and Arete, deserves to win *the model pupil prize* this year?

Questions to take you further

❖   Why did you choose who you chose?

❖   Did Deon employ any effort?

❖   Did Arete employ any effort?

❖   Does the amount of effort they each employ have a role to play in deciding who should get the prize?

❖   Is the most important thing what they are like or how much effort they put in?

The head teacher reads out some statistics about Arete and Deon's conduct for the year. By the end of the year Arete has been helpful and kind 85% of the time whereas Deon has been helpful and kind only 70% of the time. The previous year, however, Arete had also been helpful and kind 85% of the time but Deon had been helpful and kind only 25% of the time. Arete has made no improvement on her extremely good score but Deon has made a huge improvement but is still not as helpful and kind as Arete.

Start Question 2   Now that you know the statistics, who, out of Deon and Arete, deserves to win *the model pupil* prize this year?

Questions to take you even further

❖   Did the statistics in any way change your mind? Why or why not?

❖   As one 10-year-old boy said, Deon has made a 50% improvement whereas Arete has made a 0% improvement but Arete's performance is better at 85%. So, is improvement better than performance or is performance better than improvement?

Here's what will happen if Arete wins the prize:

If Arete wins the prize she offers it to Deon instead, because she would rather Deon be rewarded for her effort and it would make Arete happier for Deon to get the prize than for herself.

Here's what will happen if Deon wins the prize:

If Deon wins the prize she keeps the prize because she thinks that duty is more important than just happening to be nice. She says that she deserved to win the prize. She also thinks that she has a duty to be truthful rather than generous or polite. And she thinks that if she gives the prize to Arete she may be guilty of wanting to look good in front of people.

Start Question 3   Of Deon and Arete whom do you most admire and why?

Questions to take you even further

❖   Is it better to be naturally good or to be good out of duty?

❖   **What is duty?**

❖   Is it selfish of Deon to keep the prize?

❖   Is Deon boasting?

❖   Is Arete guilty of wanting to look good in front of people by giving the prize to Deon?

❖   Is being truthful more important than being generous or polite?

❖   If Arete has not given Deon the prize for this reason then has she acted selflessly?

❖   If Arete wins the prize, and she gives the prize to Deon, does that mean that Deon won the prize?

❖   If it makes you feel happy when you help others then are you being selfish when you help others or not?

Your Questions

❖

❖

❖

Works well with

✓   A Bad Picture

✓   Charlie's Choice

✓   Not Very Stationary Stationery

- ✓ Lucky and Unlucky
- ✓ Louis' Goodness Detector
- ✓ The Salesman
- ✓ Bobby the Punching Bag

Source: Written for 10-year-old Katrina.

Philosophy: Aristotle and virtue ethics (*arete* is Ancient Greek for 'virtue'), Kant and deontology (*deon* is Ancient Greek for 'duty').

Louis' Goodness Detector
Peter Worley

Starting age: 10 years

Louis loved fossil hunting. He often spent weekends on rocky beaches with his fossil-hunting hammer looking for rocks that hid evidence of prehistoric life. It really captured his imagination every time he opened a rock to find the remains of a long-extinct animal. He also had a metal detector for finding old coins and one day, with his metal detector, Louis hoped to find buried treasure!

Louis – with a little help from his super-scientist mum – has had a go at inventing a *good/bad-detecting machine*. It is designed to detect goodness and badness in people's behaviour in a similar way to how his metal detector is able to detect metal hidden under the ground. He hopes that this machine will help people decide exactly what the right thing to do is in any situation in which they find themselves. When he finishes building the good/bad-detector he takes it into school to try it out.

When he gets to school he hides out of sight, with his machine ready, and he watches the children in the playground. He sees a little boy minding his own business, when suddenly a bigger, older boy comes over and goes up to the little boy. For no reason, the older boy hits the little boy very hard making the little boy cry in pain. He runs to tell a teacher what happened. Louis had been holding the machine up all the while.

Start Question 1   What do you think the good/bad-detector will detect as good or bad in this situation?

Questions to take you further

- How will it detect what's good and bad?

- Louis' metal detector detects metal under the ground. What will the good/bad-detector detect? The amount of suffering? The intention of the bully? The actions of the bully? What?

- Do you think the good/bad-detector will work? Why or why not?

- Are there any facts that will determine what was good and what was bad in this situation? Or is it just a matter of opinion?

- **What is goodness?**

A little while later he sees another incident in the playground. This time a boy and a girl are playing when the boy calls the girl a name because he thought that she had been cheating. She replies by saying that she wasn't cheating. The boy says that she was and that it's not right to cheat. She insists that she wasn't cheating. The boy hits the girl and she starts to cry.

Start Question 2   What do you think the good/bad-detector will detect as good or bad in this situation?

Questions to take you further

- How will it detect what's good and bad?

- What will it detect?

- What will the machine decide if the girl *was* cheating? What will the machine decide if the girl *wasn't* cheating? What will the machine decide if the girl wasn't sticking to the rules, but only because she hadn't understood them properly?

- Will the machine detect that it was a bad thing for the boy to hit the girl? Is it wrong for a boy to hit a girl?

Finally, Louis is a good friend of Charlie and Charlie tells Louis all about his dilemma (read Charlie's Choice on page 215 to find out what Charlie's dilemma is). Louis thinks that his machine might be able to help.

Start Question 3   What do you think the good/bad-detector will detect as good or bad in this situation?

Questions to take you further

❖   How will it detect what's good and bad?

❖   What will it detect?

You probably want to know what the machine detected in each case.

Well, when Louis pointed his machine at each situation the machine seemed to malfunction and it was unable to give a clear answer. That meant that in each case Louis had to make up his own mind about what was right and wrong. He wasn't sure whether the machine had simply not worked – and therefore needed some extra work doing to it so that it *could* work – or whether there was simply nothing for the machine to detect; in other words, that it would never work, no matter how much work he did on it.

Start Question 4   Do you think the machine just needs some extra work doing to it or do you think that there is nothing for the machine to detect?

Questions to take you further

❖   Is 'what's right and wrong' a feature of the world or is 'what's right and wrong' just a matter of opinion?

❖   Are there any facts about what is right and wrong?

❖   Are some things *just right* or *just wrong* no matter who you are? What might they be?

❖   Do we already have a good/bad-detector in our heads? Do we just need to see for ourselves with our own eyes to know what is good and what is bad? (Thanks to 11-year-old Tariq for this question.)

Your Questions

❖

❖

❖

Works well with

✓   Pairs well with Louis' Beauty Detector

✓ Many of the entries in the 'Ethics' section – you could even try to use the Goodness Detector in each of the situations

✓ Immy's Interesting Invention

✓ *The If Machine:* The Ring of Gyges

✓ *Thoughtings:* Love, Goodness and Happiness

Source: An adaptation of Louis' Beauty Detector (see page 227), thought-up by 10-year-old Louis.

Philosophy: Moral realism, 'boo-hurrah' theory, emotivism, moral objectivism, Plato and 'the Euthyphro question', cognitivism and non-cognitivism.

Thoughting: Gun
Andrew Day

Starting age: 14 years   Advanced

If I had a big gun

I'd never lose an argument.

I'd have the perfect way to get your agreement.

Try saying 'Yeah, but …'

Or 'I don't think that's true'

When I'm pointing my great big gun at you!

Whatever we were arguing about,

You'd soon tell me I'd won.

No one would dare to disagree with my massive great big gun!

Start Question   Is a gun (or force) ever a good way to win an argument?

Questions to take you further

❖   **What is an argument?**

- Are there different meanings of the word 'argument'?
- What are acceptable ways to win an argument and what are unacceptable ways to win an argument?
- Is it ever acceptable to use force to make a point?
- What is power?
- In the comic book *Spider-Man,* Uncle Ben says, 'With great power comes great responsibility.' What did he mean?
- Does a gun command respect?
- **What is respect?**
- If some people have guns, do other people need them too?

Your Questions

-
-
-

Works well with

- ✓ Other entries in the 'Ethics' section (particularly Bobby the Punching Bag, Perfect People, The Wicked Which, The Good Daleks)
- ✓ *The If Machine:* The Ring of Gyges
- ✓ *Thoughtings:* Big School

Philosophy: The legitimacy of force, arguments, persuasion, the ethics of power, Nietzsche and the will to power.

The Salesman
Peter Worley

Starting age: 10 years

Imagine you are a second-hand car salesman. Someone is looking at one of your cars with an eye to buying it. They do not know much about cars and are relying on you to offer a fair price.

Start Question   Should you sell the car at a price that reflects what it is worth or should you sell the car at a price above what it is worth? If so, why? If not, why not?

Questions to take you further

❖   Would it make a difference to your decision if the person was local?

❖   What if they were not local and will never be seen around here again after today?

❖   Would it make a difference if they were a regular customer?

❖   What would be the rational or reasonable thing to do?

❖   What would be the moral or ethical thing – that is the *right thing* – to do?

❖   Is it in our best interest to be selfish or to be *not selfish* (also known as *altruistic*, meaning 'acting in the interests of others')?

❖   Should we *cooperate* with others or should we *compete* with others?

❖   Does it pay to be a criminal?

❖   Should we let others be good and then exploit them?

❖   Do we *only* act out of self-interest?

Your Questions

❖

❖

❖

Works well with

✓   The Wicked Which

✓   Arete and Deon

✓   Charlie's Choice

✓   Gun

✓   Of Fences

Philosophy: Game theory, Thomas Hobbes and contract theory, egoism and altruism.

Value: Aesthetics

Louis' Beauty Detector
Peter Worley

Starting age: 9 years

Louis loved fossil hunting. He often spent weekends on rocky beaches with his fossil-hunting hammer looking for rocks that hide evidence of prehistoric life. It really captured his imagination every time he opened a rock to find the remains of a long-extinct animal. He also had a metal detector for finding old coins and one day, with his metal detector, Louis hoped to find buried treasure!

One day, in art class at school, the teacher gave the class the task of discovering which two of four paintings were painted by the same painter. Louis wondered if he would one day be able to build a machine, like his metal detector, that would be able to detect paintings painted by the same painter. He thought it might help the police with forgeries and fakes.

[If you're doing this session with a class then why don't you set a similar task with some real paintings. Use paintings that look reasonably similar but where only two of the paintings are by the same painter.]

Start Question 1   Do you think Louis will one day be able to build such a machine? If so, what sort of things would the machine detect?

Questions to take you further

❖   Louis' metal detector detects metal under the ground. Are there any features of the painting that the machine would be able to detect in order to identify the painter? If so, what would they be?

❖   What does a person look for when trying to complete this task?

❖   Would his machine help the police with forgeries and fakes?

The following week in art class the teacher set a different task for the children. They were asked to identify 'the most beautiful' portrait of four portraits.

[If you're doing this session with a class then why don't you set a similar task with some real portraits. Use contrasting kinds of portraits for this exercise.]

Start Question 2   Do you think anyone in the class will be able to identify the most beautiful portrait?

Questions to take you further

❖   Is there any way to find out what the most beautiful portrait is?

❖   Is it 'just a matter of opinion'?

❖   Could there be any facts that would go to decide which is the most beautiful?

❖   What's the difference between the first task and the second task?

❖   Could a vote decide?

❖   Could an expert decide?

Louis wonders whether he will be able to one day invent a machine, like his metal detector, that would be able to detect beauty in an object. Then he would simply have to point the beauty detector at the four portraits in order to find out which one was the most beautiful.

Start Question 3   Do you think Louis will one day be able to build such a machine? If so, what sort of things would the machine detect?

Questions to take you further

❖   Louis' metal detector detects metal under the ground. Could there be any features in the portraits that make them beautiful or not? If so, what might they be?

❖   If you were to draw a quick 'smiley face' and then put it up next to the *Mona Lisa,* is it just a matter of opinion which one is the most beautiful?

❖   **What is beauty?**

Works well with

- ✓ Pairs well with Louis' Goodness Detector
- ✓ All of the entries in the 'Aesthetics' section.
- ✓ Rose-Tinted Speculation
- ✓ More Colour Conundrums
- ✓ The 2 Square

Source: Eleven-year-old Louis came up with 'the beauty detector'; thanks to Miriam Cohen Christofidis for the 'smiley face' question.

Philosophy: The philosophy of art, the philosophy of beauty, subjectivism, objectivism, aesthetics, Hume's 'Of the Standard of Taste', Kant and the sublime, Plato and the Forms.

Much Ado About Nothing

Peter Worley

Starting age: 8 years

On Monday, the class went on a school trip to the San Francisco Museum of Modern Art. Before they had left, the teacher, Miss No-Nonsense, said, 'Today, class, we're going to see some *real* art.' On Tuesday, as a homework assignment, the class had been set the task of producing a painting in a modern style for Thursday morning's art class. It was late on Wednesday night and Pablo still had not done his homework, having left it too late again. He had nothing. What was he to do? *Wait a minute*, he thought, *that's it! I've got nothing!*

What do you think he will do?

The next day, in art class, everyone was handing in their paintings to the teacher. When it came to Pablo, he took out a huge piece of white card and handed it to Miss No-Nonsense.

'Thank you, Pablo. I must admit, I wasn't expecting you to have done the homework and I'm pleasantly surprised,' she said taking the card from him.

She looked at the card and her smile soured.

'What's this? The page is blank!'

'It's called "Snows of Thought" or "A Blizzard of Ghosts",' announced Pablo proudly, 'you decide which title is best, depending on what you think it most looks like.'

'But it's nothing. You've done absolutely *nothing*!' shouted Miss No-Nonsense.

'I painted all the white on,' corrected Pablo. Miss No-Nonsense looked more closely and noticed that it did indeed have white paint all over it. 'But whether you painted the white on or not it's still nothing!' insisted his teacher.

'In which case,' said Pablo, who had paid attention during the trip to the museum, 'Robert Rauschenberg's *White Painting (Three Panel)* (1951) is also nothing.' He paused and waited for a response but none came, so he continued, 'And it's a *nothing* that people have paid a lot of money for and that galleries hang on their walls and that people come from all over the world to see.'

Miss No-Nonsense seethed with anger but couldn't find an adequate response to Pablo. And Pablo knew it. So did the class.

Start Question   Is 'Snows of Thought'/'A Blizzard of Ghosts' art?

Questions to take you further

❖   Is Robert Rauschenberg's *White Painting (Three Panel)* (1951) art?

❖   Is there a difference between Rauschenberg's piece and Pablo's piece?

❖   **What is art?**

❖   Miss No-Nonsense said that they would see 'some *real* art' in the museum. Does that mean that she would – or should – say that Rauschenberg's painting is real art? If so, does that mean that she has to agree that Pablo's painting is also real art?

❖   Is Pablo right – does the fact that people are prepared to pay a lot of money for a painting mean that it is art? Does the fact that it is displayed in an art gallery mean that it is art? And does the fact that people come from all over the world to see it mean that it is art? If none of these matter then what, in your view, does make something art?

❖   Is Pablo's picture just nothing? Is Rauschenberg's picture just nothing?

❖   Is Pablo's / Rauschenberg's picture of nothing?

❖   Could white *represent* nothing? If not, how could you represent nothing?

❖   **What is nothing?**

❖   What do you think Pablo's painting most looks like: 'a blizzard of ghosts' or 'snows of thought?' What would they look like?

Your Questions

* ❖
* ❖
* ❖

Works well with

* ✓ This pairs well with Music To My Ears
* ✓ A Hole Load of Nothing
* ✓ A Pageful of Nothing
* ✓ Doughnut
* ✓ Louis' Beauty Detector
* ✓ *The If Machine:* Thinking About Nothing

Source: Thanks to Sofia Nikolidaki for bringing the piece by Rauschenberg to my attention and for some of the further questions.

Philosophy: The nature of art, the definition of art, aesthetics.

'Music To My Ears!'

Peter Worley

Starting age: 7 years

Johnny doesn't like music. He thinks it's just noise that fills up the beautiful silence that Johnny really enjoys listening to. His music teacher has asked each child to compose an example of their favourite kind of music as homework. But Johnny doesn't have a favourite kind of music; he prefers silence. Then he realises that he *does* have a favourite kind of music.

When he is next in his music class each child performs their piece. He hears quite a few pieces that sound like computer-game themes, lots of people singing like they are auditioning for a television programme, he hears some simple piano pieces and a few percussion pieces. All of them are far too noisy for Johnny. Then it comes to Johnny's turn. He gets up and takes the sheet music for his piece with him. He carefully places it on the piano music stand, sits down and announces to the class that he will perform a piece he has composed called '1 Minute 33 Seconds'. He places his hand on his lap and proceeds to sit in silence for one minute and thirty-three seconds. As the seconds tick by his audience wait expectantly for Johnny to begin playing but he continues to sit, motionless. The sound of the clock ticking can be heard and, at one point, the excited scream of a boy in the hall pierces the silence. When the clock shows that one minute and thirty-three seconds have elapsed he stands up and takes a bow. Two people clap but the others remain in stunned silence, not sure what to make of Johnny's piece. The teacher says, 'But Johnny, you were just silent!'

'That's right,' says Johnny, 'Music to my ears!'

Start Question　　Is '1 Minute 33 Seconds' music?

Questions to take you further

❖　**What is music?**

❖　Is noise different from music? If so, how?

❖　Is sound different from music? If so, how?

❖　Is music the notes that you hear?

❖　Can silence be music?

❖　Is silence possible?

❖　The composer Mozart famously said, 'Music is not in the notes but in the silence between.' What could he have meant? Was he right?

[*An alternative suggestion for teachers*: You could try performing '1 Minute 33 Seconds' to your class. It is recommended to do this with a full sense of occasion. Use a real instrument, dress up for the occasion and ask your audience to attend the performance of a famous piece of music. If you can play an instrument then, by way of contrast, perhaps you could even perform some other, more conventional pieces of music as well. Once you have played it ask the Start Question above.]

Your Questions

❖

❖

❖

Works well with

✓　　This pairs well with Much Ado About Nothing

✓　　The Piano Music

✓　　The Sound of Silence

✓　　Phil and Soph and the Ice Cream

✓　　Empty

Source: John Cage's *4'33"* and his book *Silence*.

Philosophy: The nature of music.

The Piano Music
James Davy

Starting age: 7 years

Optional props: A radio, a CD, an MP3 player, a record and record player, sheet music (ideally of the same piece), a piano.

Sam hears a piece of piano music on the radio. He likes it so much he buys the CD with his pocket money. Then he decides to download it too so he can listen to it on his MP3 player. His best friend Dina gives him a copy of the piece on vinyl (what's called a 'record') from her dad's collection for his birthday. He plays it on his parents' old record player. He likes the crackles that it makes. His mum also gives him the sheet music for the piece so that Sam can play it on the piano. It takes him a few weeks of practice but in the end he can play it! He loves the fact that he can now play the piece himself whenever he wants.

Start Question　　Does he own four pieces of music, one piece of music or a different number?

Questions to take you further

❖　　How many pieces of music are there in this story?

- ❖ Is it the same piece of music in each format?

- ❖ If he copies the MP3 file does he have twice as much music?

- ❖ If he plays all five versions of the piece at exactly the same time how many pieces of music is he listening to?

- ❖ How many times can you own the same thing?

- ❖ Which is the original piece of music?

- ❖ Is the recording session different to the finished product?

- ❖ Can you 'own' music?

- ❖ When you hear music where is the music? In your head? In the air? In the player? On the CD? Or somewhere else?

- ❖ Try to find different versions of the same piece of music? Can you find:

  a. A record

  b. A CD

  c. Sheet music

  d. An MP3 file

  e. A cassette tape

  f. Can you find any more? What about singing in your head?

Your Questions

- ❖

- ❖

- ❖

Works well with

- ✓ 'Music To My Ears!'

- ✓ The Sound of Silence

- ✓ Property Thus Appalled

Philosophy: The philosophy of music, the ontology of music.

Value: Politics

Who Gets What and Why?
Anja Steinbauer

Starting age: 5 years

Tamara, Carim and Miriam decide to bake a cake together. Tamara does all the necessary shopping; in fact she spends most of this month's pocket money on ingredients. Carim puts enormous effort into making the cake – far more than his friends. He has baked before, so is very good at it as well as very enthusiastic. Miriam mostly watches and enjoys the company of her friends. Finally, the cake is done. It looks perfectly scrumptious and Miriam starts cutting it up.

Start Question 1   How much of the cake should each child get?

Questions to take you further

❖   Who should decide how to share the cake?

❖   How much should Tamara get? Since she bought all the ingredients, she might say that all the raw materials belong to her. Does this mean that she owns the cake? If so, should she decide how it is shared? Can she even claim the whole cake for herself?

❖   How much should Carim get? Since he was the one who knew how to bake and did the lion's share of the work, he might say that there could not have been a cake without him. Does this mean he has a special claim on the cake? Should he get more than everybody else, perhaps everything?

❖   How much should Miriam get? She might say that since they are all friends it would be fairest to split the cake into equal parts.

❖   What if it were Miriam's birthday? How should the cake be divided then?

- ❖ **What is fair?**

- ❖ **What is just** (as in 'justice')?

- ❖ Are 'fair' and 'just' the same?

Just as Miriam starts to cut it up, Billy Bash, who is something of a bully, bursts in and demands some of the cake. He threatens that if they won't give him any then he'll beat them all up and take it all anyway. Miriam says, 'Why should we give you any? You haven't done anything to help make the cake.' Billy replies that he's the strongest and then adds, 'The strongest always get what they want – that's just how things are! Anyway, it's my birthday.'

Start Question 2   Do the strongest always get what they want and, if so, should they?

Questions to take you further

- ❖ If Billy shouldn't get any cake, what should be done to stop him?

- ❖ What does Billy mean by 'that's just how things are'? Is he right?

- ❖ If it is just how things are that the strongest always get what they want, does that mean that it's right that the strongest always get what they want?

- ❖ Has Miriam done anything to help with making the cake? Is Miriam entitled to any of the cake?

- ❖ If it is Billy's birthday, does the fact that it is his birthday mean that he should get some cake?

Your Questions

- ❖

- ❖

- ❖

Works well with

- ✓ The Sky's the Limit

- ✓ Property Thus Appalled

- ✓ The Magician's Misery

- ✓ Of Fences

- ✓ Acorn

✓   Gun

✓   *The If Machine:* Republic Island

Philosophy: Political philosophy, distributive justice, ownership, John Locke, David Hume and the is/ought distinction/fallacy; Socrates and Thrasymachus, Socrates and Callicles.

The Magic Crown
Peter Worley

Starting age: 5 years

The magic crown is magic because whosoever wears the crown, by some strange power, becomes queen or king of all the land.

If you were to find the magic crown lying on the ground and you knew what it was and what it will do when you put it on, would you put it on?

Start Question 1   Would you put on the magic crown?

Questions to take you further

❖   Would it be good to be the ruler of all the land?

❖   Would it be fun?

❖   Are there any bad things about being a queen or a king?

❖   Does a queen or king have any duties?

❖   **What is a duty?**

Start Question 2   If you were to put the crown on and become queen or king of all the land, what rules and laws would you pass as ruler of all the land? Why?

Questions to take you further

❖   Are there any rules or laws that you should pass?

❖   Are there any rules or laws that you should not pass?

❖   **What are rules?**

❖ **What are laws?**

❖ Can a queen or king choose whatever rules or laws they like?

❖ Is a queen or a king answerable to anyone? If so, who?

Task Question 3 Is it right that whoever finds the crown and puts it on becomes the ruler of all the land?

Questions to take you further

❖ What is the right and fair way to become ruler of all the land?

❖ Is there a right and fair way to become ruler of all the land?

❖ What kind of person should rule over everyone?

❖ Should it be more than one person that rules?

❖ Should it be that nobody rules?

Your Questions

❖

❖

❖

Works well with

✓ The Wicked Which

✓ The Pill of Life

✓ Happiness and Truth

✓ Gun

✓ *Thoughtings:* What Fred Said

Source: Inspired by Shakespeare's *Macbeth*.

Philosophy: The legitimacy of rulership, the legitimacy of kingship, political philosophy.

Happiness and Truth

Anja Steinbauer

Starting age: 8 years

There was once a very rich king who led a life of joy and pleasure. In his household there was a slave whose life was miserable and filled with hardship and suffering. By night, however, the king would regularly dream that he was a poor slave, quite as wretched as his slave by day. Conversely, the king's slave would dream each night that he was a wealthy ruler, whose life was nothing but bliss and delight. Both dreams felt very real and, while they were dreaming, the dreamers would be unaware of being in a dream. In this way both men experienced an equal measure of happiness and hardship.

Start Question   Is happiness more important than truth, or truth more important than happiness?

Questions to take you further

❖   Are both lives the same?

❖   Whose life would you choose?

❖   If you could choose to dream a happy dream that would last your whole life, rather than taking the risk of unhappiness in the real world, would you do it?

❖   At the end of his life would you say that the king had had a happy or miserable life?

❖   At the end of his life would you say that the slave had had a happy or miserable life?

❖   **What is happiness?**

❖   **What is truth?**

Your Questions

❖

❖

❖

Works well with

✓   The Butterfly Dream

- ✓ The Grumpiest Poet in the World
- ✓ The Magic Crown
- ✓ *The If Machine:* The Happy Prisoner

Source: Based on an ancient Chinese story.

Philosophy: Jeremy Bentham's utilitarianism, Robert Nozick's Experience Machine, values.

The Magician's Misery
David Birch

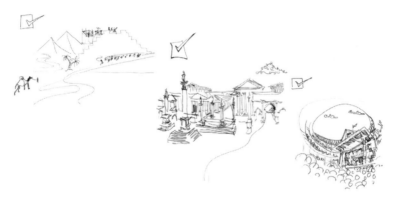

Starting age: 9 years

There was once a very old and powerful magician who had lived for many hundreds of years. Throughout his long life he had seen countless wonderful things. He had witnessed the Egyptians building their magnificent pyramids, he had strolled through Ancient Rome, he had attended the opening nights of Shakespeare's plays. But despite all the wonders he had witnessed, despite all the thrilling experiences he'd had, the old magician was feeling weary and tired. He was starting to feel very old indeed, like living this long was too much for him.

What was making him feel this way was all the violence and fighting in the world. For as long as he had lived, he had looked on as people fought, as countries waged war, as lives were lost. There seemed no end to it. But one day an interesting idea came to him.

Thinking about all the violence he had witnessed, he thought he understood why it happened. People were cruel to those who were *different* from them. Wars happened between *different* countries and *different* religions. In the 20th century even supporting *different* football teams led to conflict. And when people fought those who were similar to them, it was because they had things the other person didn't have, they owned *different* things. To put an end to all the fighting and all the conflict, the magician decided he would use his powers to make everyone the same: we would all be like each other, we would all own the same as everybody else and share the same beliefs. We would be one.

Start Question   What do you think will happen when the magician makes everyone the same?

Questions to take you further

❖   Will all the fighting stop if the magician makes everyone the same?

❖   Do you agree with the magician that *difference* is the cause of war and conflict?

❖   Should the magician make everyone the same?

❖   Should people all be the same?

❖   Are there different meanings of 'same'?

❖   If the magician makes everyone the same will everyone stay the same?

Your Questions

❖

❖

❖

Works well with

✓   Other entries in the 'Politics' section

✓   The Pill of Life (for further exploration of living forever)

✓   Pencil Person Meets Pencil Person!

✓   Perfect People

Philosophy: Egalitarianism, the philosophy of justice, political philosophy, J. S. Mill and liberalism, Isaiah Berlin and pluralism, communitarianism.

A New World
David Birch

Starting age: 8 years

The moon shines brighter in the year 1604. Its silver circumference cuts through the sky and whitens the night. Shadows are darting frantically across the darkness of a harbour while a ship waits on thick oil-like water anticipating the horizon.

Soon the harbour is still and the ship is gone. The shadows aboard will never return. Tomorrow they will be reported missing. They have left behind them a hundred shocks and empty beds. They have gone forever.

A note is found. It reads:

> We have left England for a new world, a world of our own making. We have gone in search of an island in the ocean. We could not stay. The country of our birth is a prison.

> We shall create a new country where there are no rules and no laws. We do not believe in rules. We do not believe in laws.

Start Question 1   What do you think their new country will be like with no rules and no laws?

The note continued …

> Rules and laws rob us of our freedom; they tell us what we can and cannot do; they scare us into following them; they threaten us with punishments.

> Rules and laws keep us from the things we truly want. They do not understand us; they make slaves of us. We do not believe in power; we hate to be controlled.

> We will change this. In our new world there will be no prime ministers, no police, no parents, no teachers, no judges, no courts, no prisons, no punishment. No one will tell us what to do. We will be free to do as we want.

> This new world is waiting for us. We will not look back.

The note ends with a list of carefully written signatures and four hundred years of silence. These people are never heard from again. Their island in the ocean has never been found.

Did their love of freedom, their loathing of rules, make for a better world? We can only wonder.

Start Question 2   Do you think their new country became a better place than ours?

Questions to take you further

* Do we follow laws because we have to or because we want to?

* Do laws take away our freedom?

* Is freedom more important than safety?

* By telling us how to treat one another, do laws stop us from finding out what we really feel about other people?

Your Questions

*

*

*

Works well with

✓ Phil and Soph and the Numbers

✓ Prisoner

✓ Immy's Interesting Invention

✓ Philosophical Poetry

✓ *The If Machine:* Republic Island

✓ *Thoughtings:* School Rules

Philosophy: Contractarianism, Thomas Hobbes, John Locke, Jean-Jacques Rousseau, anarchism.

The Sky's the Limit

David Birch

Starting age: 8 years

The Queen was walking with her brother, the Prince, through the palace gardens on a crisp winter's morning.

'The palace is beautiful this morning,' the Prince observed. 'Doesn't the snow make it look so very grand and enchanting.'

The Queen nodded proudly. 'You're quite right. My palace looks gorgeous today: so very expensive and *mine*,' said the Queen, stopping to admire the sight.

'I designed it myself, naturally,' she continued. 'It took over thirty years to build. The builders finished it in twenty. Twenty? Ha! I told them that wasn't big enough. I wanted a palace that was *thirty* years high and *thirty* years wide. It has so many rooms I sleep in a different one each night of the year. But I don't like to boast.'

'Yes, well, it looks truly lovely this morning,' the Prince replied. 'And the gardens are also particularly pretty today. The frost gives such a delicate touch to the leaves.'

'You're quite right. My gardens look gorgeous today: so very large and *mine*,' said the Queen. 'Of course they are the largest gardens any Queen has ever owned. I ordered for an entire forest to be chopped down to make room for them. In fact, the gardens are so large I can't see what's beyond them. Naturally I only like to see what's mine. And if an intruder breaks in, the archers are always on watch and they'll shoot the intruder through the chest in a heartbeat! But I don't like to boast.'

'Indeed,' muttered the Prince, smiling politely. 'Yes, well, the swans … '

'You're quite right,' interrupted the Queen. 'My swans look gorgeous today: so very white and *mine*.'

'I suppose they are a very rare species of swan?' enquired the Prince.

'Quite right – the rarest,' said the Queen. 'They were sent here at my request from exotic lands far away. But I don't like to boast.'

The Prince was growing rather tired of hearing about all the things the Queen didn't like to boast about. As he gazed into the sky to clear his head, he noticed how spectacular it appeared.

'Isn't the sky majestic today? The colour is almost silver,' he said, as if he were talking to the sky itself.

'Yes, well, I own the sky too,' the Queen crowed.

'You what?' gasped the Prince.

'I own it. It's mine.'

The Prince was in disbelief. 'How could you possibly own the sky?'

'I bought it, the whole thing. It wasn't cheap I can tell you. You're only looking at it now because I'm letting you. Since I own it, I could command you to stop, but I consider myself a generous person.'

'You couldn't tell me not to look at the sky,' the Prince protested. 'It's ridiculous.'

'Of course I could. It's my sky.'

'No – you have gone too far now!' raged the Prince.

Start Question   Should the Queen be allowed to own the sky?

Questions to take you further

❖   Does the sky belong to everyone or no one?

❖   Should the Queen be able to own the other things she mentions: the palace, the gardens, the swans?

❖   Is it okay for the Queen to own the swans if they are rare and therefore protected by her owning them?

❖   Should we only be allowed to own things we've made?

❖   Is it possible to own the sky (can a person own something they can't lock away)?

❖   How do you own something? What makes something 'mine' or 'yours'?

❖   Is it wrong for a person to own something that other people might enjoy or use?

❖   If you buy something from someone, does that mean that it is yours? What if it turned out that the person you bought it from had stolen it from someone else? Whose would it be then?

❖   How can something be 'thirty years high and thirty years wide'?

❖   If everything has been made by God, does God own everything?

Your Questions

❖

❖

❖

Works well with

- ✓ This pairs well with Property Thus Appalled as a follow-up to this one
- ✓ Of Fences
- ✓ Acorn
- ✓ Mind the Planet

Philosophy: Marx, Locke and private property, environmental ethics.

Property Thus Appalled
David Birch

Starting age: 7 years

Imagine you were asked to make a list of everything you own. What would you include?

[You may want to make a list before reading on.]

Start Question 1   Would you put your heart on the list?

Questions to take you further

- ❖ Can you own something you couldn't do without?
- ❖ Can you own something you've never been without?
- ❖ If something is yours, does that mean you own it?

Start Question 2   Would you put your dreams on the list?

Questions to take you further

- ❖ Who decides what happens in your dreams?
- ❖ Where do dreams come from?
- ❖ Can you own something you can't control?

Start Question 3   Would you put your parents on the list?

Questions to take you further

❖ If you don't own them, does that mean they aren't yours?

❖ Can you own something you can't control?

❖ Can you own something you couldn't have done without?

❖ Can your parents put you on their list?

Works well with

✓ This pairs well as a follow-up to The Sky's the Limit

✓ Of Fences

✓ Acorn

✓ The Piano Music

Source: Shakespeare's poem *The Phoenix and the Turtle*.

Philosophy: Ownership, autonomy, philosophy of mind, individualism.

A Fairer Society
Martin Pallister

Starting age: 14 years   Advanced

Beings from another galaxy have been studying how humans live. They cannot understand why we have created such unjust and intolerant societies. They decide to give us a chance to start from scratch and build a fairer society.

The beings transport all the earth-people to their (very big) spaceship and put them all in a special compartment called a *think tank*. When in the think tank they are stripped of all personal knowledge. They no longer know who they are; they don't know their own gender, age, race, ability, religion, social position or what their own idea of 'the good life' is. However, they are told that they could belong to *any* of the possible groups when they are taken out of the think tank. They are administered pills that give them a similarly high-level capacity for reasoning and they also know the general facts, laws and theories about the world.

Each person is then told by the beings that, bearing in mind that when they leave the think tank they could be *anyone*, they should now try to find the best way to construct society so that it is acceptable to whoever, in that society, they may turn out to be.

Start Question   Imagine that you are one of the people in the think tank. Given all that you have just been told (try hard to keep it all in mind), how would you choose society to be organised?

Questions to take you further

❖ Would the circumstances described above result in your choosing a fairer society or not?

❖ Do these circumstances show us what a fair society should be like?

❖ **What is fair?**

❖ Is the assumption of this thought experiment right: that we will choose society to be organised in such a way that is best for ourselves? Does the thought experiment solve any problems that might arise from this?

❖ How can a political system take into account a large number of different kinds of people?

❖ Should everyone have the same rights?

❖ How should wealth and resources be distributed so that persons with stronger natural abilities still have incentives to work hard?

❖ Would you make society different if you were to be a man or a woman? If so, how?

Whilst considering the Start Question, think about the following points

❖ Equal opportunities

❖ Childcare and housework

❖ Structure of the labour market

Your Questions

❖

❖

❖

Works well with

✓ Who Gets What and Why?

- ✓ The Magician's Misery
- ✓ A New World
- ✓ The Sky's the Limit
- ✓ Of Fences
- ✓ Classroom Punishment
- ✓ *The If Machine:* Republic Island

Source: John Rawls' 'veil of ignorance' from *A Theory of Justice*.

Philosophy: The philosophy of justice, political philosophy, distribution of wealth.

Of Fences
Peter Worley

Starting age: 9 years

Going back a long time, such a long time in fact that we have gone back to a time before anybody owned anything, there are simply lots of people and lots of land. Og is a caveman who has invented *fences* and he has decided that he is going to build a fence around some land to claim it as his own. He is the first human being to have done so.

Start Question 1   If nothing is owned by anyone, how can Og begin to own some land?

Questions to take you further

- ❖ How did ownership begin?

- ❖ What, if anything, will decide whether Og can claim to own the land?

- ❖ If he can't own the land, because it doesn't belong to anyone, then how can anyone be allowed to own anything?

Meanwhile, Og's wife has been out collecting nuts and berries. She has found many nuts that have fallen from trees so she's gathered them and brought them home. She prepares the nuts and berries and then, when they return to the cave, her family eats them.

Start Question 2   When did the nuts and berries become the property of Og and his wife? (Think about this before reading on.)

Was it:

1.   When she found them?

2.   When she picked them up?

3.   When she took them home?

4.   When she prepared them?

5.   When they ate them?

6.   Some other time?

7.   At no time?

Questions to take you further

❖   When is it right for someone to own something?

❖   What is ownership?

❖   What would the world be like if no one owned anything?

❖   When does something go from being owned by no one, or being owned by everyone, to being owned by only one person?

❖   When you go into a shop and buy something, what is it that makes it yours?

Your Questions

❖

❖

❖

Works well with

✓   Other entries in the 'Politics' section (particularly Who Gets What and Why?, Acorn, The Sky's the Limit, Property Thus Appalled)

✓   Phil and Soph and the Egg

✓   A Knife Idea

✓   Not Very Stationary Stationery

Source and Philosophy: John Locke and private property, Thomas Hobbes and the 'state of nature' thought experiment.

Acorn
Emma Worley

Starting age: 5 years

The class have a class hamster, called Acorn. Their class teacher bought him at the beginning of the year and all of the children have taken it in turns to diligently look after him: cleaning his cage, feeding him and generally making him as happy as they can. They have watched him grow and learn, and they are very attached to Acorn.

It is the end of the school year and the last day of term. As the children are clearing their things out of their desks, the caretaker comes in and starts to pack up Acorn's box. Their teacher says to them that now they are moving up to the next year they will have to say goodbye to Acorn, for he will stay with the teacher and her new class.

The students are in uproar: 'But Miss, he is *our* hamster. We have looked after him all year, feeding him and playing with him. He must come with us.'

Their teacher says that she bought him, and that he is her responsibility and therefore her hamster. The caretaker stops packing things away and turns to all of them: 'I feed the animals during the holidays, I look after them in the evenings, making sure they are fed and warm and well. Acorn is my friend,' says the caretaker. 'I look after her when all the classes have come and gone, I take her to the vet and play with her during the school holidays so she is not lonely. Acorn is mine,' she finishes.

Start Question   Who owns Acorn?

Questions to take you further

❖   What factors should be taken into account in deciding who owns Acorn?

❖ Can they all own Acorn? If so, who gets to take Acorn?

❖ Can Acorn own herself?

❖ Is looking after something the same as owning it?

❖ **What is ownership?**

❖ Is it possible that no one owns Acorn? Could it be that they are just looking after Acorn?

❖ Who owns the Earth?

❖ Can you think of one thing that you feel certain you own. Now say why it belongs to you – what is it that makes it yours?

Your Questions

❖

❖

❖

Works well with

✓ Other entries in the 'Politics' section (particularly Who Gets What and Why?, A Fairer Society, The Sky's the Limit, Property Thus Appalled, Of Fences)

✓ Bobby the Punching Bag

✓ Phil and Soph and the Egg

✓ Classroom Punishment

✓ *The If Machine:* Republic Island, The Ring of Gyges

Source: John Locke.

The Shop Part IV

Language and Meaning or What Can Be Said About What There Is

Language and Meaning or What Can Be Said About What There Is

Phil and Soph and the Funny Photo
Philip Cowell

Starting age: 5 years

Phil is taking a photo of Soph using his new, swish camera. Soph is dancing around and pulling silly faces while Phil takes a number of shots. Later that day they get the photos printed out and have a look at them, giggling all the while.

Start Question Why are Phil and Soph laughing?

Questions to take you further

* What is funny? What makes something funny?

* Are Phil and Soph laughing because of the photos?

* Are Phil and Soph laughing because of something in the photos?

* Are Phil and Soph laughing because of their memories of taking the photos? In which case, are they laughing at the photos or at the memories?

* Are the photos the same as the memories?

* Is it the past that is making Phil and Soph laugh?

* How can something that happened in the past make you feel something in the present?

* Can something be funny in the past that wasn't funny at the time? Why?

- ❖ Are silly faces funny? If so, why?
- ❖ Take any other example from this book that makes you laugh or that you think is funny and try to say why it's funny. Is it easy to do?

Your Questions

- ❖
- ❖
- ❖

Works well with

- ✓ Other Phil and Soph stories
- ✓ Trying to Forget
- ✓ The Girl from Yesterday

Philosophy: The philosophy of humour, time, representation, necessary and sufficient conditions.

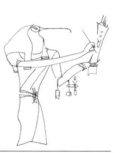

Thoth and Thamus
Claire Field

Starting age: 7 years

In Ancient Egypt there was a god called Thoth who liked to invent new things. He had already invented arithmetic, calculation, geometry and astronomy as well as draughts and dice, but his latest and greatest discovery was *writing*. Now in those days the king of the whole of Egypt was King Thamus. If Thoth's inventions were to be put to use across Egypt, they would need the King's approval. So Thoth took his inventions to the King, seeking his approval. Thoth explained all the different inventions to Thamus, and Thamus asked questions about their uses, praising some of them and criticising others. Eventually they came to writing.

Start Question 1 If you were Thoth what would you say to persuade Thamus to agree to introduce your new invention, writing, to the people of Egypt?

Start Question 2   If you were Thamus would you praise or criticise Thoth's new invention, writing?

Questions to take you further

❖   Is writing a good thing? Why or why not?

❖   What do you think life was like before writing was invented?

❖   Why do you think writing was invented?

❖   Do you think our memories are improved by writing or not?

'Writing', said Thoth, 'will make people wiser and give them better memories.'

But King Thamus replied, 'Ingenious Thoth, I'm afraid the inventor of something is not always the best judge of the value of his own inventions to the people who use them. I do not agree with you that writing will make people wiser. It will create forgetfulness in the people's minds, because they will not use their memories and they will put their trust in writing instead. Instead of remembering for themselves, they will rely on something that is outside their minds. If you give the Egyptian people this tool – writing – they will be the hearers of many things but will have learned nothing. They will appear to know everything but will in fact know nothing, and as a result they will make terrible company because they will appear wise instead of really being so.'

Start Question 3   Do you agree with King Thamus or do you agree with Thoth?

Questions to take you further

❖   Do you still know something if you need reminding?

❖   Is knowing something the same as being able to remember it?

❖   Is there a difference between wisdom and knowledge?

❖   Why does King Thamus worry about writing being 'outside' the mind? Is he right to worry?

❖   What would King Thamus have thought about Internet resources like Wikipedia? Do you agree with what Thamus would have thought?

❖   If there was no writing, would we be able to talk?

❖   Which do you think came first, language or writing?

Your Questions

❖

❖

❖

Works well with

✓ Green Ideas

✓ It Started in the Library

✓ Jack's Parrot and Wind-Spell

✓ Phil and Soph and the Meeting

✓ The Txt Book

✓ What We Talk About When We Talk About Words

✓ Who's the Philosopher?

Source: Story adapted from Plato's *Phaedrus* (274e–275b).

Philosophy: The nature of knowledge, the philosophy of writing.

The Questioning Question
Grant Bartley

Starting age: 11 years   Advanced

There was once a question: How do I know what this question means?

And the question questioned even itself. The question it asked, questioningly, was: 'How do I know what this question means?'

Now, there's a question!

Start Question   How do *you* know what this question means?

Questions to take you further

❖ What do we know when we understand words?

❖ What happens in our mind when we understand something?

❖ How does understanding happen?

❖ Where does understanding happen?

❖ **What is understanding?**

❖ When we understand something, are there two things: the 'thing' plus our 'understanding?'

Your Questions

❖

❖

❖

Works well with

✓ Other entries in the 'Language and Meaning' section (particularly Green Ideas, Jack's Parrot and Wind-Spell, It Started in the Library, What We Talk About When We Talk About Words, Itselfish)

✓ Knowing Stuff

✓ The Flying Man

✓ I'm Glad I'm Not Real

Philosophy: Reflexivity, understanding, philosophy of language.

Green Ideas
A. C. Grayling

Starting age: 10 years   *Advanced*

On the distant planet of Nomski there are two kinds of life-form: the Thoughters and the Sayers. The Thoughters communicate telepathically with thought; the Sayers communicate with speech. For a long time they have been at war but recently they have made a breakthrough, heralding the possibility of peace between the two life-forms. In an attempt to understand each other better they have decided to try to translate each of their languages into the other's language. What is thought by the Thoughters is to be translated into what can be said by the Sayers; what is said by the Sayers is to be translated into what can be thought by the Thoughters.

Start Question 1a Will each of their languages be able to be translated into the other language?

To help us answer this consider the following question:

Start Question 1b Can everything you say be thought?

The Sayers begin by sending lots of perfectly normal sentences such as 'healthy children sleep soundly' and the Thoughters translate them into thoughts without too much difficulty. But then some naughty Sayers, in order to try to confuse the Thoughters, send the Thoughters the following sentence: 'green ideas sleep furiously'.

Questions to take you further

❖   Will the Thoughters be able to form a thought of what this (perfectly grammatical) sentence says, or seems to say?

❖   Does the sentence 'green ideas sleep furiously' say anything? Is it meaningful?

❖   Can you imagine green ideas, and green ideas sleeping, and indeed sleeping furiously? If you cannot, what explains the similarity between the sentence 'green ideas sleep furiously' and the sentence 'healthy children sleep soundly'?

❖   What about the other way round?

Start Question 2 Can everything you think be said?

Questions to take you further

❖   Could you have a thought, but be unable to find any words at all to express it?

❖   If you cannot express it, have you really had a thought?

❖ Consider this. Suppose a person who is the director of a plastic toy factory owns a dog. Could the dog ever think, 'My owner is the director of a plastic toy factory?' If not, why not?

Questions to take you even further

❖ Does thought make words, or do words make thought?

❖ Do you think someone with no spoken language will have the same kind of thoughts as someone with spoken language?

❖ Can you think better if you have more words?

❖ Does someone with a small vocabulary think less well than someone with a large vocabulary?

❖ What are thoughts?

❖ What are words?

❖ Are they the same thing, or different? Why?

❖ Can you write a list of things you can think, but cannot say?

Your Questions

❖

❖

❖

Works well with

✓ Other entries in the 'Language and Meaning' section (particularly The Questioning Question, Jack's Parrot and Wind-Spell, Said and Unsaid, A Random Appetizer, Negative Nelly, The Accidental Confession, What We Talk About When We Talk About Words)

✓ Can I Think?

✓ Revelation

✓ Only Human

✓ *The If Machine:* Goldfinger

✓ *Thoughtings:* Word Wonders

Philosophy: Noam Chomsky and semantic/syntactic distinction.

Thoughting: Said and Unsaid
Peter Worley

Starting age: 14 years

Dumia[1]: This poem is not about what I *do* say

But what I leave unsaid and said anyway.

Sa'id: What do you mean, 'unsaid' and then 'said'?

There's no kind of sentence like that that I've read.

Dumia: Some things are left silent for others to *infer*

but some people miss what's *meant* to be heard.

Sa'id: What are you saying? Do I *know* one of those –

Who can't see a meaning when it's in front of their nose?

Dumia: Just that *there are* those who cannot detect

When something implicit's camouflaged in the text.

Sa'id: I still don't believe that such a thing exists.

A silent *implyment* is simply amiss.

Dumia: Maybe *you're* right, and it's *me* that is wrong,

So don't you trouble yourself, and I'll see you anon!

Start Question   What is Dumia trying to tell Sa'id?

Questions to take you further

❖   Is there anything that Dumia is implying but not saying? If so, what is it?

❖   How is it possible to mean things that we don't actually say?

❖   What does 'infer' mean? What could 'implyment' mean?

❖   Can you explain the difference between 'imply' and 'infer'?

❖   Can you 'say' something without saying anything?

❖   What does 'silence' mean?

....

1   *Dumia* is a Hebrew girl's name that means 'silent'. It is pronounced 'Dum-ya'. *Sa'id* is Arabic and means 'happy' and is pronounced 'Sie-yeed'.

Your Questions

- ❖
- ❖
- ❖

Works well with

- ✓ Other entries in the 'Language and Meaning' section (particularly The Txt Book, Jack's Parrot and Wind-Spell, Green Ideas, Negative Nelly, The Accidental Confession)
- ✓ Who Do You Think You Are?
- ✓ The Sound of Silence

Philosophy: J. L. Austin and illocutionary force.

Thoughting: It Started in the Library
Andrew Day

Starting age: 7 years

Over the door of the Library
You can see the word 'library'
So that you know it's the library.

When you get to the door
There's nothing on the door
To tell you it's a door.

But what if there were?

What if you made sticky labels
And stuck them to the doors, chairs, and tables?
And a label on every book
Saying 'book'
So you could identify it with one look.

And then you kept going

Beyond the library

To every wall and car and tree

To rocks and sand

And then the sea!

Could be hard.

It would be even harder to label birds!

You'd need a never-ending supply of labels

But you'd never run out of words.

Start Question   How do we know what something is if it doesn't have a label or a name?

Questions to take you further

❖ Are words labels?

❖ **What is a label?**

❖ **What is a word?**

❖ Will we be able to find words for everything or will some things always be beyond words and labels?

❖ Would you ever run out of words?

Works well with

✓ Other entries in the 'Language and Meaning' section (particularly C'est de l'or, What We Talk About When We Talk About Words)

✓ A Knife Idea

✓ Phil and Soph and the Ice Cream

✓ *The If Machine:* The Chair

✓ *Thoughtings:* Word Wonders

Philosophy: Words, meaning and reality, Frege and sense and reference.

Thoughting: Tralse

Peter Worley

Starting age: 7 years

If I'm not here then am I there?

And if not there then am I here?

Here, there, there, here!

Is there anywhere else I can be?

Somewhere in-between?

Somewhere squeezed in

That just can't be seen?

Start Question 1 Is there somewhere in-between here and there?

Questions to take you further

❖ **What is 'here'?**

❖ **What is 'there'?**

❖ What's in-between here and there? Anything? (See Zeno's Parting Shot for more on this.)

If it's not true then is it false?

If not false then is it true?

True, false, false, true!

Is there possibly something else

In the middle of true and false?

Could there be such a thing as

Tralse?

Start Question 2 Is it possible to have something that's in-between true and false?

Questions to take you further

❖   What does 'true' mean?

❖   What does 'false' mean?

❖   What would 'tralse' mean if the poet got his way and it became a word?

❖   Is it possible for something to be tralse?

❖   Can something be both true and false?

❖   Can something be neither true nor false?

❖   Can something be half true and half false?

❖   Can we make up words?

❖   Where do words come from?

An exercise in tralsity

With each of the examples below say whether you think they are true, false, *in-between* true and false, *both* true and false or *neither* true nor false:

a.   Zebras are white.

b.   The Simpsons is the best TV programme.

c. $2 + 2 = 4$

d.   Unicorns have two horns.

e.   Thirty grains of sand makes a heap.

f.   This sentence is false.

g.   I'm a liar.

h.   Aliens exist.

i.   God exists.

Some philosophers think that it is impossible to have a statement which is both true *and* false or that is *in-between* true and false.

❖   Why do you think they might think this?

❖   What do you think they would say about each of the above examples?

Start Question 3   Are any of the examples *tralse* (between true and false)? If not, can you think of an example of a statement that is tralse?

Your Questions

❖

❖

❖

Works well with

✓   Other entries in the 'Language and Meaning' section (particularly What We Talk About When We Talk About Words, Some Sums with Zero, Negative Nelly)

✓   Wondering About Wonderland

✓   Feelings About Fiction?

✓   Paradoxes: The Birthday Surprise, A Poem By You?, The Non-Existent Hero, A Heap of Exercises?, Zeno's Parting Shot

✓   The Duck and Rabbit

✓   *Thoughtings:* From Me To You and Puzzles and Paradoxes

✓   *The If Machine:* The Shadow of The Pyramid

Source: The many classes of children I have been in where the children have said 'half and half' or 'both' or '50-50' when talking about true and false statements.

Philosophy: Aristotle and logic, Bertrand Russell and the law of excluded middle, bivalence, paradoxes and vagueness.

Zeno's Parting Shot
Peter Worley

Starting age: 9 years

This is a famous Ancient Greek paradox and the thing to do with paradoxes is first of all to try to see *what the problem is* and then, only when you have recognised a problem, the task is *to try to solve it.*

It was the final minute of the game and they really needed to score. The ball was passed to little Zeno. Zeno was a mathematician and he didn't see the point in football but had been made to play in the team as they were short of players. Zeno stood less than ten feet from the goal with a clear shot, as all the opposition's defence – including the goalie – were not where they were supposed to be.

'*Shoot!*' shouted his team in chorus.

Zeno, being a thoughtful kind of boy, thought about it:

There's no point kicking the ball, he thought, because before the ball can reach the goal it has to travel half the distance to the goal, and before it can reach half the distance it would have to travel half of that distance too, and before it could travel half that distance it would have to travel half of its distance ... and so on ad infinitum. Zeno concluded – like a good mathematician – that the ball could never reach the goal because between here and there is an infinite series of divisions!

Well, he couldn't be bothered to explain to his teammates why there was no point in kicking the ball because it would take just as long to explain to them why the ball would never reach the goal as it would for the ball to never reach the goal!

So, Zeno simply walked away from the ball, past the goal and back to the changing rooms. His team looked on in angry amazement as he walked away without kicking the ball. And, as Zeno passed the goal, he put his hand to his mouth and said, 'Ooops!'

Start Question 1   Can you explain why Zeno thought there was no point in kicking the ball?

Start Question 2   Why did Zeno say 'Ooops!' as he passed the goal?

Questions to take you further

* Can you see a problem (the problem of the paradox)?

* If you follow Zeno's reasoning would the ball ever reach the goal?

* If he were to kick the ball accurately at the goal would the ball ever reach the goal?

* If space is infinitely divisible why do footballs reach goals?

* If you have seen the problem, can you solve it?

* Might the problem have something to do with *time* as well as space? If so, what?

* Is the world of mathematics different from the real world?

* Could there be more than one infinity between here and there?

Works well with

✓ Tralse (first part)

✓ Itselfish

✓ The Non-Existent Hero

✓ A Poem By You?

✓ A Heap of Exercises?

✓ Become a Sceptic in Three Steps

✓ *Thoughtings*: Puzzles and Paradoxes and Space, Time and Other Weird Things

Source: 'The Stadium Paradox' of Zeno of Elea.

Philosophy: The philosophy of space, time and distance, logical reasoning, experience, Georg Cantor and infinities.

Dizzy!

Peter Worley

Starting age: 7 years

Attilio and Peter are playing in Sunhill Park, a wooded park near where they live. They are chasing squirrels. The squirrels, however, are too quick for them. So they play a game where they try to run completely around a squirrel before it gets away. If one of them is able to run a complete circle around a squirrel then he wins a point. So far, they have drawn. They have both managed to run a circle around two squirrels each. It's Peter's turn. He starts running around a squirrel but the squirrel is on the other side of a tree trunk. Peter therefore runs around the tree. In order to escape Peter, the squirrel also scampers around the tree, keeping on the opposite side of the tree to Peter for safety. Once Peter has run once all around the tree he stops and says, 'Another point for me!'

But Attilio protests and says, 'No, you didn't run around the squirrel!'

'I just did. You saw me!' replies Peter.

'No, you ran around the *tree* but *not* the squirrel because you were always on its belly-side!' insists Attilio.

Peter is confused.

Note to teacher on different modes of presentation: If you are working with a class explain the situation again after reading or telling it whilst drawing the diagram on the board for all to see.

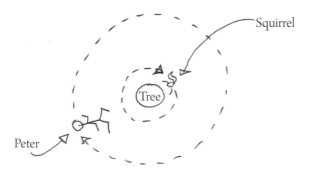

When you have drawn the diagram you should have two volunteers to demonstrate the situation for the class. Use a piece of furniture, such as a chair, in place of the tree. Make sure the 'squirrel' remains facing 'Peter' whilst they move around the tree. They could all try this in threes with a chair. Once you have made all three presentations you will have presented the problem for:

1. *Auditory* learners (those that learn best through hearing).

2. *Visual* learners (those that learn best through seeing).

3. *Kinaesthetic* learners (those that learn best through doing). This is something you may want to bear in mind with many of the stimuli you find in this book. In the cases of other stimuli, use this session as a model for thinking up different modes of presentation for other entries. For another example, see Not Very Stationary Stationery.

Start Question   Did Peter run around the squirrel or not?

Questions to take you further

❖   Do you agree with Attilio or do you agree with Peter?

❖   What did Attilio think and what did Peter think?

❖   What does 'around' mean?

❖   Do we need to stipulate a 'frame of reference'?

❖   When we say that the planets of the solar system go around the sun does that mean that the sun must be stationary?

❖   Could we understand the movement of the planets differently so that the sun is understood to go around the Earth or Jupiter or some other planet?

❖   Does the movement of the planets just depend on a particular *point of view* or not?

❖   When you are on a moving train is it possible that *you are still* and it is everything else that is moving?

Your Questions

❖

❖

❖

Works well with

✓   The Flying Man (from the point of view of movement and space)

✓   Tralse (the first half)

✓   Empty

✓   *Thoughtings:* The Other Hand, Littlest

✓   *The If Machine:* The Shadow of The Pyramid

Source: William James' *Pragmatism*.

Philosophy: Frames of reference.

Phil and Soph and the Three-Legged Race
Philip Cowell

Starting age: 5 years

Phil and Soph are best mates. They do everything together. Some people say they are inseparable. In fact, at the moment they are! Phil's right leg is tied to Soph's left leg and they are running in a three-legged race.

[Invite two children to demonstrate how it works with a piece of rope or a scarf.]

Start Question   When they take part in the race are Phil and Soph running?

Questions to take you further

❖   What is running?

❖   What's the difference between walking fast and running? Is there a difference?

❖   Who can run?

❖   Why is it called a three-legged race and not a four-legged race?

❖   What do you need in order to run?

❖   What is enough in order to run?

❖   Is this really a three-legged race?

❖   Can you have a four-legged race, a five-legged race, a six-legged race, a hundred-legged race?

❖   If only Phil and Soph are in the race, who wins?

Your Questions

❖

❖

❖

Works well with

✓   Other Phil and Soph stories

✓   Dizzy!

✓   A Heap of Exercises?

✓   The Txt Book

Philosophy: Necessary and sufficient conditions, conceptual analysis.

Phil and Soph and the Numbers
Philip Cowell

Starting age: 5 years

One day Soph walks into the room. Phil is on the floor drawing numbers onto big pieces of paper. Soph looks at the numbers: 1, 2, 3, 4, 5, 6. Phil's got some more sheets of paper and so he's clearly going to do some more. 'Oh, I see,' says Soph, 'so the next number is 7.' Phil laughs: 'Ha! No, you're wrong!'

Start Question   What is the next number?

Questions to take you further

❖   Is it possible to know the next number?

❖   Does the next number exist?

❖   What is the rule by which the number sequence works?

❖   Who knows what the rule is for this sequence?

❖   Is Phil's idea for the next number the right one?

❖   **What is 'a rule' in this sense?**

Your Questions

❖

❖

❖

Works well with

✓   Other entries in the 'Language and Meaning' section (particularly A Random Appetizer, The Accidental Confession, Jack's Parrot and Wind-Spell)

✓   Are There Cogs Beneath the Wind?

✓   The 2 Square

✓   Just Testing

✓   Some Sums with Zero

Philosophy: Wittgenstein, epistemology, ontology, prediction.

A Random Appetizer
Peter Worley

Starting age: 9 years

Take a 6-sided die and roll it to determine in which order you will do these exercises.

Random 1

Imagine that you have one jumbo jet aeroplane that has been designed and made by people. Now imagine that a whirlwind goes through a junkyard and assembles, by extraordinary chance, an object that looks and functions just like a jumbo jet so that it is indistinguishable from the other one that you have already.

Start Question 1   Are they both jumbo jets?

Questions to take you further

❖   If not, what is different about them?

❖   What are the chances of this happening?

❖   **What is chance?**

❖   Could it happen?

Random 2

Imagine you threw some Scrabble letters into the air and they randomly fell together on the ground in such a way that they made the following arrangement of letters:

> an array of letters is what you have found
>
> but is it a poem that lies on the ground

Start Question 2   Would it be a poem?

Questions to take you further

❖   **What is a poem?**

❖   If this isn't one then why? If this isn't one then what's the difference between this and a poem?

❖   What are the chances of this happening?

❖   **What is chance?**

❖   Could it happen?

Random 3

Imagine an earthquake quaked some Scrabble letters into the air and they randomly fell together on the ground in such a way that they made the following arrangement of letters:

an array of letters is what you have found

but is it a poem that lies on the ground

Start Question 3   Would it be poem?

Questions to take you further

❖   What is a poem?

❖   If this isn't one then why? If this isn't one then what's the difference between this and a poem?

❖   What are the chances of this happening?

❖   Could it happen?

❖   **What is chance?**

Random 4

Imagine that some scrabble letters were somehow thrown into the air and that they fell to make the following arrangement of letters:

ara flehinuteors iwh tyue shav efuod

btgs i apomsta nttlanie odnrttyh eaoro u

Another time the Scrabble letters are somehow thrown into the air and they fall to make the following arrangement of the same letters:

an array of letters is what you have found

but is it a poem that lies on the ground

Start Question 4   Is either of these arrangements of letters more or less random than the other?

Questions to take you further

❖   If so, which one and why?

❖   If not, why not?

❖   **What is 'random'?**

❖   The second one is meaningful to us (humans). Where does the meaning come from? Is the meaning somehow in the arrangement of letters? If not, where is it?

❖   What if the first arrangement of letters made a meaningful sentence in another (possibly alien) language? Would it be a sentence?

Random 5

Suppose there was a monkey that would never die typing randomly on a keyboard for an infinite amount of time. Just suppose.

Start Question 5   Is there a chance that the monkey would type out a play by Shakespeare by accident, or would that simply never happen no matter how long he typed for?

Questions to take you further

❖ Is there a chance that the monkey would type out the entire works of Shakespeare or is that just crazy?

❖ If you have a finite set of symbols such as the alphabet, which consists of 26 symbols, and you continue to write random words using only these symbols for an infinite amount of time, what would happen?

Random 6

Start Question 6 If you threw a die six times and threw six 6s in a row does that mean that you must have thrown a weighted die?

Questions to take you further

❖ Is it lucky?

❖ **What is luck?**

❖ Does luck exist?

❖ **What is probability?**

Your Questions

❖

❖

❖

Works well with

✓ Other entries in the 'Language and Meaning' section (particularly Negative Nelly, The Accidental Confession, Jack's Parrot and Wind-Spell)

✓ Are There Cogs Beneath the Wind?

✓ *Thoughtings:* Infinity Add One and Poems To Do

✓ *The If Machine:* To the Edge of Forever

Philosophy: The philosophy of probability and chance, the philosophy of meaning, teleology, chaos theory.

Negative Nelly
David Jenkins

Starting age: 7 years

No matter what question you ask Nelly, she always says 'no'.

We want her to admit that her name is Nelly. We cannot ask, 'Is your name Nelly?' since she will simply reply 'no'.

Start Question   How can we rephrase the question so that 'no' *really* means 'Yes, my name is Nelly'?

Questions to take you further

❖   Can 'no' mean 'yes'?

❖   If you can find a way to get her reply to mean 'Yes, my name is Nelly', even when she replies 'no', has she *admitted* that her name is Nelly? (See The Accidental Confession for more on this.)

❖   What does 'non-swimmer' mean? What does 'non non-swimmer' mean? What does 'non non-swimmer' mean if it is stammered by the speaker? Does it have the same meaning as when it is said but not stammered? (The 'non-swimmer' questions all came from 7- and 8-year-olds Marco and Patrick.)

Your Questions

❖

❖

❖

Works well with

✓   This entry is paired with The Accidental Confession and should be done first

✓   Jack's Parrot and Wind-Spell

✓   A Random Appetizer

✓   Said and Unsaid

Philosophy: Logic, syntax, semantics, meaning and intention.

The Accidental Confession
Peter Worley

Starting age: 7 years

Nigel has been pulled into the head teacher's office accused of hitting another child. Nigel protests to the head teacher: 'But I didn't do nothing!' The head teacher says, 'Well done for admitting that you were responsible for hitting Matthew. You will be punished, but not as much as you would have been if you had not admitted that you were responsible.' Matthew leaves the head teacher's office very confused. *But I didn't admit it!* he thinks to himself.

Start Question   Did Nigel *admit* that he was responsible for hitting Matthew when he said 'But I didn't do nothing'?

[You, or your class, would do well to bear in mind that it is not known whether Nigel really did what he has been accused of.]

Questions to take you further

❖   Why did the head teacher say that he had admitted it?

❖   Even if the grammar of his sentence means that he 'did do something' does it mean that he admitted responsibility?

❖   Is *admitting* logical or intentional? What's the difference?

❖   In English two negatives have the effect of expressing a positive ('she's not not here' means 'she is here') but in French or Italian, for example, two negatives provide emphasis for the negative mood of the sentence (in Italian 'Non sei felice mai' literally means 'not she is happy never', which expresses that she is *absolutely never happy*). Should a double negative mean a positive or an emphasised negative? Should language be the same as maths or logic (where two negatives always express a positive: 2 - -1 = 2 + 1)?

Your Questions

❖

❖

❖

Works well with

- ✓ This entry is paired with Negative Nelly which should be done first
- ✓ Some Sums with Zero
- ✓ *The If Machine:* Goldfinger
- ✓ *Thoughtings:* Word Wonders

Source: The many children who mean 'I didn't do anything' but express it in a double negative form: 'I didn't do nothing'.

Philosophy: Logic and meaning, syntax and semantics, intentionality.

The Txt Book
Peter Worley

Starting age: 10 years (they need to be of 'texting age' for this one)

Professor Pen and Professor Utterance are both employed by the University of Language. Professor Pen is the world's leading expert on writing and Professor Utterance is the world's leading expert on talking. With the recent introduction of 'texting' between people, using mobile phones, the university has decided to include *texting* as part of its research and would like to have a big textbook written on the subject of texting to be called *The Txt Book*. The problem that the University of Language has is to decide who should be appointed with the task of writing the textbook. Should it be Professor Pen or Professor Utterance?

Start Question   When you text, are you writing or talking?

Questions to take you further

- ❖ **What is writing?**
- ❖ **What is talking?**
- ❖ What is the difference between the two?

- If you want to text someone you might say 'I will text you.' What is the past tense of text? For instance, how should you say this sentence: 'He should have _____ me!' where the missing word is the past tense of 'text'? Is how you should say it the same as how you *do* say it?

- What about emails? Are emails writing or talking?

- When Professor Stephen Hawking speaks does he talk or write? (In order to speak he has to select each letter or word by blinking his eyes, which are connected to a sensor.)

Your Questions

-
-
-

Works well with

✓ Phil and Soph and the Three-Legged Race and Phil and Soph and the Meeting

✓ Tralse

✓ A Heap of Exercises?

✓ Thoth and Thamus

✓ Said and Unsaid

Source: Thanks to Ben Jeffrey for the question 'When you text, are you writing or talking?'

Philosophy: Vague terms.

Thoughting: Itselfish
Peter Worley

Starting age: 12 years   Advanced

A word is *autological*

if it manages to refer to itself.

A word like 'short'

is one of those words
that manages to refer to itself
Because the word 'short'
is one of those words
that happens to be *short* itself.
But the word 'long'
is not one of those words
that manages to refer to itself
Because the word 'long'
Is not one of those words
that happens to be *long* itself.

'Heterological'
is the word we use
when a word fails
to refer to itself.
So, here's a question
to ask yourself
Next time
you're by yourself:

'Is the word "heterological"
one of those words
that manages to refer to itself?
Or is "heterological" *itself*
one of those words
that *fails* to refer to itself?'

When thinking on this
You're going to have to
only refer to yourself
to make sense of what
I've asked you
As *it* can't make sense of *itself*.

Start Question   Why can't this poem make sense of itself? Can *you* make sense of it?

Questions to take you further

❖   Is the poem 'Itselfish' selfish? Why or why not?

❖   In how many different ways is this poem about itself?

❖   This poem expresses another paradox. Can you spot the paradox? Can you explain it?

❖   **What is a paradox?**

❖   Has it explained itself?

❖   Has it made sense of itself?

Your Questions

❖

❖

❖

Works well with

✓   Other entries in the 'Language and Meaning' section (particularly Negative Nelly, The Accidental Confession, Dizzy!, Tralse, The Questioning Question)

✓   The Non-Existent Hero

✓   Dis-ingenious

✓   The Birthday Surprise

✓   A Poem By You?

✓   *Thoughtings:* Puzzles and Paradoxes

Source: Grelling–Nelson paradox (also known as Weyl's paradox).

Philosophy: Reflexivity.

C'est de l'or
David Birch

Starting age: 10 years

History has forgotten King Bernard, but he was, by far, the greediest king to have ever ruled over England. A desperately jealous man, all he ever wanted was to steal from others. He stole from the rich and the poor; he stole from Scotland, Wales and Ireland; and when there was nothing more to steal, he turned to France.

At King Bernard's orders the English army crossed the Channel and tore through France. The plan was to turn the country upside down and collect whatever fell from its pockets. Most delicious of all, they would scoop clean the great Palace of Versailles.

When they arrived, as was their custom, the army used cannons rather than door-bells to work their way in. King Bernard stormed through the palace corridors hunting for gold. Hiding under an exquisitely pretty bed, he found the King of France and demanded he take Bernard to the hidden riches.

'Je ne comprendre pas,' the frightened Frenchman cried.

'Excuse me?' asked Bernard, bewildered. 'Where. Is. The. Gold?'

'Je ne parle pas anglais,' the French King persisted.

At that moment English soldiers charged in to inform the King that they'd discovered gold.

'I'm sorry, gentlemen,' Bernard said, 'but I don't believe they have gold here. I've asked this fellow, the French King, but he doesn't seem to know anything about it.'

'But Your Most Royal Excellency, we have seen it with our own eyes,' explained the General.

'Very well, take me! And bring him too,' said Bernard, pointing to the quivering Frenchman.

The General guided the King to a vast glittering room piled high with what certainly appeared to be bricks of pure, shining gold. 'Here it is,' whispered the General in awe.

'Well,' said Bernard turning to the French King, 'isn't this gold after all?'

'C'est de l'or,' replied the Frenchman.

'Oh,' blinked Bernard with surprise. 'Um. Is this gold?' he asked, trying again.

'C'est de l'or,' the Frenchman repeated.

'Well, General, I'm afraid this isn't gold. It's something called "c'est de l'or".'

The General cleared his throat and delicately said, 'I think it might possibly be the same thing, Your Most Distinguished Highness.'

'Then why does it have a different name?' asked Bernard frankly.

'Well, Your Most Intelligent Worship, I think that may just be what it is called in French,' the General explained.

'They call it that because that's what it *is*. Of course, it looks very much like gold, but I am afraid it is something else entirely. In England we don't point to gold and say, that thing is called "gold", do we? No. We say that thing *is* gold. Come now, let's return to England. I miss my cat.'

'And, erm, are we to, erm, to leave the … the *c'est de l'or* behind, Your Most … Most …' The General was feeling light-headed; words were evaporating from his tongue and gravity from his feet.

'Yes!' peeped the King. 'We are to leave it behind. What do I want with all this?' he asked, opening his arms to the room of shimmering treasure. 'I want *gold*, not this peculiar French stuff.' The General tried to nod in agreement but fainted instead.

And so, to the astonished delight of the King of France, the English left without stealing a thing. And for many years after, lest anyone repeat Bernard's mistake of seeking treasure on the Continent, it was widely taught in England that there is no gold in France.

Start Questions   Is there gold in France?

Questions to take you further

❖   If 'gold' and 'de l'or' mean the same thing, what is it they both mean?

❖   Imagine there were an Englishman and a Frenchman in the same room both looking at the same piece of gold and both arguing about what it is. The Englishman says, 'It is gold!' but the Frenchman says, 'No, c'est de l'or!' ('No, it is gold' in French). Who is right? Are they talking about one thing or two things?

❖   The Stoic philosophers of Ancient Greece and Rome thought that words were directly linked to the nature of things; for the Stoics words were not just labels. Are words separate to things?

❖   Can you say what gold is but without saying 'it is gold' (and without saying the word 'gold')?

❖   Why do different countries speak different languages?

❖   Could everyone in the world speak the same one language?

❖ **What is language?**

❖ Is perfect translation between languages possible?

❖ See if you can discover a word in one language that can't be translated into other languages.

❖ If we had a different name, would we be a different person?

Your Questions

❖

❖

❖

Works well with

✓ Other entries in the 'Language and Meaning' section (particularly Green Ideas, What We Talk About When We Talk About Words, It Started in the Library, Thoth and Thamus)

✓ A Knife Idea

✓ Wondering About Wonderland

✓ *Thoughtings:* Word Wonders

✓ *The If Machine:* The Chair, Goldfinger

Philosophy: Stoics and words and reality, semantic externalism and natural kinds, idealism, semantic holism, Thomas Kuhn and semantic incommensurability.

What We Talk About When We Talk About Words
David Birch

Starting age: 7 years

Big Dolphin and Little Dolphin – father and son – were out one bright morning catching fish for breakfast when Little Dolphin spotted a strange looking bird he'd never seen before.

'What's that in the … the …' as Little Dolphin spoke he suddenly forgot the right word. It had vanished from his mind, and since dolphins have no fingers he couldn't point to what he meant.

'In the what?' asked Big Dolphin.

'The thingy, you know, the thing.'

Big Dolphin stared at him blankly.

'The floating thing up there.'

'The sky?' asked Big Dolphin.

'Yes! The sky. What's that in the …' But the bird had already flown away. 'Oh I hate words,' huffed Little Dolphin. 'Why can't I just call things what I want? I don't even like the word "sky". It sounds yucky and wrong. I'd rather it was called "gloppy". Birds fly in the *gloppy*. The *gloppy's* awfully cloudy today. That's much better.'

Start Question 1   Can you call things what you want, using your own words?

Questions to take you further

❖   Can Little Dolphin call the sky 'gloppy' instead?

❖   Can you think of a word that seems wrong to you? If so, can you think of a replacement word that seems right? Why does it seem right and the other one wrong?

❖   Can you think of a word that seems to be the perfect word for what it describes? Why is it the perfect word?

❖   Could you change words each day to fit what seems right each day?

❖ Could you have your own private language?

'You can't just make up words. No one would understand you. Words are for other people to understand you and know what you're feeling,' said Big Dolphin.

'In that case, could I tell Ms Squid that her lessons are really boring and I wish I could be swimming instead, and could I tell you that you make me really angry when you snore at night, and could I tell mum that she embarrasses me when she wears a wig and pretends she's a human and could I …'

'Quiet!' yelled Big Dolphin.

'But that's how I feel. You said that's what words are for.'

'Forget what I said. You mustn't say those things and I don't want to hear them again. Words are *not* for telling people what you feel.'

'Well what are they for?'

Start Question 2   What are words for?

Questions to take you further

❖ **What are words?**

❖ Do words serve a purpose or purposes? If so, what?

❖ What is language? Are words and language the same?

❖ If babies don't need words, why do we?

❖ Do we need words? Could we manage without them?

❖ What would the world be like without words?

Big Dolphin paused for thought. 'Learning things,' he said, feeling rather wise. 'Yes, words are for finding things out, knowing things, asking questions and getting the answer. That's what words are for.'

'Can I ask you some questions, then?'

'Why of course you can, son,' replied Big Dolphin, settling into his poise.

Little Dolphin rushed to the surface and took a deep breath: 'Why isn't the sky called "gloppy" and why does the ocean go down rather than up and what do you and mum do when I'm not around and why do humans lock us away to make us do tricks and does that mean that humans aren't very clever because aren't we much more interesting than that and why do you get so angry when you lose at chess and does it hurt fish when we eat them and how …'

'*Quiet!*' yelled Big Dolphin once again.

'But you told me …'

'Forget what I told you,' sighed Big Dolphin. 'Words aren't for finding things out. Give me a moment and I'll tell you what they are really for.'

'You keep telling me to be quiet with words,' highlighted Little Dolphin.

'Yes, that's it!' said Big Dolphin. 'Words are ways of getting what we want.'

'There's an enormous ship coming right for us!' Little Dolphin suddenly screamed.

'*What?*' cried Big Dolphin turning.

'Made you look!' teased Little Dolphin, swallowing something as he spoke.

'Wait – where's my fish?' asked Big Dolphin.

When he wasn't looking Little Dolphin had stolen it from his fin.

'In my tummy,' said Little Dolphin, pleased with himself. 'I used words to make you look the other way and then I got what I wanted. I was using words to get what I want, see.'

'You used words to *lie!*' exclaimed Big Dolphin, feeling suddenly hungry. 'I've changed my mind. Words aren't for getting what you want. They're for telling the truth. Understand? The *truth*.'

'I think I understand. Words are for swimming up to sharks and telling them they're the ugliest things in the ocean and all the other fish hate them and wish they'd get old and lose their teeth. That is the truth about sharks.'

'No! You must never ever say that to sharks! You must always be polite to them.'

'But that would be lying. You said words are for telling the truth.'

'Well, I was wrong, okay. Wrong! I don't know what words are for.'

'But why should I use words if you can't tell me what they are for?' asked Little Dolphin, fascinated by his own question.

'From this day on,' Little Dolphin pronounced, 'unless you can tell me what words are for, I shall never say another thing.' And with that he fell silent.

'Little Dolphin, don't be so silly.'

Silence.

'Look, it's too early,' reasoned Big Dolphin, 'I'll tell you what words are for tonight.'

Silence.

'Little Dolphin, you are trying my patience.'

Silence.

'Little Dolphin, I order you to speak!'

Silence.

'Little Dolphin, if you don't say something in the next three seconds … One …'

Silence.

'Two.'

Silence.

'Three.'

Silence.

'*Grrrrrraaaaaarrrggghhhh!*' roared Big Dolphin with such rage that the ocean began to boil.

Words, it seems, had failed him.

Start Question 3   Why had words failed him?

Questions to take you further

❖   Why did silence make Big Dolphin so mad?

❖   What does 'silence' mean?

❖   What power do words have?

❖   **What are words for?**

❖   Do you ever feel that words are not enough to express what you want to express?

❖   If words are not enough, what can we do instead to express ourselves?

❖   What do you think of Big Dolphin's answers? Are words for:

    ❖   Letting other people understand you and know what you're feeling?

    ❖   Learning things?

    ❖   Getting what we want?

    ❖   Telling the truth?

    ❖   Can you think of anything else words are for?

Your Questions

* ❖
* ❖
* ❖

Works well with

* ✓ Other entries in the 'Language and Meaning' section (particularly C'est de l'or, Jack's Parrot and Wind-Spell, It Started in the Library, Said and Unsaid)
* ✓ Philosophical Poetry
* ✓ A Knife Idea
* ✓ *Thoughtings:* Word Wonders
* ✓ *The If Machine:* Goldfinger

Philosophy: See Alice's conversation with Humpty Dumpty in Lewis Carroll's *Through the Looking-Glass*; the expression 'Humpty-Dumpty-ing' is used to describe when people change the meanings of words to suit their own purposes.

Some Sums with Zero
Peter Worley

Starting age: 10 years

The teacher was very angry with Tom, Tim, Tam and Billy for being naughty in class, only the teacher had made a mistake in thinking that Billy was doing something wrong. Tom, Tim and Tam had succeeded in getting him into trouble. Poor Billy.

They were supposed to be learning about the four arithmetic operations: addition, subtraction, multiplication and division. As a punishment the teacher said, 'Right, I am going to give each of you a sum to complete. If you answer the question incorrectly then you will be kept in over your lunch break for the next week!' To confuse the children he chose to give them sums that included *zero*.

Tom was given the following sum:

'What is 6 + 0?'

Tom had not been listening during the lesson so he wasn't sure. 'Is it … 0?' he guessed.

'You are … *incorrect*!' said the teacher with a smile. 'That means that you'll have to miss your lunch break all week.'

Tim was given this sum:

'What is 6 - 0?'

Tim hadn't been listening either but he'd heard Tom say '0' and he had got it wrong, but this was a different question so he thought he should say '0' because it must be right this time given that it was wrong last time. 'Is it 0?' said Tim.

'*Incorrect*!' snapped the teacher again with glee.

The teacher turned this time to Tam. 'What is 6 x 0, Tam?' asked the teacher.

Tam had not listened either. She thought to herself, '0' was the wrong answer on both the other two sums so I won't make the same mistake they made!

'It's 6!' she said confidently.

The teacher hadn't lost his beaming smile so she knew before he told her that she was –

'*Incorrect again*!' barked the teacher.

Finally the teacher turned to Billy. *Right!* he said to himself, *What's left?* Oh yes, *division* – the hardest of them all: 'What is 6 divided by 0?'

Billy thought about it … and thought about it … and thought about it …

So too did the teacher think about it … and think about it … and think about it …

Eventually the teacher said with a very uncertain tone in his voice, 'Well … what's the answer? I mean … *what is* the answer?'

And Billy replied, 'I don't know, but you can't keep me in because you said that I would only be kept in if I answered the question incorrectly, but I don't think anyone can answer the question at all!'

With that, Billy went out to play and left the teacher scratching his head trying to answer the question. He's still there to this day and I don't think he's answered it yet.

Start Question Can the question the teacher put to Billy – 'What is 6 divided by 0?' – be answered?

Questions to take you further

❖ Are the sums the teacher asked simple sums?

❖ Is it possible to answer the question 'What is 6 divided by 0?' If so, why? If not, why not?

❖ Is there a way to find out the answer?

❖ What does the calculator say?

❖ What does your teacher say?

❖ What does a mathematician say?

❖ Does the sum work in reverse? (What is 0 divided by 6?)

❖ What do you think of the reasons Tim, Tom and Tam gave for their answers?

❖ Were their answers incorrect?

❖ If Tom had guessed the right answer would he have given a correct answer?

❖ Is a 'right answer' the same as a 'correct answer'?

Works well with

✓ The 2 Square

✓ A Pageful of Nothing

✓ Doughnut

✓ A Hole Load of Nothing

✓ Phil and Soph and the Numbers

✓ *Thoughtings:* Number Wonders

Source: Thanks to Andrew Day for the question 'What is 6 divided by 0?'

Philosophy: Undefined terms, arithmetical anomalies.

Jack's Parrot

Peter Worley

Starting age: 7 years

Parrots have an amazing ability for learning to say and repeat words and phrases. Jack's parrot, Polly, has been taught four phrases and she always says them in the same order. She lives in a cage in the kitchen and when she sees someone she always squawks 'Hello Jack'. She will also squawk the following phrases when she hears someone speak, no matter what they say: 'Hello Jack', 'I'm alright Jack', 'Pieces of eight' and 'Go away'.

So, a usual exchange between Jack and Polly when Jack comes into the kitchen sounds like this:

[Jack walks into the kitchen.]

Polly: Hello Jack.

Jack: Polly, put the kettle on.

Polly: I'm alright Jack.

Jack: Why can't you clean your own cage?

Polly: Pieces of eight.

Jack: Where's the milk?

Polly: Go away!

Start Question 1 Can Polly talk?

Questions to take you further

❖   **What is talking?**

❖   Is this a conversation?

On Wednesday this happens:

[Jack walks into the kitchen.]

Polly: Hello Jack.

Jack: Hello Polly, how are you?

Polly: I'm alright Jack.

[Jack has cut out a number '8' from a piece of paper. He rips it up and puts the pieces in the cage.]

Jack: What's in your cage?

Polly: Pieces of eight.

Jack: Can I have the pieces of eight?

Polly: Go away!

Jack: Okay.

[Jack goes away.]

Start Question 2   Are Jack and Polly talking together on Wednesday?

Questions to take you even further

- On Wednesday, when Polly says 'pieces of eight' and 'go away', is what she says true or meaningful?

- Is either of these exchanges a conversation?

- When she says 'pieces of eight' in answer to Jack's question, 'What's in your cage?', is Polly right?

- **What is a conversation?**

- Can Polly talk?

- Can Polly have a conversation?

- What does a speaker need to be doing to be talking?

- Is 'saying words' the same as talking?

- I have programmed my computer to say 'Hello, Peter' when I switch it on. Can my computer talk?

- What makes something someone says true?

- Can you say something true by accident?

Wind-Spell

Peter Worley

Starting age: 5 years

One day, Jack's little sister, Sara was out walking in the park. It was a windy day and the wind was blowing wildly. Then a big gust of wind brought some leaves and sticks swirling towards her. They fell on the ground in front of her and the way the sticks had fallen together seemed to spell the word 'ME'. 'Mummy!' she said. 'Look! The wind can write!'

Start Question   Is Sara right? Does what happened to her show that the wind can write?

Questions to take you further

❖   **What is writing?**

❖   What is needed for something to be able to write?

❖   When you write, what do you need to be able to do first?

Your Questions

❖

❖

❖

Works well with

✓   Other entries in the 'Language and Meaning' section (particularly The Questioning Question, A Random Appetizer, Negative Nelly, The Accidental Confession)

✓   Knowing Stuff

✓   Can I Think?

✓   Revelation

✓   Only Human

✓   *The If Machine:* The Ceebie Stories (particularly The Tony Test)

Philosophy: Alan Turing and the Turing test, the philosophy of artificial intelligence (AI), intentionality.

After Thoughts

Who's the Philosopher?

Nolen Gertz

Starting age: 7 years

Two friends, Nathan and Mathilda, are walking down the street. Nathan can't help but stop every few feet to ask Mathilda questions about what he sees. Nathan asks Mathilda, 'Why don't trees have names like we do, instead of just being called "Oak" or "Elm"?'

Before reading Mathilda's answer, how would *you* answer Nathan's question?

Start Question 1   Why don't trees have names like we do, instead of just being called 'Oak' or 'Elm'?

Questions to take you further

❖   Are our names different to words like 'Oak' or 'Elm'?

❖   **What is a name?**

❖   Why do we give each other names rather than just saying what we are: 'Person 1' or 'Person 37,376' for example?

Mathilda answers, 'Because trees don't need people-names, they're not individuals.' Nathan is unhappy with this answer, but he gets distracted again, and asks Mathilda, 'Do you think we'll ever invent a machine to let us talk to dogs?'

Again, before reading Mathilda's answer, how would *you* answer Nathan's question?

Start Question 2   Do you think we'll ever invent a machine to let us talk to dogs?

Questions to take you further

- Would it be possible to invent such a machine?

- Could dog-thoughts be translated into human-thoughts?

- Do dogs have language?

- **What is language?**

Mathilda answers, 'No, because dogs don't think like people do. They're of a different species, not a different language.' Nathan is again dissatisfied with Mathilda's confident reply, at which point Mathilda suddenly surprises Nathan with a question of her own. Mathilda asks, 'Nathan, why don't you just enjoy how things are instead of always obsessing over how things could be different?' Nathan doesn't answer, but just walks on in silence.

Start Question 3   Who's the philosopher: Nathan or Mathilda?

Questions to take you further

- Why did you pick who you picked?

- Who of the two are you more like?

- How did you answer each of their questions?

- Is Matilda right: is it better to just enjoy how things are?

- Why do we sometimes think about how things could be different?

- Can it be good to ask, 'What if … ?'

- **What is a philosopher?**

- **What is philosophy?**

- Are questions in philosophy different to questions in maths, science or religion?

- **What is a philosophical question?**

Your Questions

-

-

-

Works well with

- ✓ It Started in the Library

- ✓ C'est de l'or

- ✓ Nick of Time (on thought experiments)

- ✓ The Pill of Life (on thought experiments)

- ✓ The Otherwise Machine

- ✓ What Zeus Does When He's Bored

- ✓ *Thoughtings:* Are Things Always What They Seem To Us To Be?, Bliss

Philosophy: The nature of philosophy itself, thought experiments, knowledge and wisdom.

Philosophical Poetry
David Birch

Starting age: 7

For some, philosophy, like joy, is a state. It's not just an exercise or practice, not just something we do, but something we enter into. Often this state is not easily communicable and often our most absorbing philosophical discussions are with ourselves. Lucidity and sense can impoverish philosophy and thoughts made intelligible can ring out false. For some of us most of the time – and for all of us some of the time – a group discussion will not present the most fruitful conditions for philosophy. Conversation is just one way into philosophy. Poetry is another. Poetry allows us to give voice to our thoughts without having to give sense to them. For certain philosophical temperaments, the space and freedom provided by the solitude of poetry is a necessary and lovely thing.

For the following activities ask the children to write without rhyme. Rhyme is difficult and will distract them from their thoughts. The poems suggested below have a repetitive form. Again this will simplify the writing of the poems and allow the children to take each thought as it comes. Of course, if they wish to deviate from this form, they are free to – it is there as a guide only.

1. **I wonder why ...** This is a general philosophical poem which can be endlessly returned to. These poems will be revealing of the things that particularly interest the children. Ask the children to start every line with these three words. To begin with, the

children might enjoy just writing one line, then having these pooled together and read out to them as a single class-authored poem.

2. **If I could do whatever I wanted …** A poem on unbounded freedom, an extension to 'A New World'. Have this line as their first and ask the children to begin every next line with 'I would …'

3. **Comparisons**. Philosophy is full of imagery. Most famously, Plato described the world as a cave of shadows. And William Paley thought the world a giant watch. This latter image features in 'Are There Cogs Beneath the Wind?' The image of the world as an enormous snow globe is also described there. Highlight these comparisons to the children and ask them to write a comparison poem on what they think the world is like. Every line can begin with, 'The world is like …' or 'The world is as x as a …' This can serve as an extension to the session 'Are There Cogs Beneath the Wind?'

An extension to 'The Clockwork Toymaker': The toymaker describes humans as being like clockwork toys. Ask the children what comparisons they would give for themselves. Each line can begin with 'I am like …' or 'I am as x as …'

An extension to 'A Hole Load of Nothing': A poem about the dark. Ask the children to begin every line with 'The dark is like …' or 'The dark is as x as …' You might additionally ask them to write from the perspective of Mr Owl.

Something general: Ask the children to write a poem about thinking, beginning every line with 'Thinking is like …'

The comparisons philosophers make are peculiar and strange. Encourage the children to feel free to be just as peculiar and even stranger in their comparisons. To begin with it might be helpful for the children to write comparisons of and between objects in the classroom. Once they have a feel for this they can move on to the more philosophically spirited comparisons.

4. **Sometimes I look … But really I am …** A poem about our private selves, an extension to 'Who Do You Think You Are?' Ask the children to repeat this two-line structure.

5. **I don't know why I …** A poem on how we are mysterious to ourselves, an extension to 'Revelation'. Ask the children to think about the things they don't understand about themselves or their bodies.

6. **When I am by myself …** A poem on separateness, an extension to 'The Ticklish Grump'. Ask the children to think about what it is like for them when they are by themselves. What do they do? What don't they do? What do they think about? How does it feel? How is it different from being with others?

7. **We are all the same because ... We are all different because ...** This poem is an extension to 'The Magician's Misery' and is about the curious coexistence of idiosyncrasy and commonality.

Source: Kenneth Koch's *Wishes, Lies and Dreams: Teaching Children To Write Poetry*.

Writing a Philosophy Project
John L. Taylor

Starting age: 16

If you enjoy thinking about philosophical puzzles, why not try turning your ideas into a project? Project work is a great way to practise some of the skills which you need to be a good philosopher. It is also a good way of developing as an independent learner. You can do project work just for its own sake, or as part of an assessed qualification (for example, the Lower or Higher Tier Project Qualifications, or the Extended Project). Here are some tips.

Getting started

The key thing with a good philosophy project is choosing an appropriate philosophical question. Have a think about the ideas in philosophy which interest you most: this is a good place to begin. You will have to work at your project over a period of weeks or even months, and you won't find it easy to keep going unless the question is one that really interests you. Think about some of the most enjoyable discussions you have had about philosophy, or about the topics you've read about which seem most exciting. (The contents of this book may well help with this: first find the entries that most interest you and then use them for discussions with your class, friends or family.) Pick one of these as a starting point.

Once you have picked a topic area, you need to select a research question. Philosophy is all about the big questions of life – the most fundamental questions of all. Is there a God? What is the meaning of life? What is the difference between right and wrong? Am I the same person that I was when I was born? What is time? Is the mind the same as the brain? These questions are deep and challenging. It is best not to try to solve one of these within your first ever philosophy project. Instead, think about selecting a more specific, simpler question (which can still be linked to one of the big questions, but which will be easier to write about in the time you have available). The big questions of philosophy are like mountains: you are trying to find a pathway which leads you part of the way up the mountain. You're not trying to get to the very top: you are just trying to go one stage of the journey.

So, for example, suppose you are really interested in the question of right and wrong. Instead of choosing 'What is the difference between right and wrong?' as your title, you could choose to write about the question, 'Is it ever right to tell a lie?' This is a more specific question, and it would be a good one to start with. You can always go on to the bigger question later.

When choosing a question, it is a good idea to do some research to find out what topics people are arguing about. If you find a news article, a magazine feature or a blog post in which there is a debate going on about a philosophical question, this could well be a good starting point for your project. You want to choose a question which other people are arguing about, because this will give you something to research as a starting point for your own ideas.

The next step: researching your topic area

Once you have made up your mind about a question, the next step is to start doing some research. You will need to find out a bit about the history of the question. Who has tried to answer it in the past? What did they say? What different views have people held? You will also need to research the arguments which people use. Philosophy is all about argument. It is often difficult to construct your own arguments. It can be easier to find arguments that other people have created, and then think about whether you agree with them.

When you are doing research, think first of all about the types of source you will need. Most people look online, as there is lots of good, easily accessible material on the Internet. But have a think about finding other sources too. Talk to people – do interviews or questionnaires to find out more about the range of opinion on the question you have chosen. Go to your local library and try to find some books which address your question. Start making a collection of source information.

As soon as you start to find sources, begin to make notes. Don't use other people's words (apart from the odd short quotation). Try to write up what you read in your own words. If you are doing your project for a formal qualification, you will probably need to include proper references and a bibliography. There is lots of freely available guidance about this online (type 'how to cite sources' or 'how to create a bibliography' into a search engine).

Think about research as being like doing a jigsaw puzzle. First, you need to get all the pieces onto the table (this is the 'collection' stage). Then you need to have a look at all the pieces, and start to try to fit them together. It is best to try to write up your research as a story. You want to explain who has thought what – and why and when they thought it. Write up what you have found in a research report. Your aim in this section of your project should be to help someone who doesn't know much about your topic to understand what is going on.

The heart of your philosophy project: your arguments

Philosophy is a uniquely personal subject. No one else can tell you the answers to the questions of philosophy. You have to think for yourself. Once you have written up your research report, you will need to write a philosophical discussion. This is the section of your project where you give your own answer to your question. It is not easy to write this section. It can be hard to know what to think about philosophical questions, and often, the more you read, the more confusing things become. A good way to clear your head is to sit down with someone else and try to explain your ideas. You want to be able to explain:

* Your own point of view – what do you think the answer to your chosen question is?

* Your reasons for your point of view – why do you believe it?

* What arguments are there against your viewpoint?

* Can you answer these arguments?

Try to organise your ideas into a plan, then write them up in the discussion section of your project. Remember, too, that you should make use of the ideas you discovered when you were researching. Look back at your research report. What arguments did you find? Which ones help to support what you are trying to argue? Which ones do you disagree with? How can you answer the objections to your views? But don't just write about what other people have said: you need to roll up your sleeves and get stuck into the argument yourself. So you will be writing in the first person: telling your reader what you believe, and why, and how you can defuse the counter-arguments of people who disagree with you.

The end and the beginning

You have written up your research and your philosophical discussion – what next? The next step is to round out your project with a conclusion and an introduction. The conclusion should be a short summary of what you have been trying to say in your project. The introduction is a chance to set the scene and draw the reader in. Use the introduction to explain why your question is important and to explain what it means. You might be surprised that the introduction isn't the first thing you should try to write. But you can't really write an introduction to your project until you know what it is all about – and you won't know this until you've written most of it. So, although the introduction comes first, write it last.

Good writing

Always think about your reader. Your job as a writer is to make the experience of reading your work as enjoyable as possible for them. Reading your project should feel like going on a smooth, comfortable journey. If you can get rid of any jolts, and avoid sudden changes of direction, your reader will feel more relaxed about the journey, and they will be more receptive to what you have to say. So make sure that your writing flows. Put in 'signpost sentences' at the start of each new section to explain to the reader where you are going to go next. Try to connect each paragraph to the previous one with a linking sentence.

Final tips: adding the polish

- ❖ Include citations to each of the sources you have used.
- ❖ Add a proper bibliography at the end.
- ❖ Add page numbers, a contents page and a title page.
- ❖ Put in appropriate subheadings.
- ❖ Use 1.5 line spacing to make the text more readable.
- ❖ Check the whole project carefully for spelling and grammatical errors.
- ❖ Edit the project: cut out any sections which aren't relevant. It can be hard to throw away material that you have written, but remember the reader! A shorter project is often a better one.

Further Reading

More on thought experiments:

The Pig That Wants To Be Eaten: And Ninety Nine Other Thought Experiments by Julian Baggini (Granta, 2005).

The Duck That Won the Lottery: And 99 Other Bad Arguments by Julian Baggini (Granta, 2008).

Can A Robot Be Human? 33 Perplexing Philosophy Puzzles by Peter Cave (Oneworld, 2007).

What's Wrong With Eating People? 33 More Perplexing Philosophy Puzzles by Peter Cave (Oneworld, 2008).

This Sentence Is False: An Introduction to Philosophical Paradoxes by Peter Cave (Continuum, 2009).

Do Llama's Fall In Love? 33 Perplexing Philosophy Puzzles by Peter Cave (Oneworld, 2010).

Wittgenstein's Beetle and Other Classic Thought Experiments by Martin Cohen (Wiley-Blackwell, 2004).

101 Ethical Dilemmas by Martin Cohen (Routledge, 2007).

101 Philosophy Problems by Martin Cohen (Routledge, 2007).

What If?... Collected Thought Experiments in Philosophy by Peg Tittle (Longman, 2005).

More philosophy books for children:

Sophie's World by Jostein Gaarder (Phoenix, 1995).

Dead Philosopher's Café: An Exchange of Letters for Children and Adults by Nora K and Vittorio Hosle (University of Notre Dame Press, 2007).

The Philosophy Files 1 and 2 by Stephen Law (Orion, 2002/2006).

Really Really Big Questions by Stephen Law (Kingfisher, 2012).

A Young Person's Guide to Philosophy by Jeremy Weate (Dorling Kindersley, 1998).

More philosophy books for teenagers:

Genesis by Bernard Beckett (Quercus, 2012).

Philosophical Tales by Martin Cohen (Wiley-Blackwell, 2008).

50 Philosophy Ideas (You Really Need to Know) by Ben Dupré (Quercus, 2007).

The Philosophy Gym: 25 Short Adventures in Thinking by Stephen Law (Headline, 2004).

Philosophy through Science Fiction: A Coursebook with Readings by Ryan Nichols, Nicholas D. Smith and Fred Miller (Routledge, 2007).

Philosophy for Kids: 40 Fun Questions That Help You Wonder ... About Everything! by David White (Prufrock Press, 2000).

More books on poetry and philosophical poetry:

Thoughtings: Puzzles, Problems and Paradoxes in Poetry to Think With by Peter Worley and Andrew Day (Independent Thinking Press, 2012).

First Poems for Thinking by Robert Fisher (Nash Pollock Publishing, 2000).

Poems for Thinking by Robert Fisher (Nash Pollock Publishing, 2007).

Wishes, Lies and Dreams: Teaching Children To Write Poetry by Kenneth Koch (HarperCollins, 1998).

I Was Only Asking: Poems About Big Questions by Steve Turner (Lion Children's Books, 2004).

More on philosophy in the classroom:

Thinking Together: Philosophical Inquiry for the Classroom by Philip Cam (Hale & Iremonger, 1995).

Teaching Thinking: Philosophical Enquiry in the Classroom by Robert Fisher (Continuum, 2008).

Philosophy for Young Children: A Practical Guide by Berys Gaut and Morag Gaut (Routledge, 2011).

The Little Book of Thunks: 260 Questions to Make Your Brain Go Ouch! by Ian Gilbert (Crown House Publishing, 2007).

Philosophy in Schools edited by Michael Hand and Carrie Winstanley (Continuum, 2009).

Children as Philosophers: Learning through Enquiry and Dialogue in the Primary Classroom by Joanna Haynes (Routledge, 2008).

Picture Books, Pedagogy and Philosophy by Joanna Haynes and Karin Murris (Routledge, 2011).

Philosophy for Teens: Questioning Life's Big Ideas by Sharon M. Kaye and Paul Thomson (Prufrock Press, 2006).

More Philosophy for Teens: Examining Reality and Knowledge by Sharon M. Kaye and Paul Thomson (Prufrock Press, 2007).

Philosophy for Children through the Secondary Curriculum edited by Lizzy Lewis and Nick Chandley (Continuum, 2012).

Philosophy in the Classroom by Matthew Lipman, Ann Margaret Sharpe and Frederick S. Oscanyan (Temple University Press, 2006).

Transforming Thinking: Philosophical Inquiry in the Primary and Secondary Classroom by Catherine McCall (Routledge, 2009).

But Why? Developing Philosophical Thinking in the Classroom by Sara Stanley with Steve Bowkett (Network Educational Press, 2004).

Why Think? Philosophical Play from 3–11 by Sara Stanley (Continuum, 2012).

Think Again: A Philosophical Approach to Teaching by John L. Taylor (Continuum, 2012).

The If Machine: Philosophical Enquiry in the Classroom by Peter Worley (Continuum, 2010).

The If Odyssey: A Philosophical Journey through Greek Myth and Storytelling for 8–16-Year-Olds by Peter Worley (Bloomsbury Education, 2012).

More on stories for thinking:

Stories for Thinking by Robert Fisher (Nash Pollock Publishing, 1996).

First Stories for Thinking by Robert Fisher (Nash Pollock Publishing, 1999).

Thinking Stories to Wake Up Your Mind by Mike Fleetham (London Development Agency, 2007).

Once Upon An If: Storytelling for Thinking by Peter Worley (Bloomsbury Education, available 2013).

More on philosophy for adults:

Think: A Compelling Introduction to Philosophy by Simon Blackburn (Oxford Paperbooks, 2001).

Being Good: A Short Introduction to Ethics by Simon Blackburn (Oxford Paperbooks, 2002).

The Consolations of Philosophy by Alain de Botton (Penguin, 2001).

A Short Treatise on the Great Virtues: The Uses of Philosophy in Everyday Life by Andre Compte-Sponville (Vintage, 2003).

The Story of Philosophy: A History of Western Thought by James Garvey and Jeremy Strangroom (Quercus, 2012).

The Meaning of Things: Applying Philosophy to Life by A. C. Grayling (Phoenix, 2007).

An Introduction to Philosophical Analysis by John Hospers (Routledge, 1997).

What Does It All Mean? A Very Short Introduction to Philosophy by Thomas Nagel (Oxford University Press, 1987).

The History of Western Philosophy by Bertrand Russell (Routledge, new edn., 2004).

A Little History of Philosophy by Nigel Warburton (Yale University Press, 2001)

'The Philosophy Student's Beginners Pack' by Nigel Warburton:

Philosophy: The Basic Readings (Routledge, 2004).

Philosophy: The Basics (Routledge, 2004).

Philosophy: The Essential Study Guide (Routledge, 2004).

Philosophy: The Classics (Routledge, 2006).

Thinking from A to Z (Routledge, 2007).

Websites for exploring philosophy:

Stanford Encyclopedia of Philosophy: http://plato.stanford.edu/

History of Philosophy Without Any Gaps: http://www.historyofphilosophy.net/

Philosophy Bites: http://www.philosophybites.com/

Philosophy Now: http://www.philosophynow.org/

The Philosophers' Magazine Online: http://www.philosophersnet.com/

In Our Time: http://www.bbc.co.uk/radio4/features/in-our-time/archive/

About the Authors

The Philosophy Foundation (TPF) is a social enterprise and a registered charity. Its aim is to bring philosophy (the study of general and fundamental problems) to the wider community and particularly into disadvantaged schools. Philosophy teaches critical thinking and the systematic and rational approach to problem solving. By teaching philosophy at an early stage, children will develop autonomous, creative thinking skills as well as rational reasoning skills. With these skills, TPF believes that children will have a better chance of resolving problems and making better decisions for themselves as individuals, as they develop through childhood into adults.

TPF would like to thank the following authors who have given their time, creativity and knowledge to help bring this book to print and who have waived their fee for the benefit of TPF.

Harry Adamson

Harry completed his doctorate, 'Knowledge and Morality', at Cambridge in 2010. He has taught ethics, political philosophy and formal logic there for six years, and was a Teaching Fellow and Kennedy Scholar at Harvard University in 2006–7, running a seminar entitled 'Equality and Democracy' for T. M. Scanlon. He is particularly interested in the practical applications of philosophy and ethical thinking. He starts as a pupil barrister at Blackstone Chambers in 2012, aiming to specialise in public and human rights law. He also organises a weekly philosophy group on behalf of a mental health and well-being charity, which is often the favourite part of his week. The group relies on the good will of able philosophers to run it, and he would welcome anyone who enjoys this book to consider volunteering.

http://www.slt.org.uk/philosophy-forum/

stuartlowphilosophy@gmail.com

Peter Adamson

Peter is a Professor of Philosophy in Munich, and also at King's College London. He spends most of his time doing philosophy, even when he should be doing something else, and is especially interested in ancient and Islamic philosophy. He does a weekly podcast on the whole History of Philosophy Without Any Gaps which is at www.historyofphilosophy.net/.

Alfred Archer

Alfred is a Philosophy PhD student and tutor at the University of Edinburgh. His research interests are in moral philosophy. He has previously studied Philosophy and Politics at the University of Glasgow and Philosophy with Children at the University of Strathclyde.

http://edinburgh.academia.edu/AlfredArcher

Saray Ayala

In secondary school Saray was convinced that the answers to the interesting questions were to be found by analysing living and non-living matter with a microscope and scalpel. By accident she ended up doing Philosophy at the University of Murcia and realised that the questions that most interested her could not be answered like that, but with a fine-tuned conceptual framework, the result of well-trained thinking. She has taught philosophy at secondary school level and at university, and always has a lot of fun. She crossed Canada by train in 2009 and obtained a PhD in Philosophy at Autonomous University of Barcelona in 2011. She does research in the philosophy of cognitive science and sex and gender studies.

http://sarayayala.googlepages.com/

Grant Bartley

Grant is Assistant Editor at *Philosophy Now* magazine, and author of *The Metarevolution* and *Love, Solitude and Destruction*, both available from Amazon for Kindle or as downloads from www.Smashwords.com. A free download of *The Metarevolution* is also available at www.philosophynow.org/media/pdf/bartley/Metarevolution_2nd_ed_segment.pdf.

Grant is also the main presenter of the Philosophy Now Radio Show. Previous shows can be heard at www.philosophynow.org/podcasts/.

David Birch

David trained with The Philosophy Foundation in 2011 and has since worked with them at both primary and secondary schools in various parts of London.

Peter Cave

Peter read Philosophy at University College London and King's College Cambridge. He has lectured mainly in London, though also in Khartoum, and gives guest lectures throughout Europe. He currently lectures for the Open University and New York University (London Campus). Peter chairs the Humanist Philosophers of Great Britain, has scripted and presented BBC radio philosophy programmes – some too clever by one eighth – and engages in public debates. He writes grumpy letters to newspapers. His philosophy books include *Can A Robot Be Human?* (Oneworld, 2007), *What's Wrong with Eating People?* (Oneworld, 2008) and *Do Llamas Fall in Love?*

(Oneworld, 2010) – and introductions to humanism, philosophy and philosophical paradoxes. Peter lives in Soho, enjoys opera (he thinks he knows what he likes), even delights in religious music, sometimes wears raffish bow ties (only one at a time) and is often found with a glass of wine – or two …

www.petercave.com

Miriam Cohen Christofidis

Miriam was born and lives in North London. She has a BA and an M.Phil. She taught at university for many years and is currently working in schools teaching at all levels from Year 1 to A level. Her main interests in philosophy are in political and moral philosophy and she has recently become interested in how education fits into what makes a flourishing life possible. Miriam has been working with The Philosophy Foundation since 2007 and is a member of their senior leadership team.

Philip Cowell

Philip works in literature, philosophy and lifelong learning to help people of all ages explore their thoughts, ideas, memories and experiences, not to mention their dreams. He works across the life course, with everyone from children to older people, and uses different practices – philosophy as well as creative writing, reminiscence, mindfulness and clown. Visit www.philipcowell.co.uk and download your very own philosophy tablemat!

James Davy

James is a primary school teacher, currently based in city-centre Nottingham. He never had much time for three-part lessons and literacy hours, therefore he tries to avoid them wherever possible, and would much rather be getting his class philosophising, heading out to the woods to do Forest School, making films and becoming more inquisitive, resilient and independent. Amazingly, the kids seem to learn maths and English too. He also lectures on Creativity, Thinking Skills, Art, and Outdoor Learning on teacher training courses, consults on Forest Schools and Behaviour, and even finds time to do things unrelated to teaching too.

j.a.davy@gmail.com

Andrew Day

Andrew is a Senior Specialist with The Philosophy Foundation. He has written for the stage and screen, and is co-author with Peter Worley of *Thoughtings* (Crown House Publishing, 2012), a book of philosophical poetry for children. He has a degree in Philosophy and Social Anthropology, and is always on the lookout for new perspectives on education.

Georgina Donati

Georgina finished her degree in Philosophy at Leeds University where she became interested in the idea of philosophy with children. She first trained with The Philosophy Foundation at the beginning of 2009 and has worked in primary schools in East London with all age groups, with teachers and on curriculum development. Georgina now works with The Philosophy Foundation as part of the senior leadership team, helping with fundraising, business development and training, as well as teaching. Georgina has a great interest in different languages and cultures which has led her to live and work in Croatia, Spain and Central America where she co-founded and directed an international campaign working with indigenous people in the Ecuadorian Amazon.

Claire Field

Claire grew up in Stratford-upon-Avon, and like the famous playwright whose hometown she shares, moved as quickly as possible to London where more things happen. There she gained a First Class degree in Philosophy from King's College London and also became interested in teaching. Perceiving a worrying philosophy-shaped gap in the curriculum, she became a Specialist Philosophy Teacher with The Philosophy Foundation. She also teaches English as a Foreign Language to adults who have come to London from all over the world, and tutors A level, GCSE and Key Stage 2 students. Her philosophical interests include methodology, Plato and non-classical logic, and her non-philosophical interests include rock-climbing and travel.

Berys Gaut and Morag Gaut

Berys Gaut is Professor of Philosophy at the University of St Andrews, and Morag Gaut is a Chartered Teacher, teaching at Anstruther Primary School and St Andrews Nursery Centre, Fife. They are co-authors of *Philosophy for Young Children: A Practical Guide* (Routledge, 2011).

Philip Gaydon

Phil is currently (2012) doing a PhD in Philosophy and Literature at the University of Warwick. His research is centred on proving the existence and usefulness of artistic knowledge using 19th century children's literature. Part of this involves an exploration of how children engage with the thought-experimental nature of texts and how useful this is to pedagogy. Just in case this finds its way into Archbishop Hutton Primary School, Warton – tell Mrs Gaydon that Phil says hi!

http://www2.warwick.ac.uk/fac/soc/philosophy/people/postgraduates/pyrhan/

Nolen Gertz

Nolen is an Instructor of Philosophy at Delta College, Michigan, and received his doctorate in philosophy from the New School for Social Research. His research interests are primarily in applied ethics, social and political philosophy, and phenomenology and existentialism. He has published in a wide range of topics, including architecture, sports, psychoanalysis and the ethics of war, and is currently working on a project on the philosophy of J. Glenn Gray.

A. C. Grayling

Anthony is Master of the New College of the Humanities, and a Supernumerary Fellow of St Anne's College, Oxford. Until 2011 he was Professor of Philosophy at Birkbeck College, University of London. He has written and edited over 20 books on philosophy and other subjects; among his most recent are *The Good Book* (Bloomsbury, 2011), *Ideas That Matter* (Weidenfeld and Nicolson, 2009), *Liberty in the Age of Terror* (Bloomsbury, 2009) and *To Set Prometheus Free* (Oberon, 2009). In addition he sits on the editorial boards of several academic journals, and for nearly ten years was the Honorary Secretary of the principal British philosophical association, the Aristotelian Society. He supports a number of educational charities, is an Honorary Patron of The Philosophy Foundation and is a sponsor of Rogbonko School in Sierra Leone.

www.nchum.org

Michael Hand

Michael is Professor of Philosophy of Education at the University of Birmingham. He is interested in ways of teaching philosophy, politics, morality and religion, both in school and at home. His books include *Patriotism in Schools* (PESGB, 2011), *Philosophy in Schools* (Continuum, 2008) and *Is Religious Education Possible?* (Continuum, 2006). Michael didn't discover philosophy until he was an undergraduate, by which time his best years were behind him, and he's determined to ensure that the current generation of children and young people don't have to wait so long.

Angie Hobbs

Angie is Professor in the Public Understanding of Philosophy at Sheffield University. Her chief interests are in ancient philosophy and literature, ethics (both theoretical and applied) and political theory, and she has published widely in these areas. She contributes regularly to radio and TV programmes, newspaper articles and philosophy websites; she lectures and gives talks around the world. She also engages in a variety of public and political work in the UK, promoting the role of philosophy in schools and adult education and advising on academic public engagement. Angie is a Fellow of the Royal Society of Arts, Chair of the Trustees of the Institute of Art and Ideas and an Honorary Patron of The Philosophy Foundation.

David Jenkins

David is a recent graduate of Middle Tennessee State University (2012), where he earned a BA in Philosophy with minor concentration in religion. He currently resides in Costa Rica as an English teacher, and hopes to earn a graduate degree in either law or philosophy. He is also a songwriter and aspiring poet.

Milos Jeremic

Milos lives in Pozarevac, Serbia. He teaches philosophy at Pozarevacka Gimnazija (Pozarevac Grammar School). His philosophy with children approach is based on hermeneutics and he has demonstrated his workshops in Italy, Austria, Spain, France, Iran, Turkey and Russia. One of the ideas he has proposed is to motivate children for learning, reading and writing by inducing 'cognitive dissonance' and 'intellectual discomfort'. You can find out more about his work at www.philosophywithchildren. org/.

Lisa McNulty

Lisa McNulty holds a PhD in Philosophy from Kent University, and is a lecturer at Regents College London. She has taught philosophy in the British and American university systems, and has also taught English at a primary school in Thailand. It would be difficult to say which of these she has enjoyed more. Her research interests lie in the philosophy of education, philosophy of science and social epistemology, and she is an enthusiastic member of the Philosophy of Education Society of Great Britain. She lives in London and is generally in possession of a cup of tea.

www.lisamcnulty.com

Sofia Nikolidaki

Sofia has two BA and two MA degrees with honours in Education and Philosophy, respectively funded by the national Greek scholarship institution. She also holds a PhD focusing on Philosophy for Children (P4C) sponsored by the Academy of Athens. During her doctoral studies she received SAPERE's official training on P4C and further philosophical training at the universities of Montclair State (USA), Strathclyde (Scotland) and Oslo (Norway). She has worked as a teacher and a P4C practitioner in Greek and British schools. She has taught ethics to undergraduate students at the University of Wales, Newport, delivered community-based learning to adults and has trained future teachers at the University of Crete. She writes stories for children's thinking; some of which have been praised and published.

Martin Pallister

Martin was encouraged by his parents to study Philosophy at York University where he could ask the question 'Why?' as many times as possible. After his studies he left England to live in Spain with Ana, his future Spanish wife. He set up a successful

English language school with his new Spanish family, with the philosophy of looking for alternative methods of teaching the English language to children. Since then Martin has achieved a Masters in Philosophy with the Open University. His Masters, coupled with personal observations, sparked a keen interest in feminist philosophy, especially looking at the influence of gender inequality in the family and gender schemas upon society. Nussbaum, Kittay, Valian and Okin are the philosophers who have had the most influence upon him. Martin and Ana have got two fantastic kids, Ziggy and Audrey.

Andrew Routledge

Andrew is currently studying for a PhD at the University of Manchester (2012). His main research interests lie in the philosophy of mind and metaphysics. In his work, he defends a form of holism about experience, arguing that the various different experiences that we have at any time depend upon one another. He also works for the University's Widening Participation programme, a scheme that aims to increase the number of young people entering higher education from lower income families and ethnic minority groups, or who have learning difficulties or a disability.

Anja Steinbauer

Anja studied philosophy, sinology and history at the universities of Hamburg, Taiwan (National Taiwan Normal University) and London (School of Oriental and African Studies and King's College), receiving her PhD from Hamburg. Inspired by fearless thinkers in the Chinese and Western traditions, Anja is committed to combating what she believes to be the world's greatest problem: stupidity. She has lectured in university and adult education philosophy since 1997 and co-initiated the UK's only Access to Philosophy programme, which she successfully ran for almost a decade. Anja is also founder and president of one of London's most vibrant popular philosophy organisations Philosophy for All (www.pfalondon.org), works for *Philosophy Now* magazine (www.philosophynow.org) and is a co-founder of the London School of Philosophy (www.londonschoolofphilosophy.org).

Dan Sumners

Dan enjoys telling stories, facilitating philosophical enquiry, recording images and dressing up.

dansumners.co.uk

Roger Sutcliffe

Roger read Philosophy at Oxford in the 1970s, then taught a variety of subjects in both junior and secondary schools for 20 years. In the 1990s he trained in Philosophy for Children (P4C) with Matthew Lipman, and has since been a freelance trainer in P4C and thinking skills, especially critical thinking. Roger was one of the founder members of SAPERE, and was President from 2003 to 2008. He also served two terms as President of ICPIC, the international equivalent of SAPERE. He is a director of www.p4c.com, the online cooperative for philosophical resources and advice for teachers, and is on the editorial board of the Philosophy of Management journal. He campaigns for the teaching of all subjects, but especially PSHE, to become more philosophical – aiming beyond the acquisition of knowledge to the cultivation of good judgement.

www.dialogueworks.co.uk

John L. Taylor

John is a philosopher, author, teacher and curriculum developer. He has taught philosophy at Oxford University and is now Head of Philosophy and Director of Critical Skills at Rugby School. He has pioneered the use of project qualifications as a vehicle for philosophical learning, initially through the 'Perspectives on Science' course, and is now a chief examiner for the Extended Project Qualification. He is also a visiting fellow of the Institute of Education. In 2012 he published *Think Again: A Philosophical Approach to Teaching* (Continuum).

http://www.york.ac.uk/education/projects/project-qualifications/perspectives-on-science/

Amie L. Thomasson

Amie is Professor of Philosophy, Cooper Fellow and Parodi Senior Scholar in Philosophy of Art in the Department of Philosophy at the University of Miami. She is the author of two books: *Ordinary Objects* (Oxford University Press, 2007) and *Fiction and Metaphysics* (Cambridge University Press, 1999). She also co-edited (with David W. Smith) a collection of essays, *Phenomenology and Philosophy of Mind* (Oxford University Press, 2005). In addition, she has published more than 40 book chapters and articles on topics in metaphysics, metaontology, fiction, philosophy of mind and phenomenology, the philosophy of art and social ontology. She is currently working on a new book on existence, modality and the methods of metaphysics. She is also the mother of a lovely little character who is not at all fictional. She is glad she is real.

www.amiethomasson.org

Robert Torrington

Robert left his childhood home on the Isle of Wight in 2005 to study Philosophy at King's College London, then onto an M.Phil.Stud. there which he completed in 2012. He considers himself a student of Plato, especially interested in his reflections on learning and knowledge, and, within this field, the role of Socrates as an educator. All this converged perfectly with the spirit of The Philosophy Foundation, which he joined in 2007. Since then, Robert has had the privilege of facilitating their methodology in schools across the country, experimenting with it in his undergraduate tutoring at King's College and helped develop its transmission as a Philosophy

Foundation Training Director. In 2008, he met an Island girl – and philosopher, no less – Gemma Eccott. They wed in 2012.

Andy West

Andy West graduated from Heythrop specialist philosophy college in 2009 and has been teaching on behalf of The Philosophy Foundation for the last two years. He has taught at more than ten different primary and secondary schools and has been entrusted with certain schools' most promising Oxbridge candidates. As well as representing The Philosophy Foundation at last year's Philosophy Now festival, Andy has also put The Philosophy Foundation's methodology into practice when teaching adults with mental health problems. Being a conflict mediator, Andy is passionate about imparting effective communication skills. He believes that primary school philosophy can help to shape creativity through communication.

Emma Williams

Emma is the philosopher-in-residence at Rugby School where she introduces philosophy in formal and informal ways throughout the school curriculum. She also coordinates the Philosophy Zone, an inter-school partnership programme that promotes philosophical discussion both inside the classroom and online. She is currently completing a PhD at the Institute of Education, University of London for which she was very helpfully funded by the Economic and Social Research Council. She has spoken at a number of conferences on the role of philosophy in schools. She lives in Rugby where she once met a person who met Jean-Paul Sartre.

Guy J. Williams

Guy studied Theology at Cambridge and then wrote a doctorate at Oxford, specialising in spirituality in the early Church. He is now Head of Philosophy and Religion at Wellington College (Berkshire) and an examiner for IB Philosophy. Guy enjoys introducing secondary school students to the challenges and problems of philosophy, and is working with The Philosophy Foundation to develop philosophical thinking skills at Wellington.

Emma Worley

Emma is co-founder and Chief Operating Officer of The Philosophy Foundation. She graduated from Rose Bruford Drama College in 1997 and has worked as an actor for the Royal Shakespeare Company, in the West End and can sometimes be spotted on telly if you don't blink. She still continues to work in the industry when she has time, and regularly volunteers for children's charity Scene and Heard as an actor and dramaturg. She wishes she had been introduced to philosophy at school in order to bridge the gap between the sciences and humanities, both of which fascinate her. Emma studied Ancient Greek Philosophy at Birkbeck, is a Fellow of the Royal Society of Arts and has ambitions about combining theatre and philosophy in as many different ways as possible.

Peter Worley

Peter is the Chief Executive Officer and co-founder of The Philosophy Foundation. He is a Fellow of the Royal Society of Arts and is, at the time of writing, attempting to undertake a PhD at King's College London researching pedagogy in Plato. He is the author of *The If Machine: Philosophical Enquiry in the Classroom* (Continuum, 2011) and the follow-up *The If Odyssey: A Philosophical Journey through Greek Myth and Storytelling for 8–16-Year-Olds* (Bloomsbury Education, 2012). He has co-written, with Andrew Day, a collection of philosophical poetry called *Thoughtings: Puzzles, Problems and Paradoxes in Poetry to Think With* (Independent Thinking Press, 2012) and is currently working on *Once Upon An If* (Bloomsbury Education), due out in 2013. He lives in South East London with Emma and their daughter Katie.

www.peterworley.com

The Philosophy Foundation:

www.philosophy-foundation.org

The Philosophy Foundation Series

The Philosophy Foundation is a social enterprise and a registered charity. Its aim is to bring philosophy (the study of general and fundamental problems) to the wider community and particularly into disadvantaged schools.

www.philosophy-foundation.org

Thoughtings

Puzzles, Problems And Paradoxes In Poetry To Think With

Peter Worley and Andrew Day

ISBN: 978-178135087-4

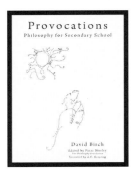

Provocations

Philosophy for Secondary School

David Birch edited by Peter Worley

ISBN: 978-184590888-1

The Numberverse

How numbers are bursting out of everything and just want to have fun

Andrew Day edited by Peter Worley

ISBN: 978-184590889-8